Transformative Teaching

Changing Today's
Classrooms
**Culturally,
Academically,** &
Emotionally

Kathleen
Kryza

MaryAnn
Brittingham

Alicia
Duncan

Solution Tree | Press

a division of
Solution Tree

555 North Morton Street
Bloomington, IN 47404
800.733.6786 (toll free) / 812.336.7700
FAX: 812.336.7790

email: info@solution-tree.com
solution-tree.com

Visit **go.solution-tree.com/instruction** to download the reproducibles in this book.

Printed in the United States of America

19 18 17 16 15   1 2 3 4 5

Library of Congress Cataloging-in-Publication Data

Kryza, Kathleen.

  Transformative teaching : changing today's classrooms culturally, academically, and emotionally / by Kathleen Kryza, MaryAnn Brittingham, and Alicia Duncan.

        pages cm

  Includes bibliographical references and index.

  ISBN 978-1-936763-38-2 (perfect bound) 1. Transformative learning. 2. Effective teaching. I. Brittingham, MaryAnn. II. Duncan, Alicia. III. Title.

  LC1100.K78 2016

  371.102--dc23

                        2015025843

Solution Tree
Jeffrey C. Jones, CEO
Edmund M. Ackerman, President

Solution Tree Press
President: Douglas M. Rife
Senior Acquisitions Editor: Amy Rubenstein
Editorial Director: Lesley Bolton
Managing Production Editor: Caroline Weiss
Senior Production Editor: Suzanne Kraszewski
Copy Editor: Sarah Payne-Mills
Proofreader: Jessi Finn
Text Designer: Rachel Smith and Abigail Bowen
Cover Designer: Rian Anderson

To all *those kids* who helped us become
better teachers and kinder human beings.
We have grown braver, stronger, and more
compassionate on our hero's journey thanks to you.

ACKNOWLEDGMENTS

Thanks to Douglas Rife, president and publisher of Solution Tree Press, for seeing the book inside Kathleen's workshop at the Hawker Brownlow conference and encouraging her to write. Thanks to Kari Gillesse and our senior editor, Suzanne Kraszewski, and all the staff at Solution Tree. You are delightful to work with, and we are grateful for your patience and understanding.

Thank you Sheila Kreichbaum for doing what you do so very well, pulling the pieces together, organizing them, and making them pretty. Thank you, Michelle Leip, for your amazing feedback and awesome ideas for weaving the hero's journey throughout the book. Thank you Mary Habich for your insights and prompt edits. Extra special thanks to Sheila Kreichbaum, Michelle Leip, Jack Naglieri, and Joy Stephens for jumping in with your superpowers and talents to save the day. We could not have done it without you. We are forever grateful.

We would like to thank family and friends, especially our dear husbands—Jack Naglieri, George Brittingham, and Noel Chrzanowski—for being there to love, nurture, and guide us. You see our greatest strengths and our greatest challenges and still love us through it all.

It took us far longer to bring this book to fruition than we anticipated, not because we are slow writers but because as we've worked on this book, we have truly been living the hero's journey in our lives—in more ways than we could ever have imagined. It is a testimony to the power of collaboration that we've managed to persevere and write this book through some of our own most vulnerable and challenging life experiences.

The support, honesty, and inspiration we offered each other helped us get through our life's challenges while also keeping the *why* of our book at the forefront of our thinking. We are deeply grateful for each other's unconditional love. We are stronger for having each other on this shared journey.

Finally, thanks to the many teachers and students we have the pleasure to work with all over the world. You will always be and are our heroes.

Anyone who does anything to help a child in his life is a hero to me.

—Mister Rogers

Solution Tree Press would like to thank the following reviewers:

Kelly Brown
Assistant Professor, College of Education
Prairie View A&M University
Cypress, Texas

Dana Cope
Educational Consultant
Summit Center
Walnut Creek, California

Mindy Fisher
Learning Support Specialist II
Waterloo Schools
Waterloo, Iowa

Savanna Flakes
Educational Consultant Services
Reading for a Better Future
Washington, DC

Jason Hooper
Academy of Reading/Mathematics
    School Coordinator
Forest Hill High School
Jackson, Mississippi

Annette Little
Associate Professor of Education
Director, Studies in Applied Behavior Analysis
Lipscomb University
Nashville, Tennessee

Christina Mayfield
Special Education Teacher
Greenville Elementary School
Greenville, Indiana

Vicki McGinley
Professor and Graduate Coordinator,
    Department of Special Education
West Chester University
West Chester, Pennsylvania

Kathy Munzlinger
Resource Teacher
Senn-Thomas Middle School
Herculaneum, Missouri

Florence Muwana
Assistant Professor, Department of
    Special Education
University of Wisconsin, Oshkosh
Oshkosh, Wisconsin

Amye Billings Scott
Advanced Learner Programs and
    Services Coordinator
English Learner Academic Specialist
Napa Valley Unified School District
Napa, California

Bonnie Taylor
Resource Teacher
McGowen Elementary
McKinney, Texas

Arlene Whitlock
Special Education Department Chair
J.E.B. Stuart High School
Falls Church, Virginia

Visit **go.solution-tree.com/instruction** to download the reproducibles in this book.

TABLE OF CONTENTS

Reproducible pages are in italics.

CHAPTER 10: Teaching With the Social-Emotional Self in Mind 123

CHAPTER 11: Teaching With the Cultural Self in Mind 135

CHAPTER 12: Teaching With the Academic Self in Mind 145

ABOUT THE AUTHORS

 **Kathleen Kryza, BA, MA,** began her journey as an educator with her Polish and Scottish parents who instilled in her strong values related to education. She was the first child in her family to complete college, and she was drawn to the field of education because of her parents' values. However, it wasn't until she stood in front of her first group of middle school students that Kathleen truly understood what a great responsibility she had taken on. Because of personal challenges she faced in high school and college, Kathleen found herself really drawn to the students who were different and didn't fit in. That road less traveled has made her journey as an educator quite interesting.

Kathleen began her career as an English teacher—her dream position. Drawn to work with students who were needy, she left after two years of teaching English to work as a teacher in a juvenile correctional facility. For three years, she taught all subjects to twelve- to nineteen-year-old boys in the criminal sex offender program. She calls this her *Tale of Two Cities* years as a teacher: they were the best of times and the worst of times! It was also at this time that Kathleen began presenting Writers Workshop to other schools and districts.

Kathleen then went back to the public schools as a special education resource room teacher and started the co-teaching program in her district. She took advantage of an opportunity to move overseas for a year and started the special education program at the American International School in Lisbon, Portugal. When she came back to her district, she coordinated the gifted program. For a couple of years, she taught special education for half the day and coordinated the gifted program the other half. This background qualified her to become a district teacher leader for gifted education and differentiated instruction.

After eighteen years in schools, Kathleen started writing books and presenting across the United States on differentiated instruction and eventually committed to working full-time with her company, Infinite Horizons. Since 2001, she has worked full-time as a consultant and coach and presents internationally on a variety of topics, such as differentiated instruction, co-teaching and inclusion, content literacy, brain-based learning, executive functioning and mindsets, and more. Her passion is to open hearts, nourish minds, and inspire teachers and students from all walks of life on their learning journey.

To learn more about Kathleen's work, visit www.kathleenkryza.com and Kathleen Kryza's Infinite Horizons on Facebook, or follow her on Twitter @kathleenkryza.

MaryAnn Brittingham, BS, MS, has a love for children that started at an early age, and she eventually became a full-time special education teacher. MaryAnn started teaching autistic and mentally disabled students and discovered her true passion and gifts were working with emotionally handicapped students.

Growing up with seven siblings enabled MaryAnn to experience firsthand the importance of a nurturing and safe environment. This became a core belief in her teaching and was the inspirational force in creating a trusting classroom environment in which students were willing to take the risk to experience, learn, and grow.

She has taught in both rural and urban schools, including a psychiatric center, a board of cooperative educational services programs, and residential schools, ranging in levels from elementary through high school. During twenty years in the classroom, she obtained a master's degree in counseling and began private counseling with students. She then began both coaching and training teachers in their classrooms. MaryAnn teaches graduate courses in the area of classroom management for students with special needs at the State University of New York at New Paltz, Marist College, and Southern New Hampshire University.

She received the Highest Achievement Award from Dale Carnegie Training in 1984, which, along with her previous experiences, was the springboard that led her to create her own national and international business. Brittingham Professional Development Seminars provides school districts with meaningful, inspirational training and consulting on respectful discipline, working with unmotivated students, and assemblies on mindsets. She offers teachers current and practical approaches to working with challenging behaviors while emphasizing the importance of their own internal responses and behaviors. MaryAnn's purpose and passion are to provide teachers, students, and parents with hope and inspiration to create a safe, compassionate environment to make personal connections and develop a joy for learning.

To learn more about MaryAnn's work, visit http://mbrittingham.com and Brittingham Professional Development Seminars on Facebook, or follow her on Twitter @BPDSeminars.

Alicia Duncan, BA, MA, has always had a love for cultural differences and found delight, even as a child, in exploring these differences as well as the fundamental similarities that all humans have regardless of color, language, or culture.

Alicia's life as an educator began as a Spanish teacher in an elementary immersion program with a focus on delivering content and language simultaneously. Later, as she moved into a general education classroom, she was drawn to the students throughout the school who were newcomers from various cultures. Her key learning year was teaching a multiage class with seven different languages and cultures represented. Although she could not speak Vietnamese, French, or Hmong, as a second-language speaker, she understood how her students' brains were processing language and content. That year, she felt her calling and began her master's degree in sociolinguistics and English as a second language (ESL) methodology.

Alicia was given the opportunity to share her love of cultures and language as a staff developer and coordinator for her school district's ESL program. The program grew from one hundred students to more than six hundred in a few short years with more than forty-two languages represented. However, the position was split, and she also had the opportunity to be the coordinator of differentiated instruction and gifted and talented services. In this position, Alicia was able to contribute to the teacher induction program by creating a yearlong study of differentiated instruction for special needs learners. She taught and coached approximately one hundred teachers per year on methods for reaching and teaching diverse learners in the general education classroom.

Alicia continues to work in the classroom as a Spanish teacher part-time. She loves being in the trenches practicing methods that she shares with her colleagues. She works with preK through high school teachers, helping them teach language minority students. Specific to English learners, her teacher education specialties include early oral language development, language acquisitions methodology, academic language development, functional linguistics for the classroom, cultural responsive instruction, and assessment of language minority students with disabilities. She also provides a cultural bridge to families through the Parent Advisory Council and continues to consult with teaching staff to assist in academic plans for gifted and high-potential learners. She shares her passion for reaching all students in her role as the professional learning community leader for her building. Alicia's passion, cofounded with Kathleen Kryza, is to open hearts, nourish minds, and inspire teachers and students from all walks of life on their learning journey.

To learn more about Alicia's work, visit www.liveit2learnit.com and Alicia's Facebook page, Live It 2 Learn It.

To book Kathleen Kryza, MaryAnn Brittingham, or Alicia Duncan for professional development, contact pd@solution-tree.com.

PREFACE

Each day as teachers, we show up at school trying our best to make a difference in the lives of the students we serve. That is our role. What we may not realize is that we are also heroes—though real and imperfect—who are on a remarkable journey amid today's educational challenges.

What is the hero's journey? In the mid-1900s, Joseph Campbell's (1968) book *The Hero With a Thousand Faces* looked at the common elements in mythic adventures and defined what he called the *hero's journey*. The hero's journey is laid out for us in Homer's *Iliad* and George Lucas's *Star Wars*. It is in *Beowulf*, *The Matrix*, and even *Spaceballs*. A version of the hero's journey also plays out daily in our teaching and in our classrooms.

The basic pattern of the hero's journey is as follows: The hero starts off in his or her ordinary world and is then called to adventure. The hero initially refuses (perhaps out of fear), preferring his or her comfortable, known way of life. Inevitably, something comes along that pushes the hero out of the known world and into the unknown. For example, in *The Matrix*, Neo receives a phone call. The caller implores Neo to escape his dreary office life and come see him. Neo refuses. Or, in *The Lord of the Rings*, Gandalf arrives at Frodo's door and tells him he must take the ring out of the Shire, despite Frodo's protests. When the hero enters into the unchartered territory, he (or she) encounters allies and enemies and faces many trials and challenges. Finally, the hero reaches the abyss, where he must face his greatest fears and weaknesses. When the hero faces these truths, he realizes he must change. As the transformation occurs, the hero finds he can meet his challenge. He grows stronger and wiser. When he returns to his former world, he brings back a new vision and gifts to share with his fellow man.

Any successful adventure of mythic proportions tends to follow the steps of the hero's journey. While we educators are not on an adventure of mythic proportions, we certainly are in a time of great shifts in education, and, like it or not, we are being called to step into the unknown to meet the challenges of today's learners. We are being confronted with many trials along the way—myriad political initiatives that sometimes seem opposed to what we know is best for kids, more and more students who don't respond to traditional ways of teaching, and common societal misperceptions of the art and science of teaching. All of these seem to be pulling us away from our most important work: developing young minds. These changes and challenges have thrust us on an adventure that may not be of our own choosing. We may want to stay comfortable in the old ways—the past structures of teaching and learning. But if we are to move forward, and we must, we will need to cross over a threshold into the unknown and shape new schools and new classrooms—new ways of connecting with *those kids* who challenge us and force us to define our world differently. We will need to develop new mindsets and skill sets that will, in turn, help our students develop the mindsets and skill sets they need to succeed.

Fortunately, we are not alone on our journey; we have an army of allies. Cognitive scientists and cognitive psychologists know so much more about how the brain learns. They offer valuable research and insights that will help us help our students learn more effectively. In this book, we look at current ideas from Carol Dweck's and Robert J. Marzano's research on the impact of growth mindsets and effort on student learning. We look at the work of Jack Naglieri on the brain and learning. We see how teaching students to self-regulate can improve their emotional and cognitive skill sets. We see that mindsets plus skill sets can equal results for both our students and ourselves. We are learning the power of systematically collecting data and using that data to inform us as to what is working and not working for students. Data collection done well supports us on our hero's journey. Strategies such as co-teaching, coaching, professional learning communities (PLCs), and lab classrooms are leading us away from teaching in isolation and taking us into each other's classroom to learn and grow. Collaboration is essential on this new hero's journey.

But change is still hard, and we don't always feel as if we have the strength of a hero. We may feel ready to crack during this time of upheaval. But poet and singer Leonard Cohen reminds us in his song "Anthem" that imperfection has its gifts. He says that although everything has cracks, that is how the light gets in.

Don't we all have a crack in some part of our being? When we are focused on these cracks and feeling our most vulnerable and broken, don't we hope the world will see the light that shines from within us through these very cracks?

We have written this book to honor the cracked parts in all of us, for when we are judging ourselves too harshly, it becomes easy for us to judge and blame our students for their cracks and imperfections. We must remember that they, too, are on their own hero's journey—thrust into overcoming a challenge, working through difficult trials, and searching for their core truth. Their journey may feel insurmountable to them as well.

As teachers, we are on a hero's journey doing the challenging work of educating students in schools. The students who come to us with learning disabilities, language barriers, or emotional needs may pose the greatest challenges for us on our journey. We may sometimes find ourselves talking about them as *those kids*, not because we don't care but because we care so much but feel unsure or unable to meet their needs with all the pressures we are experiencing. We see their cracks, we know our own cracks, and we want to see the light through it all, but where do we begin to make those kids our kids?

We wrote this book to help teachers see beyond the cracks, labels, issues, and troubles that those students present to us—to help us see into all students' souls to help them flourish and thrive. We wrote this book because we know that even though we live in times where high test scores seem more valued than developing deep thinkers and decent human beings, we can choose to do what's right for our students. We know that by creating a sacred space for learning in our schools, a place where students are safe, seen, heard, and responded to, all students will grow because they will be given space to develop into their authentic beings in mind and spirit.

We wrote this book because we trust that when we act first and foremost from a place of love for our students, and a love for learning, we will achieve what the political system requires without selling out and without doing what we know in our hearts and minds is not right for kids. We believe, as Wael Ghonim (2011), the Google executive who helped jump-start Egypt's democratic revolution, said at the end of the Arab Spring, "The power of the people is so much stronger than the people in power."

We wrote this book because we know that when we create classrooms where students honor themselves and learn to honor and appreciate others, we can come together in a community of growth despite our cultural, academic, and emotional differences. Only then can we truly see the light that shines through the cracks and see the imperfections that make us human. Only then can we learn *with* our students on a new hero's journey—not as lone heroes but as teacher heroes working together to make a difference for our students and the world.

introduction

Blaming the Lettuce

When you plant lettuce, if it does not grow well, you don't blame the lettuce. You look for reasons it is not doing well. It may need fertilizer, or more water, or less sun. You never blame the lettuce.

—Thích Nhất Hạnh

Finnuala, a nine-year-old student whose mother was in Kathleen's Inspiring Learners Institute in New Zealand, was assigned to write a descriptive poem. Her poem appears in figure I.1.

Source: Finnuala O'Higgins. Reprinted with permission.

Figure I.1: Finnuala's poem.

Finnuala's teacher, untrained in teaching students with learning disabilities, saw only the spelling errors and sloppiness of the piece and therefore gave Finnuala a low grade on the poem. Finnuala was devastated. She had worked very, very hard on the poem and had given it her all. She went home and read the poem aloud to her mother, and here's what she read:

Basking in the sun I saw it
Spread out, slumped in the heat
At first I did not see it
Camouflaged against the little grey stones
Until its swift movement caught my eye
A flick of its tail perhaps.

Extended slim body, speckled with black spots
Little claws with long toes and dragon skin
Chainmail texture glistening in the bright light
Big black, beady eyes
Staring intently into no particular place
Still as a statue, waiting.

The bendy body waddles, half runs
Wiggling, scuttles and stops by the pool
It wags its tail in a curious manner.
The water laps the edge
A blur of pink tongue shoots out
Tasting the moisture.

Hunching its chest up
On its front legs
Having a good look around
Becoming aware of its surroundings
A few steps forward and then stop
Look around and go on.

The slightest movement
And in a blink of an eye
It darted away
In and out of the shade it dashes
Then shoots up a tree like a rocket
Gone!

Finnuala's poem is an amazing, descriptive poem for a nine-year-old! Sadly, her teacher could not see past the spelling errors. It wasn't the teacher's fault; she had no background in understanding the needs of students with learning disabilities. Yet clearly the teacher's lack of understanding led her to *blame the lettuce*. Had Finnuala been given a chance to use technology or to read her poem aloud, both she and the teacher could have had a rich and rewarding learning experience. The teacher would have felt successful in teaching Finnuala to meet the descriptive writing standards, and Finnuala would have felt successful knowing that her learning disability did not stop her from expressing herself in powerful ways.

The demands placed on teachers are daunting; when we are expected to accomplish so much, often with so little, we may find ourselves wanting to blame the lettuce that is struggling to grow in our classroom environments. Furthermore, when we see the many different types of learners in our classrooms, we may feel overwhelmed, and it's easy to be frustrated when we are feeling overwhelmed, fearful, or angry. Still, we must find ways to teach *all* kids who come into our classrooms.

According to Joseph Campbell (1968), American author and mythologist, heroes give their lives to something greater than themselves. Teacher heroes have the courage to step outside of themselves to see the bigger picture in our students. When we see beyond their cracks, we do what we can to support our students on their hero's journey—imperfect as we all are.

The three of us have been on this hero's journey. We didn't enter the profession knowing how to work with the most challenging students who came into our classrooms. However, along our journey, we discovered it was not the students who sat quietly, following all our directions and completing work on time, who helped us hone our teaching skills. This made us realize that if teachers only have the "perfect" students, we might never change our teaching practices because the way we are teaching is working just fine.

When comparing notes about our varied teaching experiences, we agree that it's the students who pushed us, the students we lost sleep over, the students who didn't learn the way we taught who made us question our pedagogy, challenged us to grow our mindsets, and made us grow our skill sets as teachers. We learned that blaming the lettuce got us nowhere. However, if we became joyfully curious about the students who learned in unique ways, it would open doors to seeing the amazing potential within each of them and, surprisingly, also within ourselves. We learned that even with our limitations and imperfections, with our fears and failures, we could make a difference for students in ways we never imagined with love, understanding, and an open mindset. We hope the ideas in this book will encourage and guide you as you join us in this joyfully curious exploration.

Our inspiration for creating this book has been all the students who pushed us to grow and become better teachers. We wanted to combine our many years of experience with all types of learners to give you clear and simple ways to understand who *those kids* are. We offer the strategies we found to be most successful for including and honoring their emotional, cultural, and academic needs and supporting them in developing the mindsets and skill sets they need to succeed.

Emotional, Cultural, and Academic Needs

Throughout this book, we explore the needs of those kids in three areas: (1) emotional, (2) cultural, and (3) academic. From our experience, these three areas are interconnected facets of a student's whole self, as seen in figure I.2 (page 4). All students benefit from these three elements being addressed in the classroom; however, our most challenging learners benefit the most when we address learning needs in each domain. Without addressing all elements of the whole self, students may fail to thrive, and then we are at risk of blaming the lettuce for not growing as we expected.

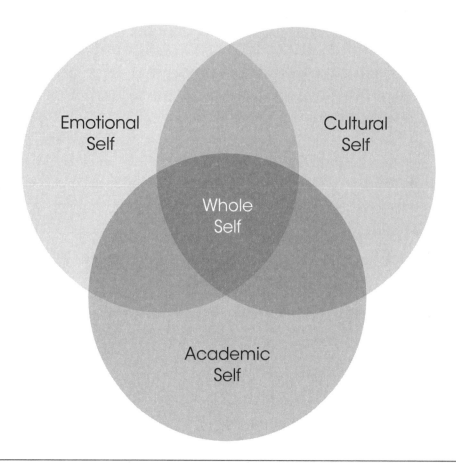

Figure I.2: The whole self—the intersection of emotional, cultural, and academic selves.

Emotional Self

Many students come to us with social and emotional challenges. Some experience stress in school because they are different. Some have home lives that are difficult in a variety of ways. Our challenge in working with these students is that academic learning is not accessible to them if they don't feel safe or if they are emotionally unstable. Recall Abraham Maslow's (McLeod, 2014) hierarchy (as shown in figure I.3). We know that functioning at higher levels, such as with critical thinking, is not possible until basic needs, such as food, shelter, and belonging, are satisfied. The brain needs to feel safe in order to work at its best. So, first and foremost, we need to create classrooms and school climates where students feel welcomed and safe.

Cultural Self

The cultural diversity in our classrooms reflects America's changing demographic. Authentic issues arise from this cultural diversity learners encounter. Ethnographic studies demonstrate that culturally responsive education can strengthen student connectedness with schools, reduce behavior problems, and enhance learning (Boykin, 1994; Kalyanpur, 2003; Solomon, Battistich, Watson, Schaps, & Lewis, 2000; Tharp, 1989).

Cultural background impacts the way students participate in our classrooms. For example, Hispanic students come from a collectivist culture rather than an individualist culture, so they see working in a community as more natural than students who may value independence more than interdependence (Kalyanpur, 2003). Some

Figure I.3: A visual of Maslow's hierarchy.

cultures value being assertive, maintaining eye contact, and asking questions, while other cultures expect more deference toward the person in authority. Our lack of knowledge about differences in culture may cause us to inaccurately judge some of our students as poorly behaved or disrespectful. On the flip side, because cultural differences are hard to perceive, students may find themselves reprimanded by teachers, but because of their worldview, they have no idea what they did to cause concern. To reach all learners, we must learn about and honor their cultural selves so they see themselves as a part of the classroom community.

Academic Self

With all the science that exists about the learning brain, educators can no longer ignore that the brain learns in varied ways. To effectively reach students academically, we need to address the differences in how they process information cognitively. Cognitive processes describe how a student thinks when doing something. Cognitive processes are relevant to learning because they influence how a student approaches tasks and how successful he or she can be (Naglieri & Pickering, 2010). The connection between cognitive processing and achievement is well documented (Naglieri & Das, 1997a, 1997b; Naglieri & Rojahn, 2004); therefore, it is of utmost importance that we support students in understanding their own cognitive strengths and weaknesses so they can learn to monitor and adjust and be in charge of their own learning.

We also know that students learn in varied modalities. In her book *Research-Based Strategies to Ignite Student Learning*, neurologist turned middle school teacher Judy Willis (2006) states, "The more ways something is learned, the more memory pathways are built" (p. 34). If we are going to effectively teach all kids academically, we must build and use a differentiated toolkit of best teaching practices to help us reach varied brains in varied ways.

Whole Self

When trying to figure out challenging learners' needs, we must remember that students' emotional, cultural, and academic selves are interconnected; we can't think of these three areas as completely separate from one another. For example, you may have a Native American student (cultural) who has anger issues (emotional) or a gifted (academic) African American student (cultural). You could have an English learner (cultural) who also has a learning disability (academic). You could have a gifted learner (academic) who has serious emotional issues (emotional).

It can be overwhelming to think about each of these components while teaching. The good news is that with some basic knowledge and understanding of each of these three areas, coupled with some quality teaching practices that teach students to build their mindsets and their skill sets, you will be able to integrate all three components in simple and doable ways. That is the goal of this book. Here you will find great strategies that work in supporting and developing struggling learners' needs. You don't need a totally separate toolkit for gifted learners, strategies for English learners, and responses to emotionally challenged students. Attending to emotional needs in your classroom is good for all struggling learners, regardless of their label. Being culturally responsive will make your classroom a safe place for all students who struggle. Planning for various academic needs will ensure all students' needs are met. These three elements woven together create a solid foundation that will meet many different learners' needs.

How This Book Works

Here's how we've structured the book to make it simple and user friendly to help you grow your skills gently and with ease and understanding. We've organized this book into three sections: (1) the why, (2) the how, and (3) the what.

Part 1: The Why

The three of us have dedicated a significant amount of time to passionately making a difference for teachers and students. This is our life purpose, our calling, our *why*. We want to do our part to contribute to a global society that raises kids to be emotionally healthy, culturally honoring, and intellectually curious. In the first chapters of our book, we will lead from our why by sharing our vision.

In chapter 1, "Understanding Our Inner Hero," we'll ask you to take a look at yourself and your own emotional, cultural, and academic background. We have found that understanding our own mindsets and our own strengths and limitations is the key to understanding what may trigger us with certain students. Understanding our own selves helps us to better deal with those kids whom we find most challenging.

Chapter 2, "Knowing *Those Kids*," will offer you key information about the most common students with special needs you will have in your classroom. We'll share misconceptions about those kids and offer some simple key ways to remember who they are and what they need.

Part 2: The How

Once we know why we are doing what we are doing, it's important to know how to do it in the most effective ways. In chapter 3, "Adopting Apprenticeship Learning," we will discuss the three hows we use instructionally to help us apprentice students into becoming lifelong learners.

1. Be intentional and transparent.

2. Model and scaffold.

3. Use deliberate repeated practice.

Part 3: The What

The why and the how form the solid foundation for what you can do instructionally to create a classroom that unites and grows your students emotionally, culturally, and academically. Chapters 4–9 will each discuss a learning foundation that unites students emotionally, culturally, and academically. These six simple yet powerful research-based ideas create a classroom that inspires and honors all learners in all three of these areas at the same time while also building the mindsets and the skill sets students need to succeed. You will also learn teaching actions you can take to make sure you achieve maximum impact for all students. Finally, in chapters 10–12, we will explore teaching with the emotional, cultural, and academic selves in mind. The ideas in these chapters of the book will make your job easier!

Nurture the Lettuce

On our teacher hero journey, we get to choose our mindset when it comes to how we will view all students who come into our classrooms. If our mindset is stuck blaming the lettuce, we are more likely to see students' deficits and challenges, and therefore, they are likely to see the same. However, if we choose to be joyfully curious about our students from different cultures, who have different needs emotionally or academically, then we have chosen to become better teachers—better selves. Like the lettuce, our challenging students are delicate vegetables to grow, but with love and the right understanding of their needs, a responsive teacher will make sure that *those kids* become *our kids*. They will not only grow but also thrive in our classrooms. We owe it to these students to be our best teaching selves.

chapter *One*

Understanding Our Inner Hero

As I teach, I project the condition of my soul onto my students, my subject, and our way of being together.

—Parker J. Palmer

Superman was born a superhero, and he chose to use his superpowers to help others. As teachers, we may not be superheroes, but, like Superman, we choose to use our gifts, talents, and strengths to help the students we teach. Remember that while Superman had amazing powers, he wasn't invulnerable. Kryptonite could debilitate him. He needed to know his vulnerabilities in order to know what he was and wasn't capable of doing.

We also need to know our vulnerabilities because we bring both our strengths and our challenges with us on our journey into the classroom. As Parker J. Palmer suggests, it is important that we as teachers study the condition of our own souls. Only then, through exploring our own vulnerability and courage, can we support students as they navigate through *their* own educational hero's journey using their strengths and understanding their challenges.

Why are we talking about heroes, and what does it have to do with teaching? By definition, a *hero* is a person who is admired for great or brave acts and fine qualities. A hero is someone who sees a need and does something about it, making a difference in the lives of others. With this definition in mind, teachers are clearly everyday heroes.

The teacher hero is an ordinary person who has intentionally developed an extraordinary knack for connecting with students. Teacher heroes help to promote and provide a safe, caring, and stable environment in an otherwise chaotic climate. They are willing to listen to their students and to accept them for who they are, where they are. They hold high expectations for their students and believe in the limitless potential in all students. Students see these teachers as mentors and heroes, and—while that is daunting, challenging, and humbling—a teacher hero is up to the task.

Teacher heroes reach out to their students and take risks personally and pedagogically without letting fear of failure prevent them from growth. Teacher heroes are grounded. They know who they are, their strengths, and their challenges. Teacher heroes know what they stand for and are strong in their convictions.

Once we have chosen teaching as a profession, we get to decide the kind of teacher we become. To become a teacher hero, we must begin by taking a close look at ourselves to see our strengths and our challenges. As wise mentor Kenny Willis told Kathleen early in her teaching career in the late 1980s, "Your greatest strength is also your greatest limitation." This kind of brave self-exploration will be essential to developing your teacher hero qualities.

Have you ever wondered why certain student behaviors bother you more than others? Isn't it interesting how your colleagues can be more patient with a student who drives you insane?

These kids can be our kryptonite but only if we let them! In order to understand why certain students trigger difficult feelings in us, we have to understand how our own hero's journey—emotionally, culturally, and academically—will impact the teacher we become. Self-awareness is essential in helping us understand and helping us teach those students who present us with the greatest challenges.

Finding the Courage to Be Vulnerable

As we begin this next part of the journey, we ask you to be courageous and vulnerable in your self-exploration. If either word, *courageous* or *vulnerable*, makes you feel uncomfortable, that's a telling sign about your journey that probably warrants closer investigation.

Let's take some time to explore the terms *courage* and *vulnerability* from the perspective of author Brené Brown, a research professor at the University of Houston, Graduate College of Social Work. She has spent ten years studying vulnerability, courage, worthiness, and shame. Brown (2007) concludes that the best definition of courage is illustrated when you tell your story with complete honesty and with all your heart.

It's courageous to look at your life journey or life story and see how it impacts the choices you make, both personally and professionally. It takes courage to be a teacher with your whole (emotional, cultural, and academic) self. We must have the emotional courage to stand before our students and honor our life story while also honoring their life stories. We must have the cultural courage to own our own heritage while also honoring the heritage of our students. We must have the academic courage to continually learn about and practice new ways of getting better at the work of educating all learners.

To truly be courageous, we must also be vulnerable. What is vulnerability? Brown (2010b) defines *vulnerability* as "uncertainty, risk, and emotional exposure. To be human is to be in vulnerability." It is human nature to defend ourselves when feeling vulnerable, yet we must tap into our own vulnerability to increase our compassion for our most challenging, vulnerable students. Courage is putting our vulnerability on the line.

We would all like to skip over the hard stuff that's involved with taking stock of who we are in our role as teachers, but it just doesn't work that way. We don't change, we don't grow, we don't move forward without doing the work. If we really want to live a joyful, connected, and meaningful life, we must talk about the things that get in our way. We must talk about the things we want to hide, forget, or pretend don't exist. The better we become at accepting others and ourselves, the more compassionate we become as teachers.

Superman was empowered because he knew how to help others despite his weakness and his own vulnerability. When we are aware of our weaknesses and strengths and they show up in our teaching, we don't deny them; we honor them and work with them. If we are not comfortable with looking at ourselves, we are likely to turn outward and blame others for our discomfort or unhappiness. We must look at our weak spots, our kryptonite, as well as embrace and enhance our "superpowers."

Learning From Our Hero Stories

Now it's time to ask you to dig deep and get courageous and vulnerable. In the appendix, you will find a journal ("Teacher Hero Self-Reflection Journal," page 162) to use to map your journey. We suggest you set aside a minimum of a half hour to do this when you feel rested and have time to think.

We have led the way for you by briefly telling you about our own emotional, cultural, and academic journeys later in this chapter. If you choose, you can read more about one or all of our stories as a way to help you get into the mindset of the experience. (Visit **go.solution-tree.com/instruction** to download these stories.) It is our intention and hope that sharing our stories with you will support you as you look at your own story. We found that taking this deep look at ourselves emotionally, culturally, and academically has given us great insights into the profound impact our life journey has had on the teachers we've become today. We all agree that the challenge and the risk taking are well worth the effort.

Once you complete your journal, it will be helpful to reflect and answer the questions in figure 1.1.

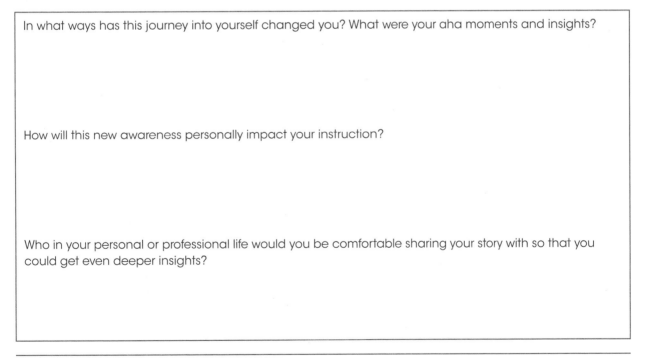

In what ways has this journey into yourself changed you? What were your aha moments and insights?

How will this new awareness personally impact your instruction?

Who in your personal or professional life would you be comfortable sharing your story with so that you could get even deeper insights?

Figure 1.1: Final self-reflection.

*Visit **go.solution-tree.com/instruction** for a reproducible version of this figure.*

Knowing Your Emotional Triggers and Personal Strengths

If you felt anything like we did after completing the personal journal, you may have come away with memories and insights that made you feel raw, scared, angry, or uncomfortable. What you have uncovered, if you were honest with yourself, are some of your emotional triggers. Knowing your triggers is the key to changing how you react to the students you find most challenging. Now that your kryptonite has been exposed, you can learn to work with it and use it to help you grow.

An *emotional trigger* is something that sets off a memory or flashback that transports a person back to an event that had a significant impact on his or her life. We all develop strengths to help us succeed and survive life's difficulties, but when something triggers a past experience or memory, many people find that seemingly irrational emotions are triggered. Triggers are very personal; different things trigger different people. Most of the time, our emotional triggers are unconscious, which is why we feel doing the journal is so important. It is a step to becoming conscious, and once you are aware of your triggers, then you have choices and can take action.

One of our greatest emotional triggers can occur when we feel someone is not honoring what makes us special. When our brain perceives that someone has taken, or plans to take, one of these important things away from us, our emotions get triggered. We react with anger or fear, and then we quickly rationalize our behavior so it makes sense. When triggered, we may lose trust in a person or a situation. We may lose our courage, or we may react in a way that could hurt our relationships in the future. The key is to catch ourselves reacting when our emotions are triggered. Only then can we discover if the threat is real or not.

We also need to keep in mind that triggers *explain*—they don't *excuse*. It's easier to forgive misbehavior in ourselves and be patient with our students once we understand this powerful connection among environment, emotion, and reaction. The more we recognize what triggers us in the classroom, the better we can begin to change our unconscious reactions.

The list in figure 1.2 includes some of the most common emotional triggers. These are common human needs that can cause a reaction when we feel as though we aren't getting, or will not get, one of these things that is very important to us. As you read through this list, note the words that invoke the greatest emotional reaction in you.

Acceptance	Respect	Approval
Understanding	Appreciation	Value
Control	Fairness	Attention
Comfort	Freedom	Peacefulness
Balance	Consistency	Order
Variety	Love	Safety
Predictability	Inclusion	Fun
New challenges	Autonomy	Certitude

Figure 1.2: Common emotional triggers.

Some of these needs will be important to us. Others will hold no emotional charge. It is critical to note that needs are not bad. These needs served us at some point in our lives. For example, our experiences may have taught us that success in life depends on maintaining control, establishing a safe environment, and having people around us who appreciate our intelligence. However, when an out-of-control student challenges or confronts these needs (making us feel out of control, unsafe, or stupid), we can have a very emotional, unconscious reaction. Our survival mechanism feels challenged, and therefore, our sense of survival feels threatened. The student who won't answer us may trigger feelings from having a mother or father who emotionally controlled through silence. The student who won't try to help him- or herself and acts inadequate challenges our coping mechanism of self-sufficiency. The student who refuses to take responsibility for completing work makes us irate because he or she triggers our autonomy that once helped us survive.

Again, the key is to catch ourselves being triggered. Once we catch ourselves, we can take time to pause and evaluate. We can then pull from our toolbox of knowledge and skills to make a choice before proceeding. That's what this book will provide.

While it's essential to know your emotional triggers, it's equally important to know what strengths and gifts you offer to your students.

What are your gifts? How do you use them to reach kids?

- Do you have x-ray vision to see beyond the walls that students build to protect themselves?
- Can your warm words melt a hardened heart?
- Do you have a soft touch that shows your compassion?
- Does your super hearing enable you to hear what is *not* being said?
- Do you have a soothing voice that guides without judgment?
- Does your patience outlast the most persistent attacker?
- Do you have the special ability to break down the most challenging concepts into understandable terms?
- Does your compassion allow students to be brave enough to be themselves?
- Do you have the creativity to present curricula in a fun and engaging manner?
- Can your super humor relax even the most anxious student?
- Is your manner so encouraging that students take risks and achieve goals they never thought possible?

Understanding Our Stories Helps Us Grow and Change

Change begins with awareness. Hopefully, after completing your self-exploration, you've had some of the same keen aha moments and insights we've experienced. We also highly recommend sharing your journey with someone you trust. You don't have to change everything on your own. In talking and reflecting together, the three of us gained much more profound insights about ourselves than we did on our own, and we came up with better ideas for how we could support one another and help each other grow. Sharing our journey has been a very rich and rewarding experience that has led us to not only be better at our work but also to become more insightful in our personal relationships.

Even though MaryAnn doesn't have a strong cultural understanding of others, she has a strong sense of caring and compassion, a desire to want others to be loved and seen for who they are. She needs to become more familiar with cultural differences, but her compassion is her teacher hero strength. MaryAnn can use her compassionate heart, her strength, to help overcome her deficit. She can joyfully seek out information about other cultures using her compassionate heart. But she has to be careful because her caring heart might sometimes allow kids to slide academically. That is where she needs Kathleen to help her give an "academic nudge" to students who need it.

Kathleen is impatient with herself and others when they don't get things quickly. She pushes kids to grow. Her strength is having high expectations for all learners regardless of background or learning differences. Kathleen wants all kids to work hard and develop to their highest potential. However, Kathleen needs to practice more patience and compassion. MaryAnn can help her learn this strength with modeling and coaching, and by giving her insights about how her pushing can be hurtful. While Kathleen was a cultural minority in her school, she still comes from a culture with deep individualist values, which makes her cultural integration easier. Alicia can help Kathleen understand how to be more inclusive of collectivist cultures—especially when the cultural differences can impact academic achievement.

Varied cultures and life perspectives fascinate Alicia. In her classroom, she brings a dynamic interaction that mixes individualist and collectivist learning styles so all students benefit. Academics came easily to her, so she often relies on the expertise of Kathleen to help her understand how different brains learn and how to keep her lessons academically differentiated. MaryAnn can offer Alicia guidance in dealing with angry students with violent behaviors and give Alicia the strategies to first deal with her own emotions so she can be mindfully responsive to students with social and emotional deficits.

The blind spots in our journeys are hardest to see, but we will never find them if we don't have the courage to look and the vulnerability to share with those we can trust to help us grow.

Taking the New Hero's Journey: You Are Not Alone

In the old hero's journey, the hero was, for the most part, on his own, except for times when allies or enemies stepped in. In much the same way, teachers have historically been on their own journey, celebrating their own successes and facing their personal fears (as well as facing their students) alone.

We know so much about the power of collaboration. We know that the brain is a social brain and learns better when safely engaged in processing with other brains (Sousa, 2006). We also have many models about the power of collaboration in other professions. Doctors watch other doctors; they do rounds together and collaborate. Lawyers study other lawyers and analyze strategies for success. Those professionals work together to share successes to create more success, and they share challenges so that they can get better at their work.

They don't let their fear of being seen as a braggart keep them from sharing successes. Can you imagine a doctor saying to herself, "I came up with this great cure for cancer, but I just don't want to brag, so I won't share"? Nor do they keep their successes to themselves for reasons of power or prestige: "I don't want to share this cure I've discovered because I want to keep all the glory to myself, because it's all about me!" They don't hang on to outdated practices for too long. No one would go to a physician who claims, "I've been treating cancer for twenty years; you can't tell me how to treat cancer. I've seen it all!" We wouldn't want our loved ones seeing a doctor who says, "So there are some new ways to treat this illness that seem to work, but I like the way I've been doing it, so I am going to keep doing what I've always done" or "Gee, I am not really sure what's wrong here, but I don't want to ask for help, so I'll sew the guy back up!" We would consider all these scenarios completely unacceptable, and yet in the teaching profession, we see teachers "close the door" all the time because of their fears of exposing their own personal vulnerabilities or their fear of being seen as arrogant.

As professionals, if we have teaching techniques and ways of working with challenging kids that work, we need to invite others to learn from us, and we need to be curious enough to watch each other do great teaching. We need to be vulnerable enough to say, "I am lost," "I don't know," "I need help," and "This kid is making me crazy—I don't know what to do with her!" Then we need the courage to reach out to help each other!

In order to do the work of teaching well, we need to risk being vulnerable with one another and be brave enough to share our greatest strengths as well as our limitations. The truth is we are not alone in being afraid. We are not alone in *not* knowing it all. We are not alone in *not* reaching all learners. We are not alone in needing help and support.

Fortunately, as we stated in the preface, education today is becoming more collaborative. While collaboration is not a new idea, the ways we use collaboration can be new and can make what we do every day feel new to us. Think of it like a book club. You read the book with intention, devour every sentence, and really enjoy the book. When you go to the book club meeting, invariably someone in the group read something in a way that was different enough from your interpretation to warrant a discussion. Ideas begin to fly around the room. People get excited. Everyone shares. That is what keeps people coming back month after month—the sharing, being part of deeper communication, the collaboration.

To help our students grow and develop into resilient learners and people, we must use these new models of teaching to work together, sharing our strengths and vulnerabilities, with an open heart and an open mind. If we see each other through a lens of judgment and comparison, we will never learn from one another. We need to move away from the mentality that "She's better than me" or "I'm better than him," which leads only to distancing, not growth. The job of teaching is too hard to do alone, and we must trust one another with our own personal kryptonite:

> Superman [giving a ring of kryptonite to Batman]: *I have many enemies who have tried to control me. And I live in fear that someday, they might succeed. If that ever should happen—if I should ever lose control, there would only be one sure way to stop me.*
>
> Batman: *Do you realize what you're asking?*
>
> Superman: *I do. I want the means to stop me in the hands of a man I can trust with my life.* (Simonson, 1993, p. 21)

To be our best teaching selves, we need to understand what it is that we currently do that gets in our way from teaching all kids. We must be vulnerable and compassionate in asking for help and in helping each other. If we don't know how to work with a student, we need to find someone who can help us. That's the beauty of co-teaching. When we pair a content specialist with a learning specialist, we double the toolkit we have for reaching and teaching all learners. So when Alicia confesses to MaryAnn that she's uncomfortable working with an out-of-control student and MaryAnn offers the amazing tools she has in her toolkit, they become a powerful team of teacher heroes, working together to do the best they can for kids. It is like Superman and Batman joining forces to make them stronger and perhaps unstoppable!

Now that you have seen the realizations that can develop from documenting your journey as an emotional, cultural, and academic learner, use the following hints and tools to guide you in making the rest of the journey more positive for all.

Using a Blueprint to Change Yourself

As you gain a better sense of yourself, your strengths, and your challenges, you will need some tools to help you make changes to how you respond to classroom challenges. The following is a toolkit of strategies that can support you on your hero's journey.

1. **Build your knowledge base:** First, you need to know and become aware of the specific behaviors or types of learners that challenge or trigger you. In chapter 2, you will find common characteristics for various learners and a guide for seeing beyond their challenges to see their gifts. To understand student behavior better, you can ask yourself the following questions about your students as learners.

    -   "Is the student behavior a result of deep cultural values that drive different actions or behaviors?" (Study the cultural iceberg in the appendix, page 166.)

    -   "Is the student behavior a result of the student's social-emotional needs?"

    -   "Is the student behavior a result of an academic challenge?"

2. **Know how to teach *those kids* any new skill they need to master:** Chapter 3 will unpack the key steps for how we teach any skill to students.

    -   Knowing how to instruct effectively is the core of working with all kids socially, emotionally, and academically.

    -   Once you have identified specific behaviors or learners you find most challenging, ask a colleague or specialist who deals with those particular issues to help you find solutions.

    -   Confer with a previous teacher who was successful with the student.

3. **Know what foundations *those kids* need to be successful:** Chapters 4–9 will give you the essential skills all students need in order to engage actively in class. When students have these skills, they are armed with the tools to bring them successfully into the classroom environment.

4. **Grow your self-care skills:** In order to respond to challenging behaviors or types of learners, we need to take care of ourselves first. We need to address our own healing and understand our triggers. Tools people use to reduce their triggers include:

   - Life balance
   - Mindfulness
   - Meditation
   - Therapy
   - Supportive colleagues
   - Books and websites on mindfulness

We are who we are; our experiences—the good and the bad—have shaped us. Our students are no different, and they come to us with all their good and bad behaviors. Once we better understand where we come from and why we think as we do, we can better understand where they come from and why they think as they do, making us more compassionate and effective for all our students. Let's make understanding each other a universal superpower!

Remember—student behavior is about the student; it isn't about us. Don't take it personally. Be calm, be smart, and choose your actions wisely. Every journey begins with a single step, and you just took your first step.

chapter *Two*

Knowing *Those Kids*

If the child is not learning the way you are teaching, then you must teach in the way the child learns.

—Rita Dunn

In the hero's journey movie *X-Men*, Professor Xavier starts his own school for the gifted. He keeps a detailed list of all students' strengths and weaknesses. He uses this information to help them achieve their highest potential as heroes (and to keep the world safe). We, too, should have such an inventory of the students in our classrooms.

However, just as a general medical practitioner will not have the depth of focused expertise that a medical expert such as a neonatal surgeon does, the general education teacher cannot be expected to be an in-depth expert on every unique type of learner that enters his or her classroom. Yet we would expect a general practitioner to have the basic skills needed to note major indicators of illness. So should general education teachers know how to recognize signs and symptoms in students that might indicate the need for additional support and learning considerations?

The goal of chapter 2 is to give you a general and easy-to-use reference tool to help you understand some of the key characteristics of the nine most common types of unique learners you may find in your classroom.

1. Learning disability (LD; table 2.1, pages 20–21)

2. Autism Spectrum Disorder (table 2.2, page 22)

3. Behavior disorder (table 2.3, page 23)

4. Gifted (table 2.4, page 24)

5. Twice exceptional (table 2.5, page 25)

6. Cognitive impairment (table 2.6, page 27)

7. Attention deficit disorder (ADD) or attention-deficit/hyperactivity disorder (ADHD; table 2.7, page 28)

8. English learners (table 2.8, page 29)

9. Students in poverty (table 2.9, page 30)

For each group of learners, you will find the major indicators of their challenge, a few key teaching strategies that will work for them, and other pertinent information, including what to be joyfully curious about when working with these students who help us become better teachers.

Under key teaching strategies, you will see that there are seven instructional ideas that are repeated in each category. These are best teaching practices that work for all learners and will be addressed in more detail throughout the rest of the book. Chapter 4 will address how to gather data about different styles.

In bold under the teaching strategies section of tables 2.1–2.9, you will find a key phrase to help you remember the most important thing about that group of learners. If you can only keep in mind one key idea about that type of student, this is the word to know!

The Individuals With Disabilities Education Act (IDEA; 2004) describes specific learning disability (SLD) as a disorder in one or more of the basic psychological processes involved in understanding or using language, spoken or written. In the classroom, students with SLD may show challenges with their ability to listen, think, speak, read, write, spell, or do mathematical calculations. In *The State of Learning Disabilities: Facts, Trends and Emerging Issues*, Cortiella and Horowitz (2014) note that while there is a decline in the number of school-aged children reported to have learning disabilities, it still remains the largest category of students served by special education (42 percent). Most students identified are male (66 percent), from poor families, and, to some degree, from minority groups. Students with SLD can be gifted and can learn effectively in our classrooms when the way we teach matches the way they learn. See table 2.1 for information about these learners.

On March 27, 2014, the Centers for Disease Control and Prevention (CDC) released new data on the prevalence of autism in the United States. Autism now affects one in sixty-eight children, and that figure is growing. Autism Spectrum Disorder occurs across racial, ethnic, and socioeconomic groups and is the fastest-growing developmental disorder in the United States. Boys are nearly five times more likely than girls to have autism. While there is no medical detection or cure for autism, we are learning and understanding more about how to reach and teach autistic children in our classrooms (CDC, 2015). See table 2.2 (page 22) for information about these learners.

Table 2.1: Learning Disability

Learner Variations	Major Indicators and Characteristics	Teaching Strategies That Work	Gifts These Students Bring to the Classroom
• Three categories of LD diagnosis are (1) writing, (2) reading, and (3) mathematics.	• Inability to follow directions and stay on task. • Trouble with reading (phonics, vocabulary, and rhyming), writing, or both.	Good for all learners: • Use graphic organizers. • Provide explicit instruction of strategies.	Early identification helps students succeed. These students may possess: • Great leadership skills • Deep-thinking skills

Learner Variations	Major Indicators and Characteristics	Teaching Strategies That Work	Gifts These Students Bring to the Classroom
• Types of SLD: perceptual disabilities, brain injury, minimal brain dysfunction, dyslexia, and developmental aphasia	• Slow to learn connections between letters and sounds • Frequent spelling errors • Reverse letter sequences • Trouble with mathematics skills • Difficulty remembering • Slow recall of facts • Problems paying attention • Poor coordination • Difficulty with concepts related to time • Problems staying organized • Impulsive behavior • Inappropriate responses in school or social situations • Difficulty staying on task (easily distracted) • Difficulty finding the right way to say something • Inconsistent school performance • Immature way of speaking • Difficulty following directions • Problems dealing with new situations • Problems understanding words or concepts	• Have students work with peers or in pairs. • Teach to different learning styles. • Teach self-responsibility. • Use alternative assessments and self-assessment. • Teach and practice a growth mindset. <u>Specific to this learner:</u> • Use feedback indicators. • Evaluate effort rather than performance. • Set short-term goals rather than long-term goals. • Create a comfortable environment. • Use visual and auditory cues. • Place students in small groups, or use one-on-one instruction. **One thing to remember is . . . build success.**	• Creativity • Intelligence • Elaborate coping mechanisms

Students with emotional and behavior disorders can create great challenges for us in our classrooms. IDEA (2004) defines a behavior disorder as:

A condition exhibiting one or more of the following characteristics over a long period of time and to a marked degree that adversely affects a child's educational performance:

• An inability to learn that cannot be explained by intellectual, sensory, or health factors

- An inability to build or maintain satisfactory interpersonal relationships with peers and teachers

- Inappropriate types of behavior or feelings under normal circumstances

- A general pervasive mood of unhappiness or depression

- A tendency to develop physical symptoms or fears associated with personal or school factors

Table 2.2: Autism Spectrum Disorder

Learner Variations*	Major Indicators and Characteristics	Teaching Strategies That Work	Gifts These Students Bring to the Classroom
• Spectrum ranges from students with Asperger's syndrome to those with severe autism	• Unresponsive to people • Perseverant • Difficulty making eye contact • Difficulty interpreting emotions • Delayed speech acquisition • Repetitive self-stimulation movements • Unusually low or high sensitivity to pain, noise, light, or crowds • Flat or singsongy voice • Sensitivity to sensory stimuli	Good for all learners: • Use graphic organizers. • Provide explicit instruction of strategies. • Have students work with peers or in pairs. • Teach to different learning styles. • Teach self-responsibility. • Use alternative assessments and self-assessment. • Teach and practice a growth mindset. Specific to this learner: • Use nonverbal communication techniques. • Allow for sensory breaks if needed. • Establish eye contact before speaking to the student. • Use applied behavior analysis. • Teach social stories to help the student respond to social situations. • Allow extra time to process. **One thing to remember is . . . set a schedule and routines.**	These students: • Can be very knowledgeable of specific topics • Are honest • Rarely judge others • Are not tied to social expectations • Are less materialistic • Have fewer hidden agendas

*With the May 2013 publication of the *DSM-5 Diagnostic Manual* (American Psychiatric Association, 2013), all autism disorders were merged into one umbrella diagnosis of ASD.

Students who come to us with behavioral challenges can create major challenges in our classrooms, so we need to create a stable and nurturing learning environment where they feel safe and can learn more effectively. See table 2.3 for more information on these learners.

Table 2.3: Behavior Disorder

Learner Variations	Major Indicators and Characteristics	Teaching Strategies That Work	Gifts These Students Bring to the Classroom
• Oppositional or defiant • Depressed • Conduct disordered • Schizophrenic • Affective disordered • Anxiety disordered	• Behaviors that interfere with the development and maintenance of reciprocal, positive, and nurturing relationships • Extremely disruptive or extremely withdrawn • Impulsive • Disregards the rules or is aggressive • Tendency to blame others • Low self-esteem • No regard for personal space or belongings • Low affect or depression • Attachment difficulties • Excessive behaviors like crying, sleeping, or eating • Self-injurious	Good for all learners: • Use graphic organizers. • Provide explicit instruction of strategies. • Have students work with peers or in pairs. • Teach to different learning styles. • Teach self-responsibility. • Use alternative assessments and self-assessment. • Teach and practice a growth mindset. Specific to this learner: • Conduct a functional behavioral assessment (FBA) to identify the motivation behind the behavior, and then introduce a positive replacement behavior. • Reinforce positive behavior. • Delay consequences. • Remain calm. • Help the student develop a self-management plan. • Role-play appropriate behaviors. • Use proactive cues before a behavior escalates. • Have consistent expectations. **One thing to remember is . . . teach self-management and coping skills.**	These students: • Are often highly intelligent • Are passionate • May be great helpers • Are empathetic

Academically gifted and talented students make up approximately 6–10 percent of the total student population in the United States, which means three to five million students nationally (National Association for Gifted Children, n.d.). Gifted students differ from typical students in terms of their learning styles, the depth and complexity of their understanding, and their potential. You may not think of gifted students as challenging to teach; however, if we don't provide the challenge and support they need, our gifted students may not, and often don't, thrive in our classrooms. Most gifted students receive the majority of their education in a regular classroom, taught by teachers who have not been trained to teach high-ability students. If we are going to truly challenge gifted learners, we must understand who they are and what they need in our classrooms. Table 2.4 has more information on these learners and shows the six domains of giftedness in the far-left column. For more information and indicators in each specific domain of giftedness, see the Malone Family Foundation website (www.malonefamilyfoundation.org/whatisgifted_identify.html).

Table 2.4: Gifted

Learner Variations	Major Indicators and Characteristics	Teaching Strategies That Work	Gifts These Students Bring to the Classroom
Students may have: • General intellectual ability • Specific academic ability • Creativity and productivity • Leadership ability • Talent in visual and performing arts • Psychomotor ability	• High achievement in domain of giftedness • Expression of spontaneous natural abilities without training • Is among top 4 percent of peers in their domain of giftedness • Highly curious • Highly self-critical • Skills developed long before peers in area of giftedness • Intensely focused on passions • Nuances of language and large vocabulary • Use of abstract ideas and concepts • Loves to learn new things	Good for all learners: • Use graphic organizers. • Provide explicit instruction of strategies. • Have students work with peers or in pairs. • Teach to different learning styles. • Teach self-responsibility. • Use alternative assessments and self-assessment. • Teach and practice a growth mindset. Specific to this learner: • Establish high standards and challenging content. • Allow for preferences. • Have a faster pace of instruction. • Create a flexible classroom environment. • Provide open-ended learning opportunities. • Offer independent projects. **One thing to remember is . . . provide appropriate challenges.**	These students have: • Unique thoughts and perspectives • Abilities to learn quickly • Unusual talents in art or music • Unique and clever solutions and ideas • A compassionate outlook about the world They bring: • Encouragement for others to find their gifts • Talent to the school environment in the domain of giftedness

Twice-exceptional students are atypical learners who have obvious areas of high intelligence but who also exhibit learning problems. Some examples of twice-exceptional learners include Alexander Graham Bell, who struggled in school and was likely dyslexic, and Temple Grandin, who is autistic. Twice-exceptional students (and often their teachers) assume that learning tasks will be easy, so they are not prepared for the learning difficulty that arises from activities in the areas of their disability. For example, they may intellectually be able to grasp a concept at a very high level, but their dysgraphia prevents them from being able to articulate their high-level thinking in writing. This leads to frustration, tension, and fear that may eventually become defensiveness. When working with twice-exceptional learners in the classroom, we need to remember to nurture and honor students' strengths while also remediating their areas of weakness or deficit. Table 2.5 has more information on these learners.

Table 2.5: Twice Exceptional

Learner Variations	Major Indicators and Characteristics	Teaching Strategies That Work	Gifts These Students Bring to the Classroom
• Gifted and learning disabled • Gifted with ADD or ADHD • Gifted with a behavioral disorder • Gifted with autism • Gifted with English as a second language	• Is gifted and has a learning difference • Giftedness masks special needs or vice versa • Tasks too easy or too difficult • Often labeled as lazy	<u>Good for all learners:</u> • Use graphic organizers. • Provide explicit instruction of strategies. • Have students work with peers or in pairs. • Teach to different learning styles. • Teach self-responsibility. • Use alternative assessments and self-assessment. • Teach and practice a growth mindset. <u>Specific to this learner:</u> • Focus on making realistic goals. • Focus on ability and strengths. • Accommodate strengths and gifts. • Accommodate weaknesses and disabilities. • Provide direct instruction. • Address social and emotional issues. • Address behavior issues. **One thing to remember is . . . nurture the strength, and remediate the weakness.**	These students are: • Talented and different • Great role models for growth mindsets, similar to Albert Einstein, Thomas Edison, Walt Disney, and Winston Churchill

A cognitive impairment is characterized by lack of development in the cognitive domain. Students with a cognitive impairment may experience difficulties with various functions of the brain, such as short-term memory, concentration, planning, and making decisions. Children with a cognitive impairment can be successful in school and lead fulfilling lives. They will need individualized help in learning new skills. Extra time, repeated instruction, and appropriate modeling will help them as they master important life skills. Each student who comes to our classrooms with a cognitive impairment will have different levels of challenges and needs and will require various support mechanisms, so we must be patient and take time to understand who these students are and find out how to support them. See table 2.6 for more information about these learners.

ADHD is one of the most common childhood disorders we see in our classrooms. The average age of onset is seven years old. The challenges of ADHD can continue through adolescence and into adulthood. ADHD affects about 4.1 percent of American adults age eighteen and older in a given year. The disorder affects 9 percent of American children ages thirteen to eighteen. Boys are four times more at risk than girls (National Institute of Mental Health, n.d.). Scientists are not sure what causes ADHD, but it probably results from a combination of factors. Researchers are looking at how genetics, environmental factors, brain injuries, nutrition, and the social environment might contribute to ADHD. Most students with ADD and ADHD can bloom and be successful in the classroom as they grow to understand their own learning needs and as we teach using methods that support their learning styles. Table 2.7 (page 28) shows information about these learners.

We are at a cultural tipping point in America. Trends in immigration and birth rates indicate that soon there will be no majority racial or ethnic group in the United States—no one group that makes up more than 50 percent of the total population (Crouch, 2012). The percentage of public school students in the United States who were English learners in 2011–2012 was 9.1 percent, or an estimated 4.4 million students, which is an increase from 2002–2003, which had 8.7 percent English learners, or an estimated 4.1 million students (U.S. Department of Education, 2014). As more and more students come to us from other countries and cultures, they will require specialized or modified instruction in both the English language and in their academic courses, so it's imperative that we learn to meet their needs in our classrooms. Table 2.8 (page 29) shows information about these learners.

More than sixteen million children in the United States—22 percent of all children in the United States—live in families with incomes below the federal poverty level: $23,550 a year for a family of four (National Center for Children in Poverty, n.d.). Students who come from economically disadvantaged families often have a very difficult time succeeding in school. Many face emotional and social instability. Young children need healthy learning and exploration to develop healthy brains. Children raised in impoverished homes often lack the physical and intellectual stimulation and the emotional stability their brains need. This lack of early stimulation can lead to poor school performance and behavior on the children's part. One of the most unfortunate results of their economic struggles is that students who live in poverty often drop out of school. Education, and therefore teachers, provides their best hope for escaping a bleak future. Table 2.9 (page 30) shows information about these students.

Table 2.6: Cognitive Impairment

Learner Variations	Major Indicators and Characteristics	Teaching Strategies That Work	Gifts These Students Bring to the Classroom
• Mild cognitive impairment (IQ of 50 to 70) • Moderate cognitive impairment (IQ of 35 to 55) • Severe cognitive impairment (IQ of 20 to 40) • Profound cognitive impairment (IQ below 20) • Can be caused by birth trauma or head injury	• IQ of less than 70 • Lack of appropriate self-care or self-help skills • Difficulty understanding social cues • Short attention span • Easily distracted by stimuli • Trouble retrieving newly learned information • Difficulty with multistep instructions • Difficulty exercising prudent judgment	<u>Good for all learners:</u> • Use graphic organizers. • Provide explicit instruction of strategies. • Have students work with peers or in pairs. • Teach to different learning styles. • Teach self-responsibility. • Use alternative assessments and self-assessment. • Teach and practice a growth mindset. <u>Specific to this learner:</u> • Use a visual system of assessment. • Use nonlinguistic representations. • Use scaffolding. • Work with manipulatives. • Reward achievement. • Use clear, simple language and directions. • Give clear objectives. • Give regular feedback. • Slowly pace language and directions. • Repeat directions. • Repeat practice of lessons and learning. **One thing to remember is . . . provide modified expectations and achievable goals.**	These students are: • Enthusiastic • Hard working • Joyful and affectionate • Innocent • Easy to please In addition, they: • Have a desire to help • Provide an opportunity for others to learn compassion

Table 2.7: ADD or ADHD

Learner Variations	Major Indicators and Characteristics	Teaching Strategies That Work	Gifts These Students Bring to the Classroom
• Predominantly hyperactive-impulsive • Predominantly inattentive • Combined hyperactive-impulsive and inattentive	• Inattentiveness • Is easily distracted by available objects • Inattention to details • Forgetfulness • Frequently switching from one activity to another • Difficulty in organizing and completing a task • Trouble completing or turning in homework assignments • Loss of possessions often • Struggles to follow instructions and directions • Hyperactivity • Trouble sitting still—fidgeting and squirming in seat • Talkativeness • Difficulty with quiet tasks or activities • Impulsiveness • Impatience • Inappropriate comments • Emotions without restraint • Actions without regard for consequences	<u>Good for all learners:</u> • Use graphic organizers. • Provide explicit instruction of strategies. • Have students work with peers or in pairs. • Teach to different learning styles. • Teach self-responsibility. • Use alternative assessments and self-assessment. • Teach and practice a growth mindset. <u>Specific to this learner:</u> • Use behavior intervention. • Give medication when necessary. • Help with organization. • Work on difficult tasks early in the day. • Do not assume laziness. • Provide a quiet area or noise-reduction head phones. • Give them the skills to move without distracting others. • Give lessons in smaller chunks. **One thing to remember is . . . one task at a time, and allow movement.**	These students have: • Creativity • Intuition • Energy • The ability to see the big picture • Innovation • Optimism • Insightfulness

Table 2.8: English Learner

Learner Variations	Major Indicators and Characteristics	Teaching Strategies That Work	Gifts These Students Bring to the Classroom
• Newly arrived students with adequate formal schooling • Newly arrived students with limited formal schooling • Students exposed to two languages simultaneously • Long-term English learners	• Is not fluent in English • Non-native speaker • English not the primary language at home • Is less proficient in English than grade-level peers • Lack of academic language (vocabulary and structures) in reading and writing • Difficulty understanding language that is decontextualized (about another time, place, or abstractions in general) • Near-native proficiency with errors that do not affect the meaning of communication	<u>Good for all learners:</u> • Use graphic organizers. • Provide explicit instruction of strategies. • Have students work with peers or in pairs. • Teach to different learning styles. • Teach self-responsibility. • Use alternative assessments and self-assessment. • Teach and practice a growth mindset. <u>Specific to this learner:</u> • Keep the environment engaging and motivating. • Encourage all attempts and approximations. • Give explicit instruction in vocabulary and language structures. • Provide opportunities for students to feel safe to attempt language. • Provide opportunities to build relationships with adults and peers (cooperative learning). • Prepare students for social interactions to assist with acculturation. • State expectations clearly. • Rephrase, repeat, or paraphrase what you want students to understand. • Get students talking. Have them speak to a prompt, paraphrase, respond to others, and clarify ideas. • Provide extended opportunities to practice until mastery. **One thing to remember is . . . keep the environment engaging and motivating.**	These students bring: • Different cultural perspectives to create a more global classroom • Joyfulness and creativity These students: • Want to belong • Can learn • May be gifted • May be learning disabled • May be twice exceptional

Table 2.9: Students in Poverty

Learner Variations	Major Indicators and Characteristics	Teaching Strategies That Work	Gifts These Students Bring to the Classroom
• Situational poverty • Generational poverty • Absolute poverty • Relative poverty • Rural poverty • Urban poverty	• Disorganization • Missing homework • Is the center of attention • Only parts of an assignment completed • Laughter at inappropriate times and in inappropriate situations • Trouble with reasoning • Trouble with authority • Verbal defiance • Lack of procedural self-talk (get started or continue to work) • Rude behavior • Lack of goal-setting ability	<u>Good for all learners:</u> • Use graphic organizers. • Provide explicit instruction of strategies. • Have students work with peers or in pairs. • Teach to different learning styles. • Teach self-responsibility. • Use alternative assessments and self-assessment. • Teach and practice a growth mindset. <u>Specific to this learner:</u> • Give opportunities to build relationships. (Students will do work if they like you.) • Link to student experiences, or create the experience for them. • Use choice and discussion as a vehicle for learning. • Provide opportunities to see the big picture and connections. • Provide a cooperative versus a competitive environment. • Use praise and positive reinforcement. **One thing to remember is … build trusting relationships.**	These students: • Are great storytellers • Have a unique sense of humor • Add to discussions • Have creative responses • Are independent • Speak their minds freely

During your teaching career, you will most likely have students from each of these groups in your classroom. The more you understand about students with unique needs, the less you will find yourself blaming the lettuce for being lazy, unmotivated, or behaviorally problematic. Once you truly understand that an unchallenged gifted learner may well act out in your classroom out of frustration from boredom and that a learning disabled student is not lazy, that he or she can learn effectively if provided the necessary time and support he or she needs, you will be able to help these students achieve success.

As noted in the introduction, this book provides you with tools and teaching techniques to help you transform your classroom into a place that honors and supports the learning needs of all students in a way that is doable and manageable. The charts in this chapter provide you with a simple overview to help you get the big picture of these learners. If you find yourself blaming the lettuce and really struggling to understand a particular student with a learning challenge or you would like more information about that student or any of the students described in the charts, visit the following websites. These are some of the top websites educators and parents use, and they can be valuable tools to help you understand the special needs learners in your classroom.

Top Websites for Getting More In-Depth Knowledge About Unique Learners

The following sites are some of the best we've found for getting quality information about the different types of unique learners we reference in this book.

Learning Disability

- LD OnLine: www.ldonline.org
- National Center for Learning Disabilities (NCLD): www.ncld.org

Autism Spectrum Disorder

- National Autism Center (NAC): www.nationalautismcenter.org
- TeachersFirst: www.teachersfirst.com
- Autism NOW: http://autismnow.org

Behavior Disorder

- Child Mind Institute: www.childmind.org
- Council for Exceptional Children: www.cec.sped.org

Gifted

- National Association for Gifted Children (NAGC): www.nagc.org
- Hoagies Gifted: www.hoagiesgifted.org

Twice Exceptional

- Hoagies' Gifted: www.hoagiesgifted.org
- Malone Family Foundation: www.malonefamilyfoundation.org/whatisgifted_identify .html

Cognitive Impairment

- American Association on Intellectual and Developmental Disabilities (AAIDD): www .aaidd.org
- Siskin Children's Institute: www.siskin.org
- Centers for Disease Control and Prevention (CDC): www.cdc.gov

Continued →

ADD or ADHD

- Children and Adults With Attention-Deficit/Hyperactivity Disorder (CHADD): www.chadd.org
- Attention Deficit Disorder Association (ADDA): www.add.org
- ADDitude: www.additudemag.com

English Learner

- Colorín Colorado: www.colorincolorado.org
- Using English (UE): www.usingenglish.com
- EverythingESL: www.everythingesl.net

Students in Poverty

- aha! Process: www.ahaprocess.com
- National Center for Children in Poverty (NCCP): www.nccp.org

Overall

- National Association of Special Education Teachers (NASET): www.naset.org

chapter *Three*

Adopting Apprenticeship Learning

*Mentors and apprentices are partners in an ancient human dance,
and one of teaching's great rewards is the daily chance it gives
us to get back on the dance floor. It is the dance of the spiraling
generations, in which the old empower the young with their
experience and the young empower the old with new life, reweaving
the fabric of the human community as they touch and turn.*

—Parker J. Palmer

All heroes have mentors who support them on their journey. Luke Skywalker was an apprentice to Yoda, Bilbo Baggins to Gandalf, and Harry Potter to Dumbledore. An apprentice gets information, guidance, and tasks to practice from the mentor until he or she has mastered a skill and is ready to take on the task alone.

We are mentors to our students. An important part of our role as mentors is to teach them skills and strategies they need to succeed in school and in life. Each section in this chapter is devoted to showing you the *how* of good teaching. These are the teaching actions that lead to successful learning—teaching that teaches students *how* to learn. In today's 21st century classrooms, teaching our students *how* to learn is as important as teaching them *what* to learn.

The way you teach makes all the difference in how students learn new skills. These three teaching actions are the cornerstone for teaching the six learning foundations you will find in chapters 4–9. Using these three teaching actions will allow you to gradually release responsibility for learning from you to your students, thus ensuring that they become masters of their learning.

The three steps to apprenticeship learning, shown in figure 3.1 (page 34), are (1) be intentional and transparent, (2) model and scaffold, and (3) use deliberate repeated practice.

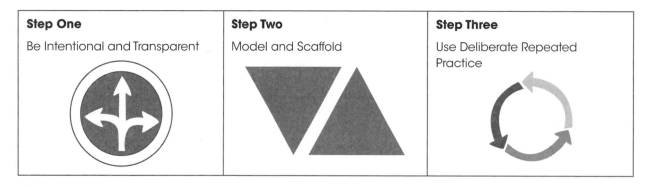

Step One	Step Two	Step Three
Be Intentional and Transparent	Model and Scaffold	Use Deliberate Repeated Practice

Figure 3.1: Three steps of apprenticeship learning.

Step One: Be Intentional and Transparent

 When we are intentional and transparent about learning goals, we learn *with* our students, rather than teaching at them. When we make our instructional strategies and our learning targets clear and visible, we provide our students with a pathway to success and make sure they know why the risk of working hard is worth taking on the challenge.

What It Means

Being intentional refers to the level of clarity a teacher has about *why* students are learning something, *how* his or her students learn, and *what* students will know and be able to do. When we are intentional, we begin with the end in mind. Beginning with the end in mind helps us plan focused instruction with formative checks for understanding along the way so students can successfully reach the destination. When we know exactly what we want students to understand, know, and be able to do by the end of our lessons and units, it drives clear instruction and allows us to effectively differentiate as needed.

Transparent teaching is when we share our intentional plans with our students. We tell students what they need to understand and know and what skills they will be developing in a lesson or a unit. Perhaps most importantly, we tell them *why* the ideas and strategies are important. We also explain to them *why* we teach the way we teach and help them understand how they are learning and how they learn best. Transparent teaching allows us to teach *with* our students—not teach *at* them. Transparent teaching invites students into the learning process by providing clarity of objectives. With a clear understanding of the lesson's objectives and instructional practices, teachers and students are better able to determine which skills and strategies to use and focus on in moving toward a common destination.

What the Research Says

We have all heard more times than we can count, usually in a whiny tone, "Why do we have to learn this?" or "When am I ever going to use this?" When students ask these questions, they are asking us to be intentional and transparent with them. Connie Moss and Susan Brookhart (2009) and others (Seidel, Rimmele, & Prenzel, 2005; Stiggins, Arter, Chappuis, & Chappuis, 2007) document that clarifying a lesson's intention is one of the most important things we can do for our students. Without a precise description of where they are headed, too many students are flying blind; they can't hit learning targets they can't see.

Perhaps the most compelling reason to share the why of learning comes from the work of Simon Sinek (2009b), staff member for one of the world's most highly regarded think tanks, the RAND Corporation. He explains through his golden circle analogy that the human brain is wired at its core to need to know why (see figure 3.2). Through analysis of various parts of the brain, he shows us that the limbic system is where decision making occurs. It drives human behavior and is what some might call *gut instinct*. But indeed, it is not the gut; it is the most primal part of our brain, and it seeks to know why. In his words, "The golden circle is grounded in the biology of human decision making and is changing how leaders and companies think and act" (Sinek, 2009a).

Figure 3.2: The human brain is wired to need to know why.

When we share the why of our lessons, we speak to the part of the brain that drives behavior. When students know the why, they are more willing to trust us and take on the risk-taking behavior that new learning requires because we have thoughtfully designed meaningful lessons that will empower them in the future. Knowing the why inspires them to try. As Sinek (2009a) says, "Those who know their why are the ones who lead. They are the ones who inspire."

How to Do It

The following are guidelines for helping you grow your skills at teaching intentionally and transparently.

Be Intentional: Know Your Why, How, and What

Knowing the why, how, and what of your lessons and units will help you discern what students need to *learn* versus what they need to *do*. Our lessons are sometimes driven by activities and not outcomes. If we follow Sinek's (2009a) advice, we want to begin with the *why* of the golden circle. The deeper understanding comes at the why level, the intentional and transparent level, of our instruction. Once our why is clear, we can focus on how students will be learning.

So, first, we need to share with students why they are learning something; then, how they will be learning that day; and, finally, what they will be learning or practicing in that particular lesson. This structure speaks to the deep motivational centers of the brain. Without this clarity, we too often just tell students what they will be doing in class, and they never know why it's important or what it looks like when they've mastered it. Use the template in table 3.1 to guide you as you think through your lesson, starting from clear learning targets that address why students are learning something (purpose), how they will be learning (modalities and groupings), and what they will be learning (knowledge and skills) by the end of the day's lesson.

Table 3.1: Planned Targets for Why, How, and What Students Are Learning

Target	Example
Why Why is this important to learn?	We are learning the different ways to greet people in Spanish. This is important because there are different ways to greet friends (familiar) and strangers (formal) in Spanish. Knowing the difference is important for interacting and will make you socially appropriate and not seem rude or uneducated.
How How will students practice this skill today?	To practice different greetings today, you will circulate around the classroom and look at cards different people present. You will choose the appropriate greeting based on whom you are talking to.
What What will students learn to do?	In order to be socially appropriate, you need to know what phrases different groups of people use.

Be Transparent: Tell Students the Why, How, and What of the Day's Lesson

It's important to write the learning objective on the board, but in age-appropriate, student-friendly language, and start your lesson each day by explaining the learning targets. Students don't care much about covering a particular standard, but they will get curious and start to wonder when they enter the room with a board that says, "Why and how did the world change forever after the invention of the telephone?" and then see an old-fashioned rotary phone on your desk.

The Framework for Explaining the Why and What of Learning Targets

We know it may seem unnecessary to create a framework for transparently articulating learning objectives to our students, but we have found that using this framework for learning targets helps us design our lessons with the *why* in mind and be completely transparent with our students. (See the learning target talk frameworks reproducible in the appendix, page 167.) Here's an example of how transparency sounds when we switch to leading with the why, how, and what:

"Today, we are learning Spanish greetings and leave-takings." (Can you hear the kids' voices saying, "Why?" "How come?" "Who cares?")

Switch that to:

"Today, we are learning the formal and informal greetings and leave-takings in Spanish. It is important to know because it will increase your social proficiency, and people who speak Spanish will respect you more because you are using greetings that make the correct social connection. You will know you got it when you are practicing with a friend and can listen and respond with the correct form of greeting or leave-taking and when you speak to Spanish speakers and see the delight in their eyes when you address them correctly."

Aha! Students now know *why* this is important, *how* they will be practicing, and exactly *what* they should know and be able to do. The intentional and transparent framework looks like this:

"It is important to [<u>INSERT SHORT EXPLANATION</u>] because [<u>REASON</u>]. Today, we will be practicing by [<u>HOW THEY WILL LEARN</u>]. You know you've got it when you can [<u>INSERT KNOWLEDGE AND SKILLS AS MEASURABLE TARGETS</u>].

Here are some other examples. The first is from elementary literacy instruction, and the second is a high school grammar example:

"It is important as readers to visualize in our minds what we are reading because it helps us make sure we understand what we are reading. Today, we will be practicing visualizing by using our whiteboards and jotting down images that we 'see' in our mind's eye when we listen to a story. You know you've got it when you can listen to a story, see pictures in your mind, and then explain to a friend what your pictures mean and how visualizing helped you understand."

"It is important to understand how grammar empowers how people perceive you and how well your message is understood. People are often judged by their grammar usage and if it is appropriate for the situation. It can be important to know the correct grammar to use with different groups to make sure people take your opinion seriously, people respect what you have to say, or people connect with how you present your ideas. Grammar gives you power to connect and be heard. Today, we are going to study models of grammar and rank their levels of formality and their objective tones. You will be working in your core groups to discuss your rankings, and be prepared to share your ideas with other core groups. You know you've got it when you can determine grammar structures that are more and less formal and distinguish grammar structures that are more objective from those that are more subjective. We have some new vocabulary terms, so let's do a quick preassessment to see what we might already know about these four key terms: formal, informal, objective, and subjective."

Note that as you move through the unit, the learning targets for the *why* and *what* of your lesson will stay the same for several days as students explore, connect, and revisit their learning. While these learning targets stay steady, *how* we do the learning will vary depending on what we ask students to do each day.

The Framework for Explaining the How of the Learning Process

Use the following framework for explaining the how of the learning process:

> *"To learn this important concept or idea, we are going to _____ in _____."*

For example:

> *"To learn this, we are going to <u>first recite phrases</u> in <u>whole groups</u>."*

In the next section, you will see a vignette of a teacher whose learning goals for why and what remain the same over several days. She revisits them daily at the beginning of each lesson, eventually drawing students into being responsible for knowing the why and what of their learning. Over several days, her goals for how will change based on what students will be doing each day to reach their learning goals.

Day One

Introduce the why and what of learning:

> *"Today, we are learning formal and informal greetings and leave-takings in Spanish. It is important to know because it will increase your social proficiency, and people who speak Spanish will respect you more because you are using greetings that make the correct social connection. You will know you got it when you are practicing with a friend and can listen and respond with the correct form of greeting or leave-taking and when you speak to a Spanish speaker and see the delight in his or her eyes when you use the correct address."*

Introduce the how of learning:

> *"To learn this important concept or idea, we are going to listen in a whole group to develop our ear for the sounds of greetings and leave-takings, and we are going to speak in a whole group to practice in a sea of voices so it's safe to make mistakes. Then you are going to use flash cards in partners to practice, practice, practice formal and informal greetings and leave-takings. Let's get started."*

Day Two

Return to the why and what:

> *"We are learning the formal and informal greetings and leave-takings in Spanish. We know it's important because it will increase your social proficiency, and you will get more respect from people because you know the difference in using casual or formal structures. Today, you will know you got it when you can listen to a conversation and identify if people are using formal or informal greetings and*

when you speak to a Spanish speaker and see the delight in his or her eyes when you use the correct address."

Explain the how and who for the day:

"To learn today, we are going to listen to a conversation between two native speakers. You will work independently to make notes about what greetings you hear. Then you will work in your core groups to compare your notes and discuss if the people are friends or strangers based on what you heard."

Day Three

On day three, you can bring in student ownership by asking the students what the learning targets are:

Teacher: *Kevin, what are we learning this week?*

Kevin: *Greetings and leave-takings.*

Teacher: *Good. Can anyone add to that?*

Dan: *Formal and informal ways to say hello and good-bye.*

Teacher: *Yes. What is it called again when we say hello and good-bye?*

Brendan: *Ooh, oh . . . I got this one! Kevin just said it . . . greetings . . . and . . . uh, leave-takings!*

Teacher: *Yes! Now, why is this important to know?*

Sarah: *Because people will respect you.*

Teacher: *Yes, and why will they respect you?*

Lexi: *Because you are using the right one for the right person, and that shows respect.*

Teacher: *Right on, Lexi. And you want to be respected, right? Who doesn't want to be respected?*

Then explain the how of the day's lesson:

"OK, we know our targets. To practice today, we are going to show what we know in writing. You will know you got it when you can fill in the blanks of a conversation that happens at a grocery store using the correct formal or informal greeting or leave-taking."

Teacher Check for Intentional and Transparent Instruction

A way to see if you are really being intentional and transparent in your instruction is to try this check-in with students. As students are working quietly, go to individual students, and ask them what we are learning and why it's important. Then listen and notice if their responses are focused on just what they are *doing* or if they can also explain *why* they are *learning* it. See the examples in table 3.2 (page 40) to note the difference in student responses when you've transparently taught from your why.

Table 3.2: Doing Versus Learning

Doing	Learning
1. We are doing a KWL (know, want to know, learned) chart.	1. We are thinking about what we already know and what we predict because good readers predict and ask questions.
2. We are making graphic organizers for our project.	2. We are connecting our thoughts and ideas to increase our understanding.
3. We are making spiders for Halloween.	3. We are learning about the differences between spiders and insects.
4. We are writing stories about our families.	4. I am using a mentor text to help me write a lead for my story because I want to write like my favorite author.
5. We are filling in missing parts of a conversation.	5. I am practicing formal and informal leave-taking so I can get respect when I speak Spanish.
6. We are doing mathematics problems.	6. I am learning how to use the Pythagorean theorem to find the length of the side of a triangle.

Jot down the names of students who do not have a clear focus on the why of a learning target. When you start your lesson the next day, use this list to give those students more clarity on the *why* of your learning targets or to hold them accountable for knowing *why* they are learning, not just what they are doing in class by asking them to explain *what* they are learning and *why*. You may want to set them up for success by asking them to review the clear learning targets you have posted on the board and tell them they will be responsible for explaining them to the class. Give them a few minutes to read, think, and talk with peers. The more the learning brain knows why, the more it is willing to do.

When we teach *with* our students, not *at* them, when we bring them into the learning targets with us, we empower them to make their own decisions about how hard they will work, whether the effort is worth the challenge, if they are going to ask for help within their community of learners, and how resilient they will be when learning becomes challenging. It shifts our teaching from stand-and-deliver to inviting students into and taking charge of their learning. That's the difference between teaching *with* your students and teaching *at* them. We become partners and advocates in their learning when we are transparent about learning targets. You can be transparent with students about the following.

- Why something is important to learn (why)
- What students will know (knowledge)
- What students will be able to do (skills)
- How they learn (learning modalities) (You will find ideas for teaching about how students learn in chapter 12 and also in Kathleen and Alicia's *Inspiring Learners* books [Kryza, Duncan, & Stephens, 2007, 2009].)
- Why we are using a specific strategy (brain research)
- How to get closer to a learning target (growth mindsets)

- How a lesson will help them in their current life (why)

- How a lesson will help them in future success (academic)

- How a lesson will help them with friends and family (social and emotional)

- How a lesson will help them be more culturally adept (culture)

Step Two: Model and Scaffold

When we model and scaffold, we are providing the small steps and supports that grow successful learners (Kryza, Duncan, & Stephens, 2010). When our students fail to thrive in our classrooms, we don't blame them; we look at how modeling and scaffolding can support their growth toward next steps for success.

What It Means

Think of a child learning to ride a bike. First, she spends time riding on the back of bikes with adults who love her. She feels the freedom and pleasure of riding a bike. She has opportunities to watch adults model the behavior and talk through the actions required to mount, pedal, steer, and break a bike. After modeling of the skill, the child will begin by practicing on a bike that has training wheels. She gets immediate feedback as she is supported in her first attempts. As the child grows more proficient, the training wheels are raised up. How perfect! The child is nearing the ability to balance alone, but if she tips just a little too far, a scaffold is in place. She is ready to go on her own. The wheels are removed, but an adult still supports and steadies the first solo attempts until the child is in a flow of ability. The parent lets go, removes the training wheels, gives positive feedback, and watches the child ride off using her new skills. This is how we model and scaffold, apprenticing a child into learning a new life skill.

It is important that we also model and scaffold as we teach students the learning strategies they will need to succeed in our classrooms. Modeling is the explicit demonstration of a skill that students need to master in school, such as how to complete a task, how to take effective notes, how to think through a problem, or how to talk to a partner. Through modeling, the teacher creates an explicit example so that students can see and hear exactly what it is effective learners do to succeed at learning tasks. Remember, in today's classrooms, teaching our students how to learn is as important as teaching them what to learn.

Scaffolding is the gradual release of responsibility. For a student to master a new skill, it is not enough for him or her to see a teacher model it and then jump in and try it. It is as silly as "teaching" the dog in figure 3.3 (page 42). Imagine allowing a child to watch you ride a bike while you describe for him or her how to use the brakes and pedals and how to steer. Then you hand the child the bike and expect him or her to replicate your actions on first try. Ridiculous, right? But far too often as teachers, we move from modeling to independent practice. Scaffolding is the intentional teacher move of allowing students to practice little by little until they are able to give it a go alone.

Figure 3.3: Teaching versus learning.

What the Research Says

After modeling, a teacher will scaffold the new skill. During this time, students need a great deal of support. As the teacher sees that students are getting it, the teacher gradually removes the support to allow students to try their new skill independently (Pearson & Gallagher, 1983). When students have yet to develop skills or become masters of new learning, we must use the gradual release of responsibility model to help move them closer to proficiency in small, well-planned steps. This, Doug Buehl (2005) suggests, will allow our students to see themselves ascending closer to the clear learning targets that we have transparently explained to them. They will know what to look for as indicators of success that will help them continue the sometimes daunting task of being resilient in the classroom. The gradual release of responsibility model of instruction has been documented as an effective approach for improving writing achievement (Fisher & Frey, 2003), reading comprehension (Lloyd, 2004), and literacy outcomes for English learners (Kong & Pearson, 2003).

The six steps for explicit teaching, modeling, and scaffolding are as follows.

1. Set a purpose for learning. Explain why what you are teaching or demonstrating is important to know. (Be intentional and transparent!)

2. Model the specific skill. (I do it.)

   - Tell students what to do step by step: "Listen to the steps for . . ."

   - Show them step by step how to do it: "Now watch me . . ."

3. Practice the specific skill as a whole class. (We do it.)

4. The whole group practices with you. You initiate each step using questions while encouraging any student who is ready, chiming in as support. Continue with the whole-class "We do it" until many students participate.

5. Practice the specific skill in small groups. (You do it together.)

   - Stepping back from direct participation, you allow students to practice the task with the support of interdependent small groups (generally two to four students) while you monitor the proficiency of each group. If needed, go back to "I do it" or "We do it" if more support is needed.

6. Practice the specific skill individually. (You do it alone.)

    *   When small groups are proving successful, it is time to move to independent practice. Each student is using the skill independently while you are monitoring the work by observing students directly and later reviewing individual student work through logs, response journals, writing, sample problems, and so on. This is also the time to have students self-assess how they are doing.

Figure 3.4 shows the gradual release of responsibility process.

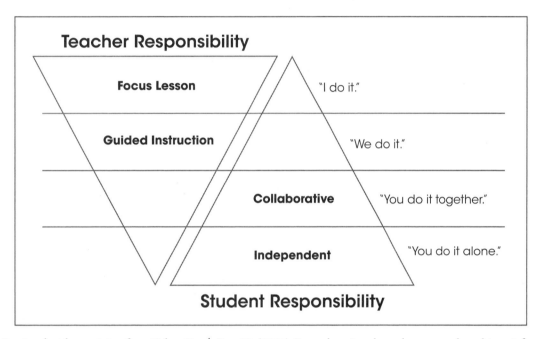

Source: Reprinted with permission from Fisher, D., & Frey, N. (2008). Better learning through structured teaching: A framework for the gradual release of responsibility. *Alexandria, VA: Association for Supervision and Curriculum Development.*

Figure 3.4: Gradual release of responsibility.

An Example: Modeling and Scaffolding Being Self-Reflective

When we are preparing to model and scaffold instruction as the second critical step of effective instruction, we need to think through these important steps.

*   Tell students what they are learning.

*   Explain why it is important (now, in the future, academically, socially, emotionally, or culturally).

*   Give a clear learning target: What will they be able to do when they've got it?

    "Today, we are going to be talking about reflecting. This skill is absolutely essential for anything you do, whether it's schoolwork, a craft or project, or even working with other people. When you reflect, you look back at your work and decide what

was working and what you would change if you did it again. You will know you've got it when you can look back at any project, situation, or conversation and analyze what was working and what needs to be done to improve it. I'm going to show you how I would reflect on my own work. Let's look at this paper that I wrote a long time ago when I was in college."

I Do It

After explaining the clear learning targets, the teacher begins the first scaffolding with I Do It to model what he or she wants the student to do. For example, the teacher could model what an effective reading practice is, the steps to complete a problem, or even how to think critically. Again, students can't hit targets they can't see. This is a time to let them see the learning made visible through your action. To begin the I Do It step, the teacher considers these actions.

- Allow students to see your work by any means possible (an overhead, an Elmo Touchboard, a SMART Board, or a chalkboard).

- Talk (think) aloud while working through the process.

- Explain what you are doing and why.

- Explain what you are thinking as you work.

- Go back to the purpose for learning, and reflect on whether your work meets the learning goal.

- Demonstrate the work.

> *"Let's look at this paper I wrote in college. As I read through it, I want you to listen as I look for what was working and what could be improved in my piece. (Teacher reads paper.) The first thing that stands out to me is the topic sentence is solid but boring. I really don't like the way that sounds now that we know so much more about strategies for writing solid and compelling topic sentences. I see it starts with the passive "There are," which I know isn't wrong, but I also know now that it's just bland writing and sets me up for using passive voice, which is not engaging for my reader. So the first thing I think I'll do to improve this piece is to write our Super Six topic sentences using the structures we've been studying (Greiner, 2012). This will stretch my thinking. I know it is a little more work, but I also know that my language gets more creative by going through the process. So I'll start there and then look for the topic sentence that has the most oomph!*

> *"Remember, our learning goal is to reflect on or look back at our writing to analyze what was working and what wasn't. Today, I looked at a piece of writing from my past and discovered what was working—good structure, strong evidence, personal experience—and what needed improvement—topic sentence, closing sentence, and variance in word choice for stronger writing."*

We Do It

We Do It is the next step in scaffolding. After students have witnessed you expertly and professionally model and talk through your thinking process, it is time to invite the whole class to participate *with* you. You are still leading the class through thinking through steps to a problem, but you are allowing students to participate based on what they have just observed. To move to the next step, We Do It, consider the following.

- Allow students to cocreate the work with you.

- Continue modeling while now asking for student participation. Ask students about their thinking based on what they have observed from the previous I Do It stage, where they witnessed strong models.

- Offer regular feedback.

  Teacher: *OK, yesterday you watched me model being self-reflective about a paper I wrote. Today, you are going to practice with me. I have a paper written by a student of mine last year. Let's pretend that this is a paper you wrote, and you are going to reflect with me on what's working and what could be improved. Let's start with the topic sentence. What do you notice about it?*

  Kevin: *It's a situation stance format.*

  Teacher: *Good noticing. Now, what do you think? Is it working, or would it need improvement?*

  Kevin: *I think it's good.*

  Teacher: *Right, it is. But what makes it good?*

  Kevin: *Well, he gives a really broad idea about how cultures all over are different; then he zooms in to tell you the two cultures in particular he is going to write about. So it's clear.*

  Teacher: *Any other ideas about this topic sentence?*

  Susie: *What transition word could he use to help make his topic sentence sound more sophisticated?*

  Kevin: *Ooooh . . . Good eye, Susie! That would definitely make this sentence stronger.*

You Do It Together—Group

Small groups are an essential step in release of responsibility because now peers, not the adult mentor, are supporting each other. As students learn new skills, there's likely to be someone in the group who has skills to help others, and this academic discourse of talking through ideas, reasoning, and explanations helps move the whole group forward.

- Increase student responsibility (as students demonstrate growing skills) by having them work together in small groups.

- Begin to diminish prompts and models.

  - Hold groups accountable for giving feedback.

  - Design checklists to help groups move through steps.

- Gradually increase complexity and difficulty of information.
- Gradually decrease student support.
  - When finished, share models of expert group work.

> *"Now that we have tried reflecting together as a whole class, it's time for you to work in your small groups to practice reflecting on your writing. Remember that Susie asked a probing question that pushed us to think and go deeper. But we also noticed that some people were not really giving specific examples in their reflection—you were being pretty general. 'It's good' doesn't tell why something's working or what's working and doesn't help the writer grow his or her skills. As you work in your small group, be aware of this, and try to ask each other to give a specific example of why it's working or why it's not. Now's your chance to help others go deeper."*

You Do It Together—Partner

Partners rely on one another, so paring down from group to partners allows an additional release of responsibility. Students still help one another, but they are more widely accountable because it is just two of them.

- Hold partners accountable for giving feedback.
- Use checklists to help partners move through steps.
- Give feedback to partners.
- Share models of expert groups.

> *"You are going to be working with your writing partner today to reflect on yesterday's homework. I'd like you to talk to your partner about how you feel you are doing. Your partner's job is to ask you questions to help you reflect deeper. Partners, you need to come up with the questions you want your partner to reflect on. Use your revision checklists to move through the steps. I'll be looking for some good models to share with the class."*

You Do It Alone

The last step in scaffolding is the step when students are ready for independent practice. Too often, we move too quickly from modeling to independent practice, and students have not yet mastered the skills they need to work independently. Scaffolds allow students to build the skills they need. To support students, teachers do the following:

- Provide independent practice.
- Provide extensive practice opportunities.
- Help students to apply and transfer the learning to new situations.

> *"OK, we've been practicing being more self-reflective as writers. I'm handing back yesterday's work, and I'd like you to write reflections about the work you've done on this 3 × 5 card. You might want to consider looking at the quality of your*

reflections or how your thinking has changed. For tonight's homework, I would like you to apply your reflecting skills to a new topic. I would like you to reflect on this question: 'How has reflecting helped you to become a better learner?' Yes, I get it. You are reflecting on reflecting!"

We can model and scaffold academic skills such as note taking, summarizing, or using the order of operations correctly. We can also model and scaffold social-emotional skills we want our students to develop, such as how to deal with frustration, or organizational skills, such as coming to class prepared. If we see that students are not getting behaviors, skills, or concepts that they need to succeed, we need to take the time to model and scaffold the skills we expect our students to use. Then we are setting our students up for success emotionally, culturally, and academically. The result is confident learners: students who accept responsibility for their learning and are capable of becoming independent learners.

Figure 3.5 offers a scaffolding planner for the release of responsibility model of instruction. Another version of a planner ("Planner for Gradual Release of Responsibility") appears on page 168 in the appendix.

Gradual Release of Responsibility	
Step	**Plan**
I do it. (Modeling)	
We do it. (Whole-class shared practice)	
You do it together. (Small-group practice)	
You do it together. (Partner practice)	
You do it alone. (Individual practice)	

Figure 3.5: Scaffolding planner.

*Visit **go.solution-tree.com/instruction** for a reproducible version of this figure.*

With the first two core instructional steps in place, communicating intentional and transparent learning goals and modeling and scaffolding, we are ready to look at the third critical step toward mastery: using deliberate repeated practice.

Step Three: Use Deliberate Repeated Practice

 Daniel, the main character (and hero) in the movie *The Karate Kid*, knew nothing about karate when he met his mentor, Mr. Miyagi. In the first few training sessions, Mr. Miyagi gave him a set of seemingly banal tasks (painting a fence, sanding a floor, and so on) to prepare him for the larger skills he would need to develop. Heroes aren't magically gifted; they hone and develop their skills through deliberate practice.

What It Means

Learning isn't always fun. Shocking, we know. Sometimes, it's just hard work. *Deliberate practice* is simply that: doing something several times in thoughtful ways with a goal of mastery. Being intentional and transparent and modeling and scaffolding instruction are the ways we introduce new ideas to our students. When it's time to really lock in the learning, then they need to know how to be deliberate in their practice.

What the Research Says

The concept of deliberate practice is not new by any means. In 1898, William Lowe Bryan and Noble Harter documented that mastery occurs after ten years of repeated practice (as cited in Hattie, 2012). We also see the work of Malcolm Gladwell (2008) who, in his book *Outliers: The Story of Success*, documents that expertise occurs after ten thousand hours of practice. Educators around the world are familiar with the book *Classroom Instruction That Works*, which determines homework and practice as one of the top-nine essential research-based strategies for improving student achievement (Marzano, Pickering, & Pollock, 2001).

Alicia's eighth-grade student Slava, a native Russian speaker studying Spanish as his third language, offers insight into the value of quality practice. Although only fourteen, he is wise beyond his years, and at times, Alicia has to interpret his deep ideas so his fellow classmates can connect. On the topic of repeated practice and developing skills, he alerted his classmates that "While practice could make perfection, it could also be your worst enemy if your practice is imperfect; you only perfect your imperfections" (Smirnov, 2012). What Slava wanted the other students to know is that if you practice something wrong, you only get better at doing it wrong! What he understood is that mastering a skill takes a fair amount of *focused* practice and reflection, not just skill-and-drill, mindless repetition. Self-assessment is critical in making deliberate practice effective (Ericsson, Krampe, & Tesch-Römer, 1993). Repetitive skill and drill is simply performing an action repeatedly without using the important thinking skills necessary to monitor and adjust practice. Students are engaged in deliberate practice when they are reflecting on their accuracy, noticing important details, analyzing their steps, using feedback, and making a plan for improved performance. As you read this chapter, you will see that this is where student self-assessment comes into play for making sure that students assess the deliberateness of their practice and make sure that practice equates with their growth.

Timing is another important aspect of deliberate repeated practice we need to consider as teachers. We need to think clearly about *when* our students are ready to move to deliberate practice. Unfortunately, Jane M. Healy (1999) reports that U.S. students tend to be engaged in a demanding practice stage before the shaping phase has occurred. In contrast, Japanese educators slowly introduce skills before deliberate practice. Healy (1999) notes:

> Whereas American second graders may spend thirty minutes on two or three pages of addition and subtraction equations, the Japanese are reported to be more likely at this level to use the same amount of time in examining two or three problems in depth, focusing on the reasoning process necessary to solve them. (p. 281)

If students are asked to enter the practice stage of learning before the shaping phase has occurred, they will not have enough background knowledge to do the important self-monitoring that will improve their practice (Healy, 1999).

How to Do It

To get your students to practice their skills mindfully and effectively, consider the following six steps for teaching students deliberate practice.

1. **Set learning goals:** Set a learning goal with your students. This is another time for using your skills for being intentional and transparent. The goal should not be about time or quantity of repetition but rather what skill students will master after practice. For example, it would sound like this in Alicia's Spanish class: "Today, we have studied the pattern for -*ar* verbs in the singular forms; after today's practice, you will be able to conjugate any regular -*ar* verb to match the pronouns yo, tú, él/ella/ud." Clearly defined learning goals allow students to engage effectively in the important practice of self-assessment.

2. **Plan:** Ensure that students have had enough instruction so that they can actually think through their deliberate practice. For example, you should not ask students to memorize any of their times tables before they really understand multiplication.

3. **Require attention:** Practice items should require students' mental engagement at higher levels of thinking to increase the skills required to lock in learning. Repetition that a student can do without thinking about the correct answer will not yield results. For example, if Alicia's learning goal in the previous example had students practice the verbs in order consistently, students would no longer have to think about which pronoun matches which verb form. Varying the tasks and activities helps students think about their learning.

4. **Give feedback:** Keep feedback timely and specific. The optimal time would be while students are practicing. This allows for taking advantage of just-in-time teaching that helps students continue moving ahead. Also, make sure feedback is corrective in nature; tell students how they did in relation to the specific learning goal. A simple "Nice job" doesn't

help a student see his or her learning progression. Specific feedback informs students of what they have mastered and what they need to do next, such as, "Marissa, I see you have the *yo* forms correct on your practice sheet, and with the *tú* form, there is only one error. See if you can find it and if you know how to correct it." Feedback is essential for mastery, and it has a motivating effect that helps students continue to exert effort in improving their skills.

5. **Allow for self-assessment:** It's also essential to teach students to self-assess and assess with their peers because you can't be the sole assessor of a large class of students, and even more important, learning to self-assess empowers students to make good practice plans and decisions when you are not around. (See chapter 8, page 101, on self-assessment.) Encourage students to lead a feedback session with a question such as, "So, what do you know you've mastered, and what do you need more practice with?" This is a great way to lead them into the last step.

6. **Determine next steps:** Self-assessment helps students see what they've mastered and what their weaknesses might be. In order to address their deficiencies, students need to make a plan for improvement. What will they do next? Do they need to do something different? Do they need to set a duration goal? Do they need to change their method of practice? What goal are they shooting for?

Deliberate Practice for Teachers

Now it's time to think about your own practice as you develop new teaching skills. As we learn to use new instructional strategies in our classrooms, we also need to keep these three key steps in mind: (1) be intentional and transparent, (2) model and scaffold, and (3) use deliberate repeated practice. If you are implementing research-based strategies proven to make a difference for students and they don't seem to be working for your kids, most likely you've missed one of these three steps.

Too often as teachers, we do not give ourselves time to practice a new strategy to get good enough at teaching it. When students seem unsuccessful, we scratch the strategy off the "tried it" list and look for another solution. You need to allow yourself time to practice, practice, practice a quality teaching strategy until you and the students are good at it. It is hard work, but it will help you and your students lock in their learning until all become experts. This is how transfer occurs so that students have skills for life, not just to get through your class. It is best to teach fewer strategies with more depth so that students are really apprenticed into lifelong skills, not simply doing cute, fun activities that we found online. Studies have found that students who study fewer subject matters with greater depth have an advantage over students who study many topics with little depth (Schwartz, Sadler, Sonnert, & Tai, 2008).

The more we deliberately practice new classroom instructional practices, the better we get at them. So, as we move forward, remember the following six steps for yourself.

1. **Set learning goals:** What will it look like and feel like when you and your students have mastered a new strategy?

   • Students will be comfortable talking in small-group partnerships.

   • Student talk about the content will deepen over the course of the school year.

- Students will be more successful, and that will feel great for all of us!

2. **Plan:** Select a skill your students really need to build to be better learners in your classroom.

   - Consider the importance of student talk.

   - For the first marking period, your goal may be to have students learn to talk with a *chat chum* or *talk partner*.

   - You are committed to having them practice, practice, practice talking with their chat chums or talk partners until they (and you) are good at it.

3. **Require attention:** Think while you practice your new teaching strategy. What's working, what's not working, and what could you do differently? Consider the following self-talk.

   - "If the talk partner groups aren't going well, maybe it's because I didn't explain *why* talk is so important to the learning process (being intentional and transparent). I need to give students information about the learning brain and the importance of making meaning through talk."

   - "I assumed they know how to talk effectively with each other. I need to model and scaffold how to talk effectively, and they need to see lots of quality examples of good talk." (See chapter 7, page 91, on student talk.)

   - "I have not created solid procedures and routines for how students find their talk partners and how they need to sit together to talk. In the workshop, Kathleen said to teach the kids to go 'knee to knee, eye to eye.' Tomorrow, I'll assign partners and have them practice the body language of quality conversation."

4. **Give feedback:** The scariest but most effective feedback you can get is in the room with you every day: ask students how something is going. Not only is this the most authentic feedback, but it also builds trust while you model being a risk taker and a lifelong learner.

   - "OK, class, you know how much I believe in the value of quality talk in our classroom, and you've been practicing for a few weeks now. Before you leave class today, I'd like you to fill out an exit card giving me feedback on the following questions.

     a. What's working for you with your chat chums?

     b. What's not working for you?

     c. What could I, you, or we do differently?"

5. **Allow for self-assessment:** Remember to honor what went right. Too often as teachers, we focus on instruction that was less than perfect. If you tried something new, that alone needs to be honored as a first step.

   - "I was so nervous about having kids in these talk groups, but I had a growth mindset, and I tried it. Yay for me!"

6. **Determine next steps:** What needs to change next time to move you closer to your goal?

- "Next time, I'll start by being intentional and transparent. The students really responded to hearing about how the brain learns through talk and collaboration. I think if I lead with that, I'll get more buy-in from the beginning."

If we want our students to be joyfully engaged in the learning process with us, it will be essential for us to grow and practice *our* skills at being intentional and transparent, modeling and scaffolding, and making sure we offer time for deliberate practice. Remember that our students don't come to us already knowing how to learn; we must plan to apprentice them, to teach them in ways that make the learning and thinking process visible and that draw on their innate sense of wonder and curiosity. Our students will go forward with us if the way we teach matches the ways their brains learn.

chapter *Four*

Learning Foundation One: A Safe Learning Environment

All kids need is a little help, a little hope and somebody who believes in them.

—Earvin "Magic" Johnson

Some of the greatest heroes of our time have been inventors, writers, and thinkers. If we reflect on the environment that led to their success, we will have a good idea of what our students need to be successful in the classroom. Thomas Edison worked with a team of people who had one thousand failed attempts before finally inventing the lightbulb. They expected mistakes, and they were encouraged to take risks. Under these circumstances, the team was able to deepen its understanding and achieve world-changing results.

What It Means

A safe environment is not limited to physical parameters. Students must not only feel safe in the classroom physically but also emotionally, culturally, and academically. You must provide and maintain an environment where students feel free to take risks. When the relationship mystery is replaced with clear expectations, the teacher and student are free to proceed and interact with mutual trust and respect. Debra Sugar, a school social worker, notes the following:

Emotional safety means being able to act, think and feel without fear. It means being able to try activities I'm not good at, express my ideas without censoring them, display my feelings and have them respected, question my teachers without fear of punishment. It means being able to take risks and expose what I don't know. It means being valued for who I am instead of how well I perform. It means that the teacher is interested in me, in my ideas and experiences. (as cited in Bluestein, 2001, p. 8)

Educational consultant Rita Mercier (as cited in Bluestein, 2001) describes a safe school as creating a learning environment that allows all students to achieve their potential academically, socially, and personally, regardless of mental ability; language; culture; race; appearance; physical differences; economic status; emotional, social, or physical challenges; learning styles; temperament; gender; or other diversity. A school would be a most effective guardian, then, if it were to remove all barriers that categorize students by the adversities they face rather than the potential they hold.

The importance of a safe learning environment cannot be underestimated and is not attained accidentally. One must be deliberate when teaching what a safe environment looks like and feels like; simply encouraging participation is not enough. Modeling is the first step to creating this atmosphere; creating norms and consistently revisiting these norms are keys to maintaining the group's emotional safety. Having a motto such as that in figure 4.1 and actually having it play out in the classroom is a start to a safe learning environment.

Figure 4.1: Class motto.

Author and educator Jane Bluestein (2001), in her book *Creating Emotionally Safe Schools*, believes an emotionally safe classroom provides the following: a sense of belonging, a sense of being welcomed and valued, treatment with respect and dignity, and acceptance.

An emotionally safe classroom means having:

- One's own unique talents, skills, and qualities valued, recognized, and acknowledged

- The freedom to *not* be good at a particular skill, make mistakes, forget, or need additional practice and still be treated respectfully and with acceptance

- The freedom to make choices and influence one's own learning, pursue personal interests, and control various factors in the process of learning . . .

- The freedom from prejudice, judgment, and discrimination based on academic, athletic, creative, or social capabilities; modality or learning-style preferences; temperament . . .

- The freedom from harassment, intimidation . . . and the threat of physical harm from adults or peers (Bluestein, 2001, p. 10)

Why It Works

An emotionally safe classroom is necessary for students' cognitive learning, growth, and creative expression. Students can't learn if they don't feel safe. We know this from studying Maslow's (1943) hierarchy of needs model, which, if you recall, is divided into basic and growth needs. This hierarchy of requirements, or needs, is arranged according to their importance for an individual's survival, starting with physiological, then safety, belonging, esteem, and ending with self-actualization. We have little control of what happens to students at home; however, we *can* create a safe haven for students physiologically, we can provide safety, and we can create a sense of belonging in our schools and classrooms so that students can learn while they are with us. Until students feel a sense of belonging in our classrooms, they will have greater challenges learning reading, writing, mathematics, and science. A student's readiness to learn is not solely dependent on existing knowledge and skills. As educators, we can assist students in moving up Maslow's hierarchy by understanding that each student brings his or her own unique emotional, cultural, and academic background to the classroom.

Emotionally

Our emotional state has the potential to influence our thinking; we need to create a safe classroom that feels secure for students with emotional challenges. The classroom can be transformed into a safe haven for students facing emotional challenges (Boekaerts, 1993; Darling-Hammond et al., 2003; Oatly & Nundy, 1996). To achieve this, teachers must connect with their students on an emotional level in order to effectively communicate with them. In doing so, they provide the necessary support and help these students need, thus guiding them to overcome their fears and insecurities so that future challenges can be faced with a new enthusiasm and an eagerness to learn.

Emotions such as anger, anxiety, and sadness have the potential to distract students' learning efforts by interfering with their ability to attend to the tasks at hand. When our emotions are heightened, we use up our intellectual resources, which causes difficulty learning for some students because their minds are cluttered with distracting thoughts or memories. A student might be thinking so much about an abusive or neglectful situation that occurred at home that there is little mental room left to think about other things such as schoolwork, and therefore, he or she has insufficient resources available to engage in learning.

Culturally

We may not always understand the cultural variations of what safe feels like to our students who come from other cultures. It might seem as if *safe* is universal but only if we are looking through our own lens of what safe feels like to us. As we examine more parameters of cultural norms and community behaviors that make students feel safe, we will begin to see there are many different needs in our classrooms to attend to. Whether students feel safe because they are working in groups, safe because they feel individually successful, or safe because their cultures are represented in the classroom, students from varied cultural backgrounds need to have their cultures recognized, respected, and understood in order to feel safe, as if they belong, and as if they are empowered in the classroom.

Academically

We want to create a classroom that honors and acknowledges that people learn in different ways. If students are secure in knowing how the classroom functions and if they develop successful skills for learning, they are able to take risks, make mistakes, learn together, and readily welcome a challenge or new situation. In order to do this, teachers need to create a risk-taking, mistake-making classroom environment.

What the Research Says

When students feel positive about their learning environment, the brain releases endorphins. Endorphins produce a feeling of euphoria and stimulate the frontal lobe, thereby making the learning experience more pleasurable and successful. Conversely, if students are stressed and have a negative feeling about the learning environment, the brain releases cortisol. Cortisol is a hormone that travels throughout the brain and body and activates defensive behaviors, such as fight or flight. Frontal lobe activity is reduced to focusing on the cause of the stress and how to deal with it. Little attention is given to the learning task. Cortisol appears to interfere especially with the recall of emotional memories (Kuhlmann, Kirschbaum, & Wolf, 2005; Tollenaar, Elzinga, Spinhoven, & Everaerd, 2009; as quoted in Sousa, 2006, p. 89).

Learning occurs more easily in environments free from threat or intimidation. Whenever a student detects a threat, thoughtful processing gives way to emotion or survival reactions. Experienced teachers have seen this in the classroom. Under pressure to give a quick response, the student begins to stumble, stabs at answers, gets frustrated or angry, and may even resort to violence (Sousa, 2006).

It is often as frustrating for the teacher and other students in the room when a student begins to stumble and stammer and search for the right answer. Imagine how powerful it is to have a classroom full of cheerleaders instead of a group that snickers and sneers. Allowing for mistakes, indeed, encouraging risk taking, can make the most withdrawn students want to participate because even when they are incorrect, they are still growing and searching for knowledge.

Classroom Practices for a Safe Environment

The following classroom practices help to create a safe environment for students.

Build a Trusting Relationship

Based on work published in 2008 by Robert J. Marzano, one can then conclude that in order to establish a high-functioning classroom, a coherent and adherent trust must be formed between the teacher and students:

> Both research and common sense tell us that many of the problems among today's students are rooted in the fundamental desire of individuals to belong to a group—a group where they are depended on, respected, and supported. Children who don't belong, who feel anonymous, isolated, or neglected, will disengage from the contexts where we hope to influence them, leaving us powerless to affect them either academically or socially. (Bunn, 2000, p. 13)

Coaches and generals understand this better than anyone. It is no surprise that the winning team is always the one with the best teamwork. We have been teaching that individuality is so important for so long that teamwork has gone by the wayside. There needs to be a balance. The three Musketeers said it best: "All for one, and one for all!" This statement means we can celebrate each student's unique talents while utilizing individual strengths for the benefit of the group.

Imagine a shaggy but beautiful stray dog came to your house one day. Your heart went out to it, and you decided to help it. You put out some food, which it ate, but it refused to let you approach. Every time you tried, it would shy away and stay out of reach. For one reason or another, it did not trust you. Who knows what its history was. It trusted you enough to eat your food, but that was as far as it went. Given a few weeks, you could have built a relationship of trust with that dog—but, unfortunately, it moved on.

Students who come to our classrooms have much in common with that dog: unless they trust us, they are unapproachable. We earn our students' trust by showing them respect, and part of that respect comes in the form of meaningful, challenging, and rewarding learning activities that are worthy of their time and best efforts. Students often work harder for teachers with whom they have a trusting relationship. It's been our experience that students don't *care* what we *know* until they *know* that we *care*.

In order to build a trusting relationship, consistently strive to interact in ways that positively contribute to the relationship. It's easy to be positive when times are good, but the challenge is making positive contributions when times are difficult. Putting curriculum before relationships is like a farmer planting valuable seeds in infertile soil. Building relationships is the sunlight and rain to the seed. You cannot just tell a student to trust you; you have to show a student that he or she can trust you through your consistent, caring actions. For example, for students with emotional challenges, have a two-minute conversation every day for twenty-one days. The topic can be anything *except* behavior, academics, and attitude.

Here are some other caring actions you can start taking.

- Recognize effort—"Thank you for making it to class today" or "I noticed you have been staying after for extra help to improve your grades."
- Create positive nicknames—Wise Wenting, Terrific Tamiko, Fantastic Fred.

- Give encouragement, not praise.

- Write encouraging notes on the student's paper, even if the grade was low: "This is ten points higher than the last test! You are getting it!" or "You remembered to include an introduction and a closing paragraph."

- Remind students of past successes.

- Stop by to watch a student in a sporting event or concert.

- Concentrate on the individual's strengths, and invite him or her to share his or her talents with the group (for example, a sense of humor, knowledge about a particular topic, artistic or musical talent, or strength).

- Share topics in which the student is interested (like cars, movies, or fashion).

- Smile, and call students by name.

- Acknowledge or celebrate birthdays. Write, "Happy birthday!" on the board, sing "Happy Birthday," and give students happy birthday pens or stickers.

- Recognize when students are absent. Sincerely welcome students back, rather than just reminding them of the assignments they missed. Perhaps even call students at home when they are sick for an extended period of time.

There needs to be an unconditional acceptance of the student as a person—regardless of his or her behavior.

Get to Know Your Students

To create a safe environment, it's important that we learn as much about our students as possible early in the year. We want to be intentional about gathering data about our learners' strengths and interests and then manage the data so we can be proactive in meeting our students' needs. It is critical to understand who our learners are and then differentiate the pathways that will help all learners reach the same goal.

An efficient way to learn more about our students is by collecting data from surveys, questionnaires, and inventories. Summarize these data on an index card so you have them at your fingertips. You may want to survey your students throughout the year to gain a greater perspective on them. You can survey your students in areas such as:

- Learning style or multiple intelligence

- Learning preference

- Student interests

- Cultural experiences

Create a Community of Belonging

The need to belong is universal. As educators, we need to be aware of students' need to feel a connection to school. It doesn't really matter whether they would like to belong to a school club, athletic team, or community organization; they need to feel that they belong to a group of people who accept them unconditionally—a group that will welcome them simply for who they are, not for what they have accomplished in the past or what they might accomplish in the future. Belonging gives everyone, especially students, a sense of what it feels like to be part of a community and to be an active participant in that community, and it lets him or her know that he or she is valued.

What happens when you feel you don't belong in a particular situation? A simple example is if you were to go into the teachers' lounge and no one spoke to you or sat next to you. Would you continue to put yourself in that situation? Well, when students feel they don't belong, they may drop out of school, fail subjects, or fall in with the wrong crowd because they feel that group accepts them for who they are, not who society thinks they should be.

It's important to allow students to experience different ways in which they are comfortable learning, and it is equally important to allow them to respectfully express their unique opinions and feel comfortable showing their strengths and weaknesses without fear of ridicule.

Keep in mind that belonging is a mindset and a philosophy. A school does not need to change or add any programs in order to foster the condition of belonging. If you, as a teacher, understand the need to belong, you can then choose which actions you will employ to reflect that spirit of belonging. Just think what a difference it will make for all your students.

Students look up to teachers as role models, so it is critical that we convey a clear message that we celebrate their individuality and seek to learn from them just as they learn from us. Our goal is to create a positive emotional tone in our classroom and to create a space where it is OK and normal to be different—a space that recognizes that everyone has something special to offer. We can start by:

- Modeling for our students so they see the ways in which we honor others' gifts and celebrate everyone's contributions

- Providing literature on topics of belonging, being part of a community, working together, and honoring others' differences

- Creating a pleasant physical environment in which to enjoy the learning and offering various options to suit different learning preferences (lighting, music, spatial preferences, and so on)

- Having materials available for all means of learning and exploration (paint, paper, manipulatives, and so on) to reinforce acceptance and promote independence by saying, "I welcome you and all your talents to our room. Help yourself."

- Teaching fair versus equal (Many educators have heard the phrase "Treating everyone the same is unfair." We must recognize that students need different, personalized treatment, and being the caring educators we are demands that we acknowledge students' individuality.)

One popular educational cartoon shows a monkey, a penguin, an elephant, a fish, a seal, and a dog standing in a line with a tree behind them. A man behind a desk says to them, "For a fair selection everybody has to take the same exam: please climb that tree." As educators, many of us believe what the cartoon portrays, especially when it comes to testing. However, on a daily basis, we often forget and insist that students do and act the same. Believing that *fair* means treating everyone equally, or the same, is not true. In fact, this is the most unfair thing a teacher can do. If the difference between fair and equal is not clear in your mind, you will have a hard time giving students what they need and will conduct your classroom as one size fits all. Take time to examine your belief systems regarding your rationale for different treatment so you will not become susceptible and fall into the trap of treating everyone the same because you fear others perceiving you as unfair. It is our hope you will individualize your instruction and handling of behavior; therefore, it is important to teach your students about fair versus equal. See the appendix (page 169) for a list of books that can help you teach about fair versus equal in your classroom.

How often have you heard questions similar to these?

- "Why does he get to go on the computer first?"
- "Why does she get to have someone write the class notes for her?"
- "Why doesn't he get suspended when he curses in school?"

These questions generally mean one of two things: students are genuinely confused as to the rationale behind the different treatment, or they don't like the consequences and want us to change our mind. In other words, they are trying to guilt us into giving them what they want or to taking a consequence.

When the student says, "Why does he get to use a calculator and I don't?" or "Why did she win first place in the science fair and I didn't?" what he's really saying is "My reason for bringing this up is I also want to be able to do or to have that." An appropriate response to the second statement would be "You really wish you had won first place and are disappointed that you didn't. Would you like to hear the criteria for getting first place in the science fair?"

A colleague of MaryAnn's believes the reason students say, "It's not fair," is because they are disappointed. There is a difference between disappointment and unfairness, and there is a need for students to process this difference.

- Teach your students about need versus want. We give you what you need, not always what you want (such as with handicap parking).
- Help students to understand invisible handicaps. Just because you can't see the handicap, it doesn't mean it doesn't exist. Everyone knows a student in a wheelchair can't take the stairs because the disability is visible and it is understood that the student needs an elevator. When a student with two hands who can write needs help taking notes, his or her disability is not so clear. This student may have a tracking disability, not a physical disability.
- Have students create and post signs in the classroom that read:
  - FAIR ≠ SAME
  - I will be fair, not equal.
  - Treating everyone the same is the most unfair thing I can do!
  - I will give you what you need but not always what you want.

In the appendix (page 171), there are additional sayings you can put on a poster to hang in your classroom.

Establish Classroom Norms

Classroom norms define the behavioral expectations or rules of the class. Class norms inform us how we are expected to behave toward each other and toward the materials we use in school. They also help ensure that students indeed understand the classroom community's expectations and provide the rationale for them to monitor and change their own behaviors. "Not knowing what is expected can cause insecurity, discomfort and self-consciousness" (Weinstein, 2006, p. 54). Clear norms minimize confusion and prevent loss of instructional time.

It is not enough to state norms for general conduct and expect students to understand or remember them. Instead, you need to define terms as clearly as possible, discuss rationales, and provide examples. "Students who are partners in composing class norms are more likely to experience a level of ownership, participate in instruction, and engage in mutually respectful and cooperative relationships" (Weinstein, 2006, p. 55). It is helpful to involve students in generating the rules in order to promote student ownership of the rules and more student responsibility for their own behavior.

Student involvement can take many forms, such as discussing the reasons to have rules and clarifying particular rules' rationale and meaning. It is useful for students to generate concrete examples of the kinds of behaviors a particular rule covers. Many teachers begin the process of developing classroom rules with a whole-class discussion. During this discussion, the students and teacher suggest possible rules for the classroom, and the teacher records each suggestion on the board. After all suggestions are recorded, the suggestions are arranged in broad categories, and then the teacher and students develop a title for each category. This title becomes a classroom rule. Role playing at the elementary level is helpful to have students understand the rules. You may choose to have students draw pictures of themselves following the rules. Once the list is complete, you may find it helpful to have all the students sign the rules, demonstrating their commitment to following them. Keep in mind it is also best to emphasize the positive "do" parts of the rules rather than just their negative counterparts; for example, say, "Walk in the classroom" instead of "No running." Figure 4.2 (page 62) illustrates some real-life examples.

Here are some suggested guidelines for creating classroom rules.

- Create the rules together as a class.
- Rules need to apply all day or all period long. ("No talking" does not apply all day.)
- Rules should be observable and specific. (Can you see it or hear it?)
- Use words students understand.
- State the rules in the positive (when possible).
- Rules should be in the best interest of the students (a win-win).
- Include a maximum of five rules.
- Teach the rationale for each rule.
- Do not include academic rules.
- Post the rules, or send home a handout with the rules.
- Teach and review the rules for three to five days.
- Give students a quiz or test on the rules (for documentation purposes).
- Practice the rules for a week before enforcing consequences.

Group Norms

* Encourage each other.
* Provide constructive feedback.
* Contribute equally.
* Stay on task.
* Be respectful.
* Listen genuinely.

Our Class Constitution

We, the students of room 54, in order to have a more perfect class, promise to respect all ideas and people. We will always be sure to promote the general welfare, listen well for a tranquil classroom, work our hardest and never give up, care for each other as a team, and keep our classroom clean. We pledge to make this year a success and to be the best class we can be. We ordain this constitution for the class of room 54.

Figure 4.2: Examples of classroom rules.

Describe behaviors that are necessary for your class to be a safe place to work. Here are examples of traditional classroom rules to pull your own rules from.

- Follow directions.

- Respect yourself, others, and school property.

- Let one person speak at a time.

- Raise your hand, and wait for your turn to speak.

- Keep your hands, feet, and objects to yourself.

- Be seated when the bell rings.

- Walk in the classroom.

- Use materials as instructed.

- Stay seated unless given permission to get up.

- Come to class prepared, or bring all needed materials to class.

Successful teachers interact with students in ways that provide encouragement, support, and a positive learning environment for their students. The methods in this chapter provide the basis for creating adult-student relationships that support student learning and emotional safety. One of the major distinctions between highly successful and less-successful teachers is the degree to which they anticipate and arrange for what they want to happen in the classroom. In the next chapter, we will look at the fundamentals of planning routines and procedures in order to get more of what you want from your students.

chapter Five

Learning Foundation Two: Procedures and Routines

Babe Ruth, like many other athlete heroes, followed a routine. Every time he came in from the outfield, he had to touch second base on his way in. If he missed it, he would go back out and make contact before the next inning started. Tennis player Serena Williams ties her shoes the same way before each game and bounces the ball exactly five times before every serve. Though these routines are seen as quirky superstitions, the psychology behind their use is similar to that behind classroom routines. Predictability feels safe and comfortable and frees students' minds to focus on more important tasks.

What It Means

Procedures and routines enable you and your students to carry out housekeeping tasks (like taking attendance, distributing materials, and collecting homework) smoothly and efficiently so that the time for learning and teaching is maximized. The *Merriam-Webster* (2015) dictionary defines *procedure* as:

1. An established or official way of doing something

2. A series of actions conducted in a certain order or manner

For example, when students arrive in the morning, do they need to hang up their coats, go immediately to their desks, and take out a book? May they chat quietly with neighbors, sharpen pencils, and play games? Certain procedures may look so basic or obvious that they are easily overlooked, but lessons can fall apart if you don't have a procedure to distribute or collect papers. Take nothing for granted. Intentionally and transparently teach students what you want them to know and do.

Once procedures are in place, they must be rehearsed repeatedly until they become routine. Routines are what students do automatically.

Procedure + Practice = Routine

Think of procedures and routines as railroad tracks that need to be laid down so the train (content) can run smoothly. Your destination is learning the content. In order to get there, you need to stay on the track. The track is always the same. It doesn't change. Therefore, the train can follow it automatically and get to its destination on time.

When planning procedures for your class, consider independent learning and interdependent or group learning. When working independently, students need to know the procedures that will help them be self-sufficient. Within groups, student roles and specific responsibilities need to be established. Group procedures give each student a purpose and direction; students know they are an integral part of the community and their contribution is valued.

Why It Works

Many parents set a bedtime routine for their children, knowing children feel more secure and find emotional comfort in this nighttime ritual. Likewise, a structured classroom provides psychological safety for students. By clearly defining established processes, procedures, rules, and practices, we eliminate students' fear of the unknown. By gaining knowledge of the classroom's expected dynamics, the student gains more control of his or her environment simply by being aware of what is going to happen before it happens. Think of an airline crew going over the safety procedures before takeoff. This procedure gives the passengers a sense of confidence and a feeling of safety to know what to expect in an emergency and how to respond.

It is helpful for students to have common expectations—even if they don't come from common backgrounds. Because procedures that become routines are ways of doing things, they are often visible. Students with limited English skills can learn from observing other kids who are modeling them. Procedures and routines for independent work are essential. American schools, as part of an individualistic culture, value independent work and independent success. Students raised in a typical individualist American culture are more comfortable working alone. However, students from collectivist cultures are most comfortable working in groups to complete a task. If all students are to be successful and self-reliant when learning alone, the explicit instruction of what to do when learning independently needs to be taught. However, procedures and routines for interdependent work are equally important. While many of our students who come from collectivist cultures are more comfortable working in groups, it isn't necessarily a skill that comes naturally for all students. Even if students are comfortable being in groups, how to *learn* in a group is a different skill, one for which all students need procedures and routines to help them be successful.

Simply said, procedures and routines give us more teaching time. Without a procedure to help students transition or to do housekeeping tasks, what could take almost no time (attendance, for example) could waste ten precious minutes of instruction. With more time for instruction, the teacher is able to be more responsive to student needs; it allows for time to do more interactive activities and projects, to work with small groups, or to spend time giving one-on-one formative feedback. We all complain about not having enough time to get students where they need to be; procedures and routines give us the structure we need to not lose precious instructional time.

What the Research Says

Common sense and our teacher instinct tell us that procedures and routines are necessary in class, and we can see how they will help our students emotionally, culturally, and academically. Research supports the imperative nature of these classroom structures.

It is possible to form a strong and viable engagement between student and teacher when both are performing at their highest levels of achievement and working coherently with one another (Wong & Wong, 2001). Likewise, Jere Brophy and Carolyn Evertson (1976) document the inevitable failure of a classroom teacher in their findings:

> Almost all surveys of teacher effectiveness report that classroom management skills are of primary importance in determining teaching success, whether it is measured by student learning or by rating. Thus, management skills are crucial and fundamental. A teacher who is grossly inadequate in classroom management skills is probably not going to accomplish much. (p. 27)

In short, we know in our core that procedures and routines are essential for classroom management, and research supports that when used consistently, they are indispensable to student success.

Classroom Practices for Procedures and Routines

Following are some tips for teaching procedures and routines.

- **Teaching procedures will take some time:** Keep in mind that teaching procedures will take some of your academic time in the beginning of the school year, but it will save you time the rest of the year. You will avoid a year of chaotic transitions, lost instructional time, and irresponsible students. The only way you can have responsible students is to teach expected procedures and routines.

- **It is best to teach procedures as they naturally arise during the day:** To teach all classroom procedures at one time would be overwhelming and decrease the chances the students would retain the process of each procedure. Therefore, a few minutes before dismissal, go over the procedure for exiting the class at the end of the day or period. Before beginning a lab or art project, teach how to share materials and ideas. Teach the procedure as it is needed so students can engage in natural practice. Start with "Class, today we will be going to the library. Let's talk about the procedure for going to the library."

There are five steps to teach procedures and to avoid confusion.

1. *Explain*—Inform students of the exact steps in the sequence you want them to follow.

2. *Model*—Visually demonstrate the procedure.

3. *Role-play* (when task- and age-appropriate)—For elementary students, it helps to have a couple of students demonstrate the steps while the teacher is stating the steps. Providing

auditory and visual support will increase the chances of understanding. You can also engage students to "Find the flaw!" by having them intentionally *not* follow the procedure and then see who can figure out what's wrong and how to fix it.

4. *Practice*—Allow everyone to do the procedure before it is actually needed.

5. *Review*—Remind students of processes after weekends, after vacations, or when they are not following procedures.

To clearly demonstrate the five steps to teaching procedures, we have listed examples of the two most commonly needed procedures: manage materials and get help. Please keep in mind that step three (role-play) is only used when age- or task-appropriate.

Manage Materials

The examples here demonstrate two ways to provide directions depending on the type of activity (interdependent versus independent). Interdependent procedures are needed when groups or students are mutually dependent on one another. This differs from independent procedures, where students are responsible for themselves or for doing a task on their own.

Independent

1. **Explain:** Explain the importance of being able to find all your learning materials. "Imagine a football team ready for kickoff, but it cannot find the football! The clock is ticking, and the teams are not able to play. They are wasting valuable time. It's the same with our school supplies, books, papers, and pens. We need to have them organized and available so that we can spend our time learning and having fun instead of wasting our time looking for them."

2. **Model:** Demonstrate how to organize students' binders and where to place books, pens, and homework assignments.

3. **Role-play:** Give two students worksheets for different subjects, and have them place the worksheets in the correct spot in their binder or in their desk.

4. **Practice:** Spend at least a week rehearsing. At the end of each lesson, take a few minutes to have students place all materials in the correct spot.

5. **Review:** When students are frequently forgetting the procedure or have returned from vacation, review the process. Have the students tell you, model, and explain where their supplies and papers belong.

Interdependent

1. **Explain:** "Imagine going to play your favorite Wii game and you can't find the disc or the remote because your younger sibling did not put it back in the correct place after last using it. Not only are you annoyed, but you've also now spent your playing time looking for it! We will be sharing materials in our classroom and in our small groups; we need to use the

materials respectfully and return them to their proper places so they are there and in working condition for the next classmate."

2. **Model:** Show students how to use various types of equipment—microscopes, scissors, iPads, glue sticks, and calculators—and where to return the materials when finished.

3. **Role-play:** Have one or all students demonstrate proper use.

4. **Practice:** Just before the materials need to be returned, stop the class, and question students on what needs to be done with the materials, and then have them do it.

5. **Review:** After weekends, after vacations, or when students are not following procedures, review the process. Have a student teach it to peers and new students.

Get Help

Students may need help while the teacher is busy working with small groups. The following procedures are to help students get their questions answered with minimal disruption to the teacher.

Independently

1. **Explain:** "When you are working independently and have a question or need help, please raise a *silent hand*. You will use your fingers to give me a signal of what you need. Hold up one finger if your question is urgent. Hold up two fingers if you are stuck on the assignment and can't move forward without help. Hold up three fingers to let me know you need clarification on the assignment but that you can still keep working." (Discuss what you think an urgent question is. Fingers can be replaced with color-coded cards or cups.)

2. **Model:** Put a worksheet on the SMART Board, and pretend you are a student doing work on the worksheet. Do your thinking aloud so students can hear your thought process as you model the finger symbols and what an urgent question is while thinking aloud. "I have to go to the bathroom." Hold up one finger. "I don't know what to do on this whole section." Hold up two fingers. "I am stuck on this one, but I get how to do the next problem." Hold up three fingers.

3. **Practice:** Give students scenarios, and have them hold up the correct number of fingers: "My pencil broke, and I can't continue to work until it is sharpened. Show me how many fingers to hold up."

4. **Review:** After weekends, after vacations, or when students are not following procedures, review the process. Have a student teach it to peers and new students.

Interdependently

1. **Explain:** "There are times I will be working with small groups or individuals and may not be readily available to help you. So we will use the *three before me* rule. When I am working with another student or teaching in a small group and you need help, you should look around your desk to the person in front of, behind, or on either side of you for help and ask him or

her for help using a whisper voice. If the first person does not know the answer, ask someone else. If you don't have the answer by the third person, raise your hand to ask for help, or put up your help card requesting the teacher's assistance." Each student has a folded card on his or her desk. On one side, this card reads, "Help me." The student turns the help side to the front when he or she needs help.

2. **Model:** Sit in a student's desk, and model the previous behavior. Ask the students, "Who should I turn to ask my question?" Point to the students in front of, behind, or on either side of you instead of across the room. Use your whisper voice.

3. **Practice:** Call on a few students to demonstrate whom they will ask for help, the voice volume used for asking, how to raise a quiet hand, and when to use their help card.

4. **Review:** If students are frequently forgetting or it's after vacation, it is time to review.

Use Anchor Activities

Students finish their work at different times, or they may be waiting for the teacher to work with them. During these downtimes, it is critical that you have anchor activities for the students to do while waiting. The absence of anchor activities is an invitation to chaos.

Anchor activities are a collection of assignments or projects that students can work on when they finish the immediate assignment. They do not require the teacher's help or interaction. Here are a few ideas. Students can:

- Check their work for errors, asking themselves, "Can I make it better?"

- Read a book

- Write in their journal

- Play file-folder games (paper game boards laminated inside a file folder and then placed in a large ziplock bag with game pieces needed and used to review academic skills for different subjects)

- Listen to audiobooks

- Play desktop games or use manipulatives

- Work on a fun packet (packets that contain fun worksheets for students to work on when they finish work early, such as word searches, riddles, coloring sheets, and picture puzzles)

- Write a story

- Catch up on some homework

- Offer to help out another class (after checking with the teacher first)

- Study for a test

- Draw on the back of their paper

- Read a book to or with someone else who is also an early finisher (after checking with the teacher first)

Post approved anchor activities in the classroom. It is helpful to preteach about these activities. Consider:

- When to use anchor activities
- Where to find materials
- The voice volume, if any, during the activity
- Where to do the activity (such as on the floor, at a desk, and so on)

Use the following five steps to teach students about anchor activities.

1. **Explain:** "I understand that you all work at a different pace. There may be times when you finish before other classmates or before we are ready to move on to the next assignment. It can be tiring to just sit and wait, so when you finish early, look at the anchor activity chart, and select an activity to do."

2. **Model:** Demonstrate each activity on the anchor chart, including where it can be done, where the materials are, and the voice tone and volume to use while doing it.

3. **Role-play:** Have one or two students demonstrate an activity.

4. **Practice:** Have students all select an activity and practice how it is done.

5. **Review:** After weekends, after vacations, or when students are not following procedures, review the process. Have a student teach it to peers and new students.

Use Transitions

Teach and use specific directions for transitions. In order for students to move fluidly from whole-class, independent, and interdependent groupings, we need to teach them specific procedures. Again, this will clarify the behavior that you expect while doing a procedure.

It is helpful (and fun) to use a signal word for transitions. The purpose of a signal word is for students to remain still until all directions have been given and are understood. Use the signal word only for transitions and for no other purpose. It should be a word that is not often used—for example, "Yabba dabba doo!" This lets students know it is time to transition. Use the same signal word all year long. Speak the signal in the same voice and tone you want students to use.

The following types of transitions need classroom procedures.

- Leaving the room
- Returning to the room
- Ending the day
- Getting ready for an activity
- Moving into and out of group work and interdependent work
- Moving into and out of independent work
- Finishing classwork early

How to Teach Transitions

Using specific directions is a helpful way to prepare students for transitions. Lee Canter (2010) suggests that specific directions relate to three main areas: (1) mouths, (2) bodies, and (3) materials. A fourth direction is added when needed: what to do when you finish (or anchor activities). The following are some options for each of the three main areas.

1. **Mouths**

   - "Be silent." (Avoid using *quiet*, as it is vague.)

   - "Use your whisper or indoor voice."

   - "Raise your hand, and wait to be called on."

   - "Let one person speak at a time."

2. **Bodies**

   - "Face forward."

   - "Keep your eyes on the speaker."

   - "Stay seated."

   - "Walk."

   - "Put all six legs on the floor (yours and the chair's)."

   Have fun with your students; try some of the following ideas, even with middle school students.

   - "Walk with your left hand on your hip and your right hand in front of your mouth to remind yourself to be silent."

   - "March with your hands at your sides."

   - "Be supermodels on the catwalk."

   - "Tiptoe with your arms folded."

3. **Materials:** Remember to tell students what to do with their materials before transitions.

   - "Bring designated materials."

   - "Return materials to the proper place."

   - "Leave materials where they are—none is needed."

How It Will Sound

Table 5.1 is a blueprint with specific directions for any transition in your classroom or between classrooms. Following table 5.1 is an example of how to teach specific directions using the mouths, bodies, and materials structure. Additionally, figure 5.1 (page 74) provides a template for writing specific directions for these and other activities.

Table 5.1: Scaffolding Giving Specific Directions

First Two Weeks	Third Week	Fourth Week
• Name the activity. • State: "When I give the signal, which is . . ." • State the directions regarding mouths, bodies, or materials. • Ask the students questions regarding comprehension of mouths, bodies, or materials. • Role-play. • Ask: "Any general questions?" • Give the signal. • Use positive repetition.	• Name the activity. • State: "Wait for the signal." • Ask students to repeat the directions regarding mouths, bodies, or materials (or ask them to show you). • Ask: "Any general questions?" • Give the signal. • Use positive repetition (not as frequently).	• Name the activity. • Ask: "Any questions?" • Give the signal.

Source: Adapted from Canter, 2010.

Teacher: *It is time to transition. When I give the signal, you will: mouths—use an indoor voice; bodies—use walking feet to get to your place in line; materials— bring your lunch or lunch money. Sarah, how will we go to the line?*

Sarah: *Walking feet.*

Teacher: *Tom, what kind of voice will you use while lining up?*

Tom: *Indoor voice.*

Teacher: *Jamel, what do you need to bring with you to the line?*

Jamel: *Lunch money or lunch.*

Teacher: *Tamika, please show the class how we will be lining up for lunch.*

(Teacher states what the student is doing.)

Teacher: *Are there any questions?* (Waits, scans the room, and answers any questions.)

Teacher: *Yabba dabba doo!* (Uses an indoor voice.)

Teacher: *I see three people using walking feet. I hear indoor voices being used. I notice two tables of students have their lunch in hand.*

Teachers can prevent a great deal of misbehavior by establishing and teaching classroom procedures, transitions, and rules. It is critical to anticipate and arrange for what you want to happen in the classroom. By defining in advance what you want to occur, you're able to minimize off-task behavior and help students develop skills that lead to greater success.

In the next chapter, we will explore how dedication and hard work can change student performance by changing mindset. We will share ideas for ways to build a growth mindset with your students.

Write Your Specific Directions for Each Activity

My signal word: _____

Example: Test taking

1. Mouths: Be silent; raise your hand if you have a question.

2. Bodies: Stay seated; keep your eyes on your own paper.

3. Materials: Clear your desk of all materials, except for a pen or pencil.

4. Anchor activity: Turn your paper over, and draw without talking.

Transition in the class: _____

1. Mouths: _____

2. Bodies: _____

3. Materials: _____

4. Anchor activity: _____

Dismissal: _____

1. Mouths: _____

2. Bodies: _____

3. Materials: _____

4. Anchor activity: _____

Arrival to the class: _____

1. Mouths: _____

2. Bodies: _____

3. Materials: _____

4. Anchor activity: _____

Activity: _____

1. Mouths: _____

2. Bodies: _____

3. Materials: _____

4. Anchor activity: _____

Figure 5.1: Template for writing specific directions for activities.

*Visit **go.solution-tree.com/instruction** for a reproducible version of this figure.*

chapter *Six*

Learning Foundation Three: A Growth Mindset

Probably, one of the most promising aspects of the research on effort is that students can learn to operate from a belief that effort pays off even if they do not initially have this belief.

—Robert J. Marzano, Debra J. Pickering, and Jane E. Pollock

Although most of our on-screen superheroes are born with special powers, modern-day, real-life heroes build those powers with effort and practice. Michael Jordan, the NBA hero, was cut from his high school basketball team. He trained diligently and was then chosen as a starter the following year, received a full scholarship to college, and, well, we all know the rest of the story. Dr. Seuss had his scripts rejected twenty-seven times before he was finally published. Real heroes don't make it by magic—they work hard! As Mahatma Gandhi said, "Heroes are made in the hour of defeat. Success is, therefore, well described as a series of glorious defeats."

What It Means

In her pivotal research, Carol Dweck (2006), author of *Mindset: The New Psychology of Success*, notes that humans can develop one of two types of mindsets: (1) fixed mindsets or (2) growth mindsets. These mindsets impact the internal messages that play out in our minds as we face challenges.

Fixed mindset thinkers live by the following internal messages.

- Intelligence and talent are fixed, innate traits.
- Talent alone creates success.

- When learning something new, either you get it or you don't.

- Effort does not make a difference.

The internal message for students with a fixed mindset is "I need to look good at all costs." Students with a fixed mindset may act as if they don't care about school or learning or their teachers. This internal message may play out with external behaviors such as having their head down on their desk or refusing to do work. They might say, "This is stupid" and "You're stupid!"

Growth mindset thinkers, on the other hand, develop the following internal beliefs.

- Most basic abilities can be developed through dedication and hard work—brains and talent are just the starting point.

- A love of learning and resilience are essential for great accomplishment.

- Effort and determination pay off.

The internal message for growth mindset students is "I need to learn at all costs." They are not afraid to ask for help, ask questions, or try again. They are ready and willing to work hard and to learn what they need to succeed. In her book *Mindset*, Dweck (2006) outlines the dramatic effect that these opposing beliefs have on learners, as shown in table 6.1.

Table 6.1: Fixed Versus Growth Mindsets

Fixed Mindset	Growth Mindset
Wants to *prove* intelligence or talent	Wants to *improve* intelligence or talent
Avoids challenges for fear of failure	Engages challenges to improve
Gives up in the face of tough obstacles	Persists in overcoming obstacles
Avoids hard labor	Sees labor as the path to success
Treats criticism as an attack	Treats criticism as an opportunity
Feels threatened by others' success	Feels inspired by others' success

Source: Dweck, 2006.

What Dweck's (2006) research says is that virtually all successful people have a growth mindset. The good news for educators (and parents) is that, according to Dweck, we can help our students develop a growth mindset, and we can grow our mindset as well!

Why It Works

Helping students regulate behavior involves not only developing their ability to control their actions but also shaping their internal messages to allow them to think flexibly and respond appropriately to academic challenges. Dweck's (2006) research and insights offer teachers ways to build essential, self-regulatory executive-functioning skills into daily classroom instruction.

Developing growth mindsets can help students who have emotional and social challenges. Many students who deal with emotional and social challenges feel they have no control over their emotions or their ability to handle social challenges—they have fixed mindsets. ("When things go wrong, I always act this way.") But if they work to shape their mindsets about their emotional stability and social skills, they can make positive changes in their emotional lives. They do have control, but they have to believe this before they can make changes. Research shows that practices such as teaching students mindfulness and cognitive behavioral strategies can have a positive impact on helping them develop social-emotional skills (Davis & Hayes, 2011).

Many students coming to us from other countries or cultural backgrounds have a *fatalistic cultural perception* (Añez, Silva, Paris, & Bedregal, 2008). This means they are more likely to believe that they must accept life situations as they are. ("This is what life has dealt me, and I can't change that, so I'll just have to accept it.") They may have a fixed mindset about how they fit in or about their performance in school or the classroom. Students who have this fatalistic cultural perception can benefit from learning about mindsets and the mind's ability to change. Showing them ways to develop a growth mindset can help them shift their perspective.

Academically, we know that many gifted students have developed a fixed mindset, believing that learning should always come easily. Oftentimes, teachers and parents inadvertently perpetuate that belief by overpraising students' intelligence over their effort. ("You're so smart!" versus "You worked hard to make this happen.") Many gifted students go through their entire school career earning "lazy As." They have never had to work hard, and they leave our schools under the false delusion that learning will always come easily for them.

Students who come to us with learning challenges often develop learned helplessness or fixed mindsets about themselves as learners: "I can't do math; even my parents say they can't do math!" These mindsets become cemented with each passing year that they are taught in a manner that does not work for them. Dweck's (2006) research shows that until we change students' mindset, strategies alone won't be enough to help them see new results. Dweck (2006) notes:

> It's no wonder that many adolescents mobilize their resources, not for learning, but to protect their egos. And one of the main ways they do this is (aside from providing vivid portraits of their teachers) is by not trying. . . . In fact, students with the fixed mindset tell us that their main goal in school—aside from looking smart—is to exert as little effort as possible. . . . This low-effort syndrome is often seen as a way that adolescents assert their independence from adults, but it is also a way that students with the fixed mindset protect themselves. They view the adults as saying, "Now we will measure you and see what you've got." And they are answering, "No you won't." (p. 58)

Students with fixed mindsets may lack all or some of the executive-functioning behavioral regulation skills of inhibition, shift, emotional control, and initiation.

What Dweck's (2006) work says to us as educators is that if we are going to change our students' emotional, cultural, and academic *skill sets*, we also need to develop or change their *mindsets*. We need to focus on noticing and praising students' efforts and not their abilities or their intelligence. Whether a student fails or succeeds, we need to learn to give feedback about specific effort given or strategies used—what the student did wrong and what he or she could do now or next time. Dweck's research shows that specific praising of effort is a key ingredient in creating students who value success that comes through hard work. Wouldn't we like to be a part of developing a nation, a world, filled with growth mindset humans!

You can learn more about Dweck's research at her educator website, Mindset Works (www.mindsetworks.com).

What the Research Says

As noted, according to Dweck (2006), the human brain can develop a growth mindset. In one of the studies referenced in her book, Dweck took two groups of seventh graders who were struggling in mathematics. Group one received quality instruction in study skills to support mathematics learning. Each time Dweck's researchers replicated the study, they saw no statistically significant change in students' academic growth. Participants in group two received intentional and transparent information about how the brain worked and learned how they had the power to shape the messages in the brain. They were taught about fixed versus growth mindsets. They learned about how their brains worked and the difference that effort makes in growing neural connections. Then they were given the same study skills training as the group one learners. Each time Dweck's researchers replicated this study, the group two students' academic scores improved in statistically significant ways.

Marzano et al. (2001) find similar results in their research for *Classroom Instruction That Works: Research-Based Strategies for Increasing Student Achievement*, stating:

> Not all students realize the importance of believing in effort. Although it may seem obvious to adults—particularly successful ones—that effort pays off in terms of enhanced achievement, not all students are aware of the fact that the effort they put into a task has a direct effect on their success relative to the task (see Seligman, 1990, 1994; Urdan, Midgley, & Anderman, 1998). (p. 50)

The implication here is that teachers need to be intentional and transparent in explaining and exemplifying the "effort belief" to their students.

Classroom Practices for a Growth Mindset

What Dweck's (2006) and Marzano et al.'s (2001) research says to us as educators is that if we are going to change our students' skill sets, we need to develop or shape their mindsets at the same time. Students' mindsets play a key role in the development of their executive-functioning skills. Dweck (2006) finds that when students are intentionally and transparently taught about how their brains learn and how growth mindsets make a difference, they realize that they have control of their own learning and take empowering actions to change the way they approach learning and life.

Since Dweck's research shows that we should see results if we intentionally teach about mindsets, then it is imperative to find doable ways to embed explicit instruction about mindsets into the daily school routine. Alicia practices the following strategies with her students, and Kathleen and MaryAnn have modeled them in classrooms around the world.

At the beginning of the year, we ask students what they know about their learning brains. Once we have some background, we teach students about mindsets and their learning brains. Since we know that students learn in varied ways, we offer them experiences and activities that help them "feel" their mindsets, feel-it activities that help them learn from others' mindsets and support them in changing their fixed mindset self-talk into growth mindset talk. The goal of this transparent teaching is to help students develop the internal messages and executive-functioning skills they need for successful learning.

We suggest teachers spend one full class period doing the feel-it activities that follow and teaching students about mindsets. The feel-it activities are designed to have students feel how they respond when learning gets hard for them. Then follow up with a few ten- to fifteen-minute minilessons about mindset talk throughout the next week. The time you take at the beginning of the year will lay the foundation for how you talk to your students for the rest of the year. If you "go slow to go fast," your students will have the time to develop their mindset muscles into growth mindset muscles, and you will see more empowered and responsible learners.

Teach About the Learning Brain

The following are steps we recommend implementing in your classroom at the beginning of the year to help students see how they feel and respond and what they say to themselves when learning gets hard.

- To begin, introduce the idea of building brain matter by showing how neurons are activated in learning and how new connections can be made (see figure 6.1).

- Next, teach students the phrase "Neurons that fire together wire together." Have them chant it three times while making motions with their hands for firing and wiring. Remind them that this means the more they put forth effort and practice learning tasks, the better their brains make and grow connections.

- Explain to teenagers that this time in their life is pivotal and that if they don't work hard in school now, they will lose the chance to grow stronger neural connections in academics later. The teenage brain will prune away information that doesn't get used. So the phrase "If you don't use it, you'll lose it" is true for adolescents.

- After you do the feel-it activities, teach your students about fixed and growth mindsets.

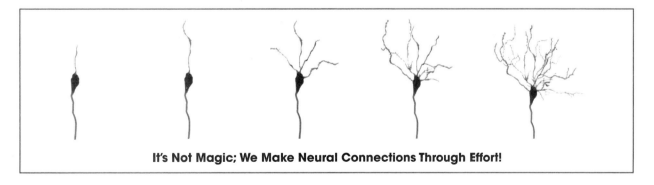

It's Not Magic; We Make Neural Connections Through Effort!

Figure 6.1: Growing dendrites.

Teach Strategies for Developing a Growth Mindset

Much of our learning is tied to our emotional reactions to events and situations. Eric Jensen (1998), an educator who has done extensive research on neuroscience, reminds us that the brain is most alert when there is a physical or emotional change. In order for students to move from fixed mindset thinking and negative self-talk to growth mindset thinking and self-encouragement, they need to understand what messages are playing in their brains when faced with challenges.

The following activities are designed to have students feel and experience their own mindsets so they can learn to recognize them when they are activated and adjust them toward more growth mindset reactions. Plan one classroom period to do the feel-it activities. You can choose to do one or two of the activities with your students. Another fun way to do the activities is in stations, with a different feel-it activity at each station. Students can then rotate through the stations and note their response to each station.

Remember the goal of this experience is to move students away from fixed mindset thinking and negative self-talk toward growth mindset thinking, giving them the vocabulary and experience to talk growth mindset talk and shape growth mindset behaviors. To start, opening the lesson may sound like this: "We are going to test our limits, patience, and determination today. Let's pay attention to the messages our brain is sending as we tackle a difficult task. First, let's try _____."

Using Feel-It Activities

The following are possible activities you could use to have students feel their mindsets (Kryza, Stephens, & Duncan, 2011).

- **Take a quiz (linguistic or logical):** Give students a surprise quiz on what they've been learning in your class.

- **Try toothpick puzzles (logical):** Have students try to solve a toothpick puzzle. Visit Toothpick World (www.toothpickworld.com/kids) for examples and solutions at various levels.

- **Tie knots (visual and tactile):** Provide rope and written directions with no pictures, and have students try tying knots.

- **Complete visual word puzzles (visual and linguistic):** Give students word puzzles to complete within a given amount of time.

- **Solve tangrams (visual and tactile):** Have students solve tangram puzzles within a set time.

- **Build a tower of cards (tactile):** Challenge students with criteria that make the tower of cards more difficult, such as holding a brick for five minutes.

- **Do riddles (linguistic):** A quick search for student riddles will help you locate several resources of linguistic challenges to help students feel it in a limited time.

- **Do Sudoku (mathematical):** For some students, Sudoku is a treat; for others, it is a major challenge! This provides a great way to enter into a discussion about how it feels to be frustrated when others are enjoying a task.

- **Run an obstacle course or scavenger hunt (kinesthetic):** Many resources are online for creating a simple obstacle course using everyday items. Again, for some students, this will be an easy challenge, while others will struggle. It will really help students feel what happens in their brains when they take on a new challenge. Do they feel like quitting? Do they feel inspired and excited?

After an activity, ask students to respond to the following questions.

- "How did you feel before you started this activity? What were you saying to yourself?"
- "What did you feel during the activity? What were you saying to yourself during the activity?"
- "How did you feel after the activity? What were you saying to yourself after the activity?"

Students then discuss which comments are growth mindset comments and which are fixed mindset comments. Keep notes of what students share. The discussion generated from the feel-it activities will lead into the following talk-it section.

Using Talk-It Activities

Language is so pervasive in our lives we are often unaware of the powerful effect it can have on our socializing, our teaching, our thinking, and most certainly our learning. Peter Johnston (2004) notes in *Choice Words: How Our Language Affects Children's Learning*:

> If we have learned anything from Vygotsky (1978), it is that "children grow into the intellectual life around them" (p. 88). That intellectual life is fundamentally social, and language has a special place in it. Because the intellectual life is social, it is also relational and emotional. To me, the most humbling part of observing accomplished teachers is seeing the subtle ways in which they build emotionally and relationally healthy learning communities—intellectual environments that produce not mere technical competence, but caring, secure, actively literate human beings. (p. 2)

By focusing on the language or talk in a growth mindset classroom, we choose to make the invisible visible. Some educators may be naturals at using powerful language in the classroom—understanding the implications that our words can have socially, intellectually, and academically. However, most of us have to study, work hard, and practice talking the talk. (Get your growth mindset ready!)

The following are activities that create classroom talk and help students develop growth mindsets (Kryza et al., 2011). You can teach these activities in short minilessons and then reinforce the message throughout the school year. Alicia and her students made a list of fixed mindset phrases that they were saying during a feel-it activity. They worked together to flip those messages from fixed to growth mindset messages. ("I can't" becomes "If I work hard, I can!" or "I can't *yet*.") Alicia posted their new growth mindset phrases on an anchor chart in the classroom. Anytime students used fixed mindset talk, Alicia or their peers kindly reminded them that they could choose better self-talk from their anchor chart to change their mindset. It became a fun way to support each other throughout the year.

- With lower elementary (K–2) students, choose a self-talk phrase or a teacher-to-student or student-to-student phrase from the talk-it resources (figures 6.2, 6.3, and 6.4, pages 82–83), and practice choral chanting with the whole class. This can be the phrase of the day or the phrase of the week to help students start building the language of growth mindsets. For example, the charter K–2 school KIPP Ujima Village Academy in Baltimore, Maryland, has students gather together every morning in the cafeteria, and (among other things they do to start their day in a calm and routine way) they chant, "We're here to get some knowledge so we can go to college."

Before Learning
• Today, you might find there are some things that are new to you, and you are going to get to grow from trying them.
• Does this remind you of something you've done before? How can you use that experience to help you with this new learning?
• Looking at today's work, what part do you think will be the most challenging for you? What can you do when learning gets to the good part (the hard part) to help you continue learning?
During Learning
• What parts are going well? What parts are making you grow?
• Why do you think this part is challenging for you? What do you need to help you? Do you need more information? More practice? A different way to practice?
• Have you done something like this before? What did you do when it got hard? Can you do it again?
• What do you know about yourself as a learner that can help you continue learning?
After Learning
• How did you grow as a learner?
• Did you learn something new about yourself and how you learn?
• How can you use that in the future when something gets tough?

Figure 6.2: Teacher-to-student talk-it resource.

*Visit **go.solution-tree.com/instruction** for a reproducible version of this figure.*

Before Learning
• My plan for this learning is _____.
• I think the hardest part for me might be _____, and I'm going to _____ to help myself.
• _____, I can help you when you get to _____ if you can help me work through _____.
During Learning
• You know how to do this! Remember when you _____.
• You worked really hard on that!
• This is just like _____. Use what you know from when we did that.
• You just need more practice. Let me help you.
After Learning
• You worked really hard on that!
• You never gave up!
• You used lots of resources and effort to keep going.
• I saw you _____ when you got frustrated, stuck, or overwhelmed.

Figure 6.3: Student-to-student talk-it resource.

*Visit **go.solution-tree.com/instruction** for a reproducible version of this figure.*

Before Learning
• OK, let me make a plan for myself.
• I am going to need _____ to help me through _____.
• I've done something like this before; let's see if I can figure it out.
• Oh! Something new! Yay!

During Learning
• I just have to take it one step at a time.
• I get all this information. I just need to know _____.
• I have all these skills. I just need to be able to _____.
• I've gotten this far—I'm not stopping now.
• I'll know I got it when I can _____.

After Learning
• Wow. I learned so much!
• I grew a ton. Before, I didn't know _____, and now I know _____.
• Before, I couldn't _____, and now I can _____.
• Based on what I learned from this, next time, I am going to _____.
• One thing I learned about myself as a learner is _____.
• Next time I try something like this, I will _____.

Figure 6.4: Student-to-self talk-it resource.

*Visit **go.solution-tree.com/instruction** for a reproducible version of this figure.*

- Alternatively, you can sing this song that Kathleen wrote for younger students to the tune of "Twinkle, Twinkle, Little Star." (Adding motions makes it more fun and makes it stick in their brains!)

     When I work hard, my brain grows.

     All my effort really shows.

     I love learning; I love school

     When I use my mighty tool.

     When I work hard, my brain grows.

     All my effort really shows!

- Have students reflect on an aspect of their life where they already have a growth mindset. For some students, this can be when playing video games, taking a dance class, or working on a hobby or sport. Have them notice their self-talk when they are doing something that they enjoy practicing. Ask them to write down those messages and apply those same messages when they are working on an academic skill that feels more challenging for them.

- Students can work in pairs to restate their fixed mindset messages as growth mindset messages.

- Post growth mindset phrases (as shown in the anchor chart in figure 6.5) in the classroom for students to use as a resource when they find themselves thinking in fixed mindset ways. Also, post a chart of metacognitive strategies they are learning throughout the year that they can use when they are feeling stuck (see figure 6.6). Then, when they see the messages every day, they remind them, "Mindsets plus skill sets equals results."

<u>When things are challenging for you, what do you say to yourself?</u>

* Think! Think!
* I'm not leaving this school until I get it!
* This looks impossible, but I can do this!
* Slow down! Try to figure these things out.
* Keep trying!
* I tell myself what I need and observe the challenge!
* Come on! You can do it!
* You've done this before. It is not that different!
* I can't do it . . . yet!
* What are some other ways to do it?
* Get it done!
* What do I already know about this?

Figure 6.5: Growth mindset phrases for self-talk during challenges.

*Visit **go.solution-tree.com/instruction** for a reproducible version of this figure.*

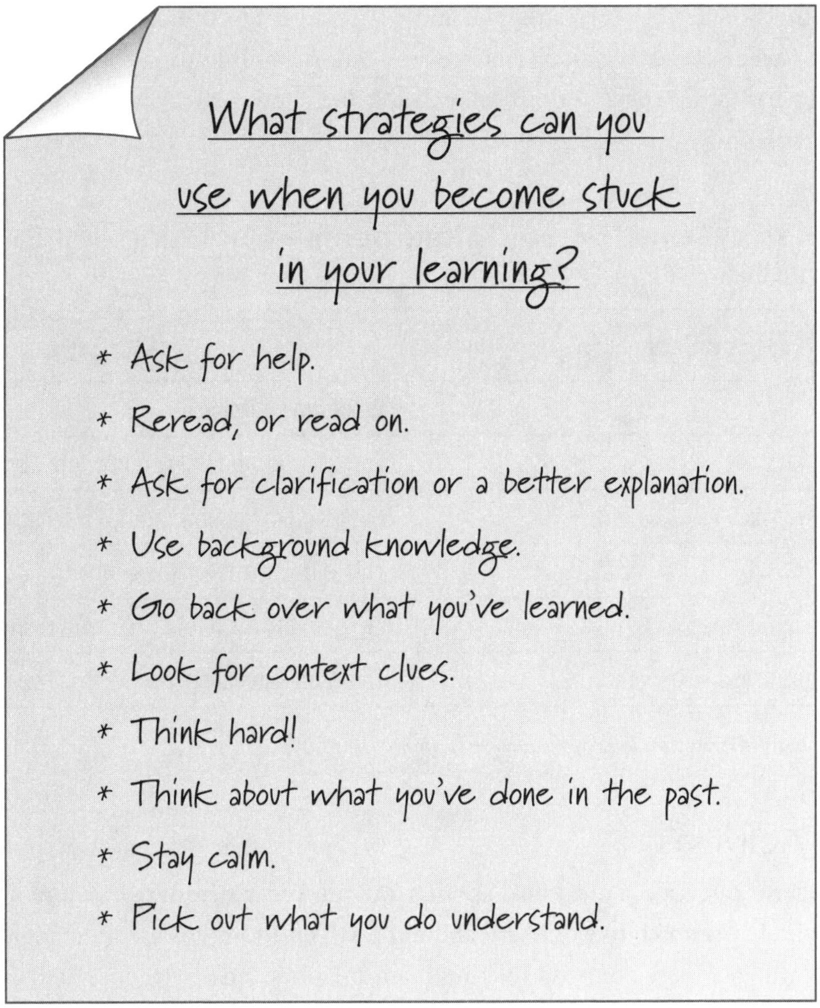

What strategies can you use when you become stuck in your learning?

* Ask for help.
* Reread, or read on.
* Ask for clarification or a better explanation.
* Use background knowledge.
* Go back over what you've learned.
* Look for context clues.
* Think hard!
* Think about what you've done in the past.
* Stay calm.
* Pick out what you do understand.

Figure 6.6: Metacognitive strategies to get unstuck.

*Visit **go.solution-tree.com/instruction** for a reproducible version of this figure.*

- On a T-chart, have students jot on one side a list of phrases or statements they recall that have stopped them from wanting to try harder. These can be messages from teachers, peers, parents, or themselves. On the other side of the T-chart, have students write a plan for how they will respond if they hear those phrases again. (After all, not all teachers, family members, or friends will be making the shift to a growth mindset, so students need to be prepared to defend themselves as learners who are working hard!)

- Close the day, or a class period, with feedback to students about working hard. The feedback can be from you or between students. Remember that empty praise or feedback without specific input about behaviors does not have a significant impact on learning (Marzano et al., 2001). It's not enough to say, "Nice job" or "Great effort!" Feedback needs to be focused on behaviors that can be noticed and named. Calling attention to specific actions such as asking for help, starting over, taking a deep breath, or staying focused is what helps students understand the behaviors that contribute to their success.

- Share with students your own struggles and what you say to yourself to keep your effort and drive up. Remember, beyond affirmations, self-talk is about knowing what we know and knowing what to do when we don't know. Table 6.2 shows how you can combat negative self-talk with positive self-talk.

Table 6.2: "Don't Say" and "Do Say" Statements—Changing Self-Talk From Negative to Positive

Don't Say	Do Say
"I'm so stupid."	"What am I missing?"
"I don't know what to do."	"I got started, and I am on the right track."
"I just can't do mathematics."	"I'm going to train my brain in mathematics."
"This is too hard."	"This is going to take some time."
"She's so smart; she makes me sick."	"I'm going to figure out how she's doing it."
"It's fine the way it is, and yours isn't any better."	"That's an interesting idea for improvement."

Visit **go.solution-tree.com/instruction** *for a reproducible version of this table.*

Using See-It Activities

Teachers and students can learn a great deal about growth mindsets from stories and examples of people, real and fictional, who have chosen to work hard and put forth effort, often against great odds. Bringing these stories and people into your classroom and making them mentors and role models will guide your students on this journey of personal and academic growth.

The following are activities that can help students develop growth mindsets by learning from role models (Kryza et al., 2011). Growth mindset stories should be shared in small moments throughout the school year. Alicia showed some videos about people with growth mindsets at the beginning of the year and then interspersed the stories and examples throughout the year, especially when she saw students were facing new challenges and their growth mindsets needed a boost. Sometimes, students brought in their own examples, which Alicia then shared with the class.

- Start the week with some growth mindset inspiration—Mindset Mondays! Read stories and show movies or read excerpts about real or fictional people who exemplify growth mindsets. (The movie *Rudy* is a great true-life example of a growth mindset person.) After viewing or listening, ask students to reflect on what they learned from the examples. Ask how they can apply this knowledge to their own lives. If you go to Kathleen's Infinite Horizons YouTube channel (www.youtube.com/user/KsInfiniteHorizons), you will find a great collection of short videos that focus on growth mindsets.

- Make class commitments to "live what you learned" from a role model. For example, when teaching about revision in writing, share how Ernest Hemingway rewrote the ending of *A*

Farewell to Arms thirty-nine times. Then make a classroom commitment to "Rewrite until it feels and sounds right!" Post your saying, and chant it from time to time.

- Have students select someone they admire who has grown in positive ways through mindsets and skill sets. Then have them study the person and create a project about what they learn from that person. (In the content areas, have them select a person from those fields of study. Jennifer in Bedford, Michigan [personal communication, September 2010], had her high school students study a scientist and create a poster about the scientist, including all the ways he or she failed before reaching success.) Make it a choice project. They can write a song, poem, or reflection; paint, draw, or create a model; make a video, VoiceThread, or photo journal—anything that they are inspired to create from what they learn.

- Create a bulletin board of role models, and let students add pictures and personal reflections. Let them change and grow it over the year. (Remind them to look for role models in their friends and family members too!)

- Have a share time once a week for the last five to ten minutes of class. You and your students can take turns sharing your story or role model and then have a class discussion. The students then discuss what growth mindset ideas or talk they took away from the people or characters, and then those new ideas are added to the anchor charts on growth mindsets. (See figure 6.5, page 84, for an example of a growth mindset anchor chart.)

- Collect and play songs that have growth mindset messages.

Keep Mindsets Alive

Here are some ideas for keeping the idea of growth mindsets alive throughout the school year.

- Nourish growth mindsets by creating a risk-taking, mistake-making environment. (Visit **go.solution-tree.com/instruction** or Kathleen's website, www.kathleenkryza.com, to download a free 8 × 10 poster about mindsets.) Mindsets exist within a larger classroom culture. In your classroom, shift the focus from proving to improving, from product to process. An inquiry-based approach to learning facilitates the growth mindset by embracing challenges, obstacles, and criticisms as chief drivers of learning. Failure can be a great teacher if it is approached not as judgment but as opportunity. That mental shift frees you up as well. If you take some missteps as you are trying to shift the classroom culture, don't be embarrassed. Be empowered to improve.

- Celebrate mindsets. Some ideas include individual and collective celebrations, such as a classroom "car wash" celebration. Once a week, students nominate someone in the classroom whom they see demonstrating a growth mindset (either academically or socially). The student who gets the most votes by Friday gets to go through the car wash, which is two lines of students who cheer and hug and support the student as he or she goes through the line. At the end, the student shares a tip that helped him or her maintain a growth mindset. That tip is added to the growth mindset bulletin board of tips of the month, and the student gets to record his or her tip in the classroom success book for growing a growth mindset. Provide each student with a printed copy of the book at the end of the year.

- Give out two growth mindset learner (GML) awards each week. (See figure 6.7 for an example of a growth mindset award certificate.) All week, anyone in the school can nominate someone for respectful behavior or growth mindset behavior inside and outside the classroom. The school leaders from the mindset team collect nominations, and each week, winners are selected for the GML award. The winners are announced each Friday. The principal presents an award certificate to the students and adds their names to a GML award poster in the school's entryway.

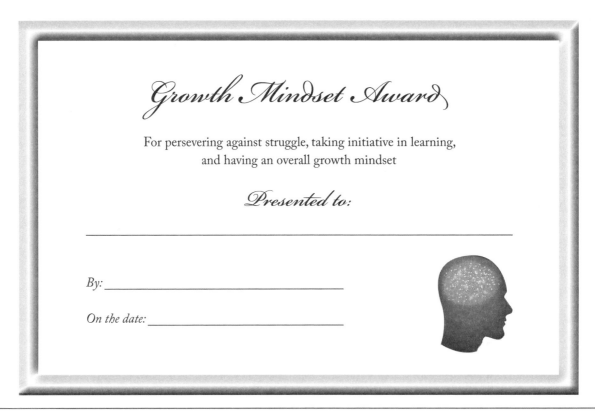

Figure 6.7: Sample growth mindset award.

Visit go.solution-tree.com/instruction for a reproducible version of this figure.

In wrapping up this important foundational skill, remember that students who've been taught about growth mindsets and how their brains learn made gains over students who were not taught this, and those gains continued over a year (Dweck, 2006). We have also collected many personal stories from teachers who are teaching about mindsets in their classrooms. One of the teachers Kathleen worked with in Watertown, New York, shared that one of her student's parents asked her what she was teaching her students. The teacher asked why. The parent shared that her high-school-age son was in the backseat of the car complaining about how bad he was in mathematics. After a time, her fifth-grade daughter, who was in this teacher's class, chimed in to tell her brother that if he kept talking like that, he was bound to develop a fixed mindset. But if he started telling himself to work hard on his mathematics, he would succeed, develop a growth mindset, and start doing better in class (personal communication, February 2015). When you hear stories like this from teachers all over the world, as we do, you know teaching mindsets is essential. Teaching students about growth mindsets and the power they have within them to literally change their minds will have lasting results for your students. Oh, and an added benefit is that because you are always reminding them to have growth mindsets, you'll find you develop your growth mindset skills alongside them.

chapter Seven

Learning Foundation Four: Student Talk

Whoever is doing the talking is doing the learning.

—David Sousa

Heroes talk with their allies to gain wisdom and to get help in making sense of the journey. In *The Matrix*, Neo reluctantly needs time to think and talk to Morpheus, Trinity, and the Oracle to put the pieces of the Matrix together. Harry, Hermione, and Ron often talk together to solve the mysteries they encounter in the *Harry Potter* series. The hero of every mystery show works with a partner or team to solve a case. Similarly, students need time to talk while learning, and there is great value in taking the time to teach students how to talk.

What It Means

Student talk is an essential tool for enriching classroom interactions and facilitating deeper learning and retention. Student talk should happen in varied groupings in our classrooms, including peer to peer, small group, and whole class, and in something very important—student self-talk. Student talk can occur in many formats in the classroom, such as metacognitive conversations about how learning occurs, presentations, debates, listening, writing, and critiquing others' work. What is most important is that students have many opportunities to process and interact using academic vocabulary. This is especially essential for students who come from other cultures or from homes where there is an absence of deep conversation.

Why It Works

Academic discourse is not something that comes naturally or easily for most students, and yet taking the time to teach our students to talk effectively gives them tools that will benefit them throughout their learning lives. Meloth and Deering (1999) maintain that high-quality talk is unlikely to emerge naturally, so teaching students to dialogue together is very important. In order for students to process new learning more deeply, teachers must explicitly teach, model, scaffold and allow opportunities for deliberate practice so that students learn how to effectively engage in academic discourse. When we provide opportunities for students to talk about their learning, we are providing an emotionally safe community where pondering, grappling, and synthesizing information are encouraged. Practicing academic discourse shifts the focus from asking one or few students to give the correct answer to fostering a community that discusses ideas and whose members learn from one another.

Culturally, students who come from a collectivist background will tend to feel comfortable in group conversations. However, it's also important to think about students who come from cultures where they are not encouraged to engage in academic discourse. By providing opportunities and supports, we offer these students the scaffolds needed to begin to deepen their discourse. Finally, at the academic level, if we want our students to be deep and critical thinkers, we must intentionally give them ample opportunity to practice deep discussions around academic topics.

What the Research Says

There are many ways that academic discourse benefits all learners in our classrooms. Alina Reznitskaya, Richard Anderson, and Li-Jen Kuo (2007) find that oral discussion is one of the best ways to develop critical-thinking skills. When students engage in thoughtful discussion in the classroom, they are able to practice articulating their ideas and also to learn about varied perspectives from others. This time to practice helps them develop their critical-thinking skills. Student discourse also helps build academic language, which is the language that describes complex ideas and concepts in academic settings. Jeff Zwiers and Marie Crawford (2011) note that student talk fosters all three language learning processes: listening, talking, and negotiating meaning with others. When students talk with one another in purposeful ways, they build skills in all these areas, thus promoting and deepening the use of academic language. Keep in mind that purposeful and focused talk also helps to bridge the gap between adolescents' social needs and the learning need of acquiring and using academic language (Fisher, Frey, & Rothenberg, 2008).

Another important reason to teach students to speak academically to one another is to consider the thirty-two-million-word gap. Betty Hart and Todd Risley's well-known research reveals:

> Children in professionals' homes were exposed to an average of more than fifteen hundred more spoken words per hour than children in welfare homes. Over one year, that amounted to a difference of nearly 8 million words, which, by age four, amounted to a total gap of 32 million words. (as cited in Shenk, 2010, p. 38)

If students are not exposed to rich language, from casual to formal, they will have less access to the content. Everyone benefits from learning academic discourse, but our most disadvantaged students will not thrive without it. In addition, research from David Sousa (2010) reminds us that our brains learn best in groups engaged in discourse. Ned Flanders (1970) reports that teachers of high-achieving students spend about 55 percent of class talking, whereas teachers of low-achieving students spend about 80 percent of class time doing the talking.

When students do the talking, we are able to listen to their thoughts and gain a better understanding of their depth of knowledge. When we hear from so many more voices in the classroom, we are able to mutually construct even deeper conceptual thinking. Consider this common question-and-answer format typical to our classrooms:

> Teacher: *What did the Sumerians use to control the twin rivers, the Tigris and Euphrates? (Initiate.)*
>
> Justin: *Levees? (Respond.)*
>
> Teacher: *Right. (Evaluate.) And why did the Sumerians want to control the twin rivers? (Initiate again.)*
>
> Justin: *To travel? (Respond.)*
>
> Teacher: *Right again. Next question.*

The problems inherent in this type of approach to talk in the classroom are multiple. In the previous example, only one student has an opportunity to talk, and that talk does not even require the talker to speak in a complete sentence, let alone extend to deeper discourse. If our goal is to create a classroom where students analyze, synthesize, and evaluate, we should quickly see that this type of interchange doesn't engage them in critical thinking. Instead, they may become frustrated as they struggle to guess what's in the teacher's head or become disengaged as they listen to the "popcorn patter" of teacher question, student response, teacher question, student response, and so on. If we want students to learn, *they* need to be doing the talking.

Learning and practicing academic discourse builds the social fabric in our classrooms that allows students from different backgrounds, with different opinions and different levels of understanding, to build communication skills and deepen thinking using common language and common language structures.

Classroom Practices for Student Talk

When explicitly modeling, scaffolding, and allowing opportunities for deliberate practice of academic discourse, there are several practices to consider that will support students and ensure they are successful. Consider the following steps to grow your students' discourse skills.

Establish Classroom Norms for Student Talk

Productive talk happens when students and teachers respond to and build on what others in the classroom have said. It is focused, meaningful, and mutually beneficial to the speaker and listener. When talk supports learning, both the speaker and listener use skills (ask questions for clarification, rephrase ideas, and use appropriate body language and eye contact). They have responsibilities to share opportunities to speak, respectfully challenge ideas, and come to consensus as a learning community.

To get started on this path to deep discourse with your students, have them brainstorm what effective talk and listening skills look like and sound like. Note all their thoughts and ideas, and create an anchor chart with the heading, "What does effective talk look like and sound like?" A second chart would read, "What does an effective listener look like and sound like?" Now the whole class can see visible reminders that explicitly state what we act like and sound like when we are speaking and listening to one another in a responsible learning way. These charts set an established routine of expectations for what academic discourse should look like and sound like, whether students are talking with a partner, with a small group, or as part of a whole-class discussion.

Assign Roles in the Small Group

Have students take on specific roles for the discussions, such as the questioner, clarifier, recorder, speaker, or facilitator. Define the roles you choose, and hold the students accountable for taking their roles seriously.

Provide High-Level and Visible Talk Prompts

If we want deep talk, we need to ask deep questions, so we should be sure to design questions that go beyond regurgitation of facts. For example, rather than ask, "Who fought against each other in the War of 1812?" deepen student engagement and push student thinking by asking, "What factors led to the start of the War of 1812? What side do you think you would have stood for, and why?" The prompts should be aligned to and beyond the level of thinking students are required to do in your state standards. Don't just say aloud what you want students to talk about; make sure your prompts are visibly posted where students can see them and refer back to them.

Use Talk Protocols

As students are learning how to do academic discourse with each other, offer them protocols that support and help them develop their talking skills. One simple protocol for building talking skills is called Save the Last Word for Me (adapted from Buehl, 2014). This is a great activity that allows students time for rehearsal of what they will share when practicing their academic discourse skills. List the following five steps on a bookmark for students to reference as needed to structure their talk for learning.

1. Reread the text, and find five passages you like.

2. Record your five passages and the locations of your passages in the text on index cards or in your reader's notebook.

3. On the back of your cards, jot down why you chose your five passages.

   * Why did the passage appeal to you?

   * What did it make you think of?

   * How would you extend the idea presented by your passage?

4. Sharing one passage at a time, in your core group:

   * The reader listens to all other thoughts about his or her chosen passage.

   * When all other thoughts are shared, the reader shares his or her thoughts at the end.

5. The reader of the passage always gets to "Save the Last Word for Me."

See page 172 in the appendix for a reproducible example of secondary and elementary bookmarks with the steps of Save the Last Word for Me on them.

You can also use the Three Levels of Talk protocol with students. This protocol takes time to teach and have students really use, but it is a powerful protocol for supporting the deepening of student talking and thinking.

1. **Say-anything comments:** A say-anything comment is how you get students started talking to *each other* in the classroom—not just answering the teacher's questions. All comments are welcome when we start out with say anything. All comments are acknowledged, and gratitude is expressed for participation. This establishes a safe environment for students to learn to listen and honor one another's comments. Spend about a week asking students to say anything about what they notice, what they feel, or what they think.

2. **Connecting comments:** After approximately a week of practicing say-anything comments and honoring all thoughts and comments, you can begin to model and scaffold the next level of talk: connecting comments. A connecting comment has to be related to the information presented or to what another student has said. We teach and model phrases such as, "I agree with . . .," "I disagree with . . .," and "I'd like to add . . ." Now in student discourse, we are welcoming both say-anything comments as well as asking students to make connecting comments, which pushes students to really listen to one another, think, and build important academic conversations.

3. **Deeper comments:** When you feel students have become comfortable with making connecting comments, it is time to model and scaffold how to extend their thinking with deeper comments. Deeper comments encourage students to clarify their thinking, extend ideas, process, and stimulate conversation among peers. We begin to model academic stems that will support students talking with one another, such as, "An example might be . . ." and "I used to think _____, but now my thinking has changed. I now think . . ." or stimulating conversations with questions for others, such as, "Why do you think . . . ?"

Remember that students will need time to develop these levels of discourse. However, if we don't explicitly teach them how to have discussions for learning, they will never learn the skill. Our students' depth of knowledge will only go as far as one-word iterations without us applying what we know about *how* to teach; be intentional and transparent about the skills they need to develop, model and scaffold those skills, and allow time for deliberate practice until students reach mastery.

Use Anchor Charts to Support Levels of Talk

As students are learning to do the levels of talk, provide talk prompts at each level to help them build their language skills. Creating an anchor chart (see table 7.1, page 96) as students are practicing each level of talk is a great scaffolding tool to make thinking visible and to help support students as they learn to talk deeply about their learning. You can add to the chart as students practice new ways to move through the levels of talk. The chart will remind them of what the different levels are (say-anything comment, connecting comment, and deeper comment) and will also provide them with academic talk stems (prompts) to support them as they begin developing their thoughts and building their discourse skills. Eventually, you will have a great anchor chart posted in the room that students can reference that looks like table 7.1. This tool is constantly visible in the classroom and used as a reminder and support for helping students to deepen their thinking through talking. Another version of a levels of talk chart ("Levels of Talk Processing Guide and Prompts") appears in the appendix on page 174.

Table 7.1: Talking to Think and Learn Anchor Chart of Three Levels of Talk

	Level of Talk	**What It Is and How to Get Started**
Teach first level of student talk.	Say-anything comments	All comments are welcome—any thought, any comment. All voices are heard and honored—"I noticed . . .," "I like . . .," "I feel . . .," or "I thought . . ."
Teach second level of student talk.	Connecting comments	Say something back to someone. Say something about the topic. Add new information about the topic. Add to the current conversation. • "I agree because . . ." • "I disagree because . . ." • "I'd like to piggyback on that and say . . ." • "I'd like to add . . ." • "Another way . . ." • "That reminds me of . . ." • "That connects to . . ." • "I'd like to ask a question . . ."
Teach third level of student talk.	Deeper comments	**Clarify:** Explain your thinking. • "What I really meant was . . ." • "What I'm trying to say is . . ." • "Let me add that . . ." • "An example might be . . ." **Extend:** Lengthen your ideas. • "I want to tell you more about . . ." • "Let me explain more . . ." **Process:** Explain how your thinking has changed. • "Before, I thought _____, but now I think . . ." • "My thinking has changed. . . ." • "Thinking about what _____ said, now I'm thinking . . ." **Stimulate:** Ask for ideas, invite discussion, and ask for perspectives. • "What was your thinking?" • "I wonder why . . ." • "Why do you think . . . ?" • "How would you . . . ?"

*Visit **go.solution-tree.com/instruction** for a reproducible version of this table.*

To help students reflect on how deeply they are talking, we can help them reflect on their conversations. As the facilitator of talking for learning, we can chart comments that students make in class. Students can analyze the script of their discussions to see how deeply they are thinking and talking. A nice touch is to color-code each level, making their talk very visible. You will hear comments such as, "Wow, we had mostly connecting comments and only two deeper comments. We need to start going deeper with our conversations!" And now you have created a community that is safe emotionally to grow and think together and one that is vital and alive in which students have the desire to be deep thinkers, great communicators, and lifelong learners.

Let Students Lead

When teaching students to talk, it's important that we start to remove ourselves from the conversation. If we keep becoming part of the conversation, many students may come to rely on us and not get going on their own. We can help facilitate and prompt talk, but we need to let students lead. In the following example, the teacher gives prompts to stimulate the depth of the conversation. As students get more adept with academic discourse, the teacher should begin to remove her- or himself from the conversation as much as possible and let the students lead:

> Teacher: *OK, class, let's practice deepening our talking skills today as we discuss the first two chapters of our read-aloud book. Can someone get us started with a say-anything comment about the beginning of* Stargirl *by Jerry Spinelli?*
>
> Betsy: *A new girl has come to the school, and everybody wonders who she is.* (Say-anything comment—write in green.)
>
> Teacher: *Would anybody like to add to this?* (Prompt for connecting comment.)
>
> Calvin: *Yeah, I'd like to add to that. She's weird, and everybody's curious about her. So am I. Playing the ukulele at lunch? Too weird!* (Connecting comment—write in blue.)
>
> Teacher: *What do you think might be going on with her?* (Prompt for deeper comment.)
>
> Juanita: *I think she might be crazy, like, mental. Like, maybe she escaped from somewhere and showed up at the school.* (Deeper comment to clarify—write in black.)
>
> Charles: *I disagree. I think she just comes from a different background. She was homeschooled, and maybe she just doesn't know how to act like other kids do. I have a friend who is homeschooled, and he's kinda different.* (Connecting and deeper comment, extending—write in black.)
>
> Teacher: *Is anybody wondering about what happened in the opening chapter?* (Prompt for deeper comment.)
>
> Noel: *Yeah! Why would the author include that opening chapter about the guy getting the mystery porcupine tie in the mail if it wasn't somehow connected to this Stargirl character? There's a mystery going on here. What do you guys think?* (Deeper comment, stimulating—write in black.)

Teaching our students to grow their academic discourse skills is essential if we want them to think deeply and feel safely connected in a community. It takes time and practice to learn to share ideas, to listen to one another, and to ponder, wonder, and build curiosity and connections in learning. We can make it happen, but, as with all the foundational skills we are sharing in this book, it is critical that we plan to intentionally and transparently model and scaffold the skills students need and allow opportunities for deliberate practice of structured academic talk.

Make Student Talk Accountable

Usually, having students talk isn't a problem. Getting them to be focused on talk that's connected to a learning target is sometimes the challenge. When talk supports learning, all members of a conversation are accountable for their contributions to the conversation, achieving the goals of the conversation, and assessing whether the goals have been reached.

Once students have the basic skills and responsibilities for student talk for learning, make certain to move between groups and monitor them. In Japan, they do *kikan-shidō*—teaching between desks. This is an essential technique for holding students accountable for their talk and is a great formative assessment tool for you to learn what students need to help them grow. After small-group talk time, share models and examples of productive talk that achieve the class expectations. You might note what students say to move the talk to deeper comments. For example:

> *In one group, I heard someone intentionally take the talk deeper by asking a wondering question to the group when she said, "I wonder what would happen if the rate of mammalian DNA replication were different. What do you think?" In another group, I saw respectful listening and disagreeing. In this group, I noticed that the idea, not the person, was the focus of disagreement when I heard someone say, "While I agree with most of that statement, the one thing that I disagree with is . . ." This is a wonderful example of respectful talk based on confronting an idea and not a person.*

You can also leave students notes as you walk around the room commenting on quality talk and making suggestions for those who are struggling. Students love this and can't wait to read what you wrote. Students may actually overdo their talk to impress you when they see you coming to listen to and analyze their academic talk. This is a good thing! Like with any skill, we overpractice until it becomes natural.

You can also focus student talk and make students accountable by having them think and process together around a product they have to create, such as a graphic organizer, annotated quotation, or placemat where they have to synthesize their ideas as they talk and think together. Their product becomes a record of their conversation and can be used for assessment information.

You can design a simple rubric to help you assess students and help them self-assess on the talking skills they are building. For example, if you want them to self-assess the levels of talk they are developing, you could create a rubric like the one shown in figure 7.1.

Levels of Talk Rubric

Rate your ability to make the three types of comments: say anything, connecting, and deeper.

1 = I'm not using this type of comment, and 5 = I can do it!

Name: _____

I know how to make a say-anything comment.

1   2   3   4   5

Here's an example: _____

I know how to make a connecting comment.

1   2   3   4   5

Here's an example: _____

I know how to make a deeper comment.

1   2   3   4   5

Here's an example: _____

Figure 7.1: Levels of talk rubric.

*Visit **go.solution-tree.com/instruction** for a reproducible version of this figure.*

Time and Practice

Teaching students to talk at deep levels takes time and practice. But, over time, once you have modeled and scaffolded how to talk; displayed an anchor chart to remind students of what the levels of deepening discourse look like and sound like; and practiced, practiced, practiced, you will see students' talking skills begin to take hold and blossom. When Kathleen was coaching teachers in Milford, Michigan, she observed fourth graders talk for forty-five minutes in their book club groups unprompted by the teacher. When Kathleen asked the teacher how she achieved this, the teacher credited patience. In October of that school year, she had felt really frustrated and had wanted to quit, but if she had, she would not have seen the amazing results that occurred by March. The payoff for patience in teaching students to talk is worth the effort and will change the level of thinking in your classroom to that deep, rich talk you've always imagined.

chapter *Eight*

Learning Foundation Five: Student Self-Assessment

We must constantly remind ourselves that the ultimate purpose of evaluation is to have students learn to become self-evaluative. If students graduate from our schools still dependent upon others to tell them when they are adequate, good, or excellent, then we've missed the whole point of what self-directed learning is about.

—Arthur L. Costa and Bena Kallick

Real heroes must continually self-reflect on their journey. Abraham Lincoln, Nelson Mandela, and Mahatma Gandhi all wrote and reflected about their life journeys. As Socrates said, "The unexamined life is not worth living."

What It Means

Student self-assessment is the process of students gathering information about and reflecting on their own learning. It is the students' own assessment of personal progress in knowledge, skills, processes, or attitudes. Self-assessment leads students to a greater awareness and understanding of themselves as learners. Self-assessment is the key to becoming a metacognitive thinker and learner. Students can self-assess individually, and you can also teach them to self-assess as a group.

Why It Works

The ability to self-reflect and monitor your actions is essential in all three areas of the learning triad: (1) emotional, (2) cultural, and (3) academic. Self-assessment is metacognition, which is the ability to think about your own thinking and plan, monitor, and adjust your approach to problem solving as needed. "Developing strong metacognitive strategies and learning to teach those strategies in a classroom environment should be standard features of the curriculum in schools of education" (Bransford, Brown, & Cocking, 2000, p. 21).

Social-emotional self-assessment is self-regulation, and it is a taught skill. Students need to be aware that they have behaviors that aren't working for them or perhaps others (you and the rest of the class) and that they have the power within them to shape and change their behaviors in ways that will help them better succeed in school and life. Self-assessing and learning better strategies for coping are paramount to developing better social-emotional skills.

Culturally, students need to be aware of their own cultural norms and how they connect or don't connect with community norms. They need to self-determine which actions from their culture might have a challenging impact on fitting in with the school culture, and they also need to observe, notice, and respect the cultural norms of the country they live in. For example, Kathleen loves chewing gum, but when she was doing workshops in Singapore, where gum is not acceptable, she chose to honor the country's cultural norms and leave her Chiclets at home! Another example would be if students are from a culture that does not use direct eye contact but they now live in one that does. They need to self-assess when to use their own culture's expectations (at home, with others from their culture) and when it would be in their benefit to use the cultural expectations of the community in which they now live. Cultural self-assessment helps students fit in and can also help them explain to their teachers and others what the norms are for their world so that others become more aware and understanding.

Academically, teachers should support students practicing self-reflection starting in age-appropriate ways as soon as they enter school. Students who self-assess academically know where they are in the learning process, they know what's working, and they know what to do when things aren't working for them. It's important for teachers to have clear learning targets (objectives) so students know where they are going and what they should be self-assessing. The clearer we are about where they should be heading on the academic journey, the more realistic our students can become about themselves as learners. For example, Kathleen was having pairs of first graders assess themselves on how well they were working together. One group gave itself smiley faces for being cooperative, even though the students hadn't been very cooperative. When Kathleen was honest with them, saying, "I wouldn't give you a smiley face there," the one little girl looked at the other and said, "See, I told you we shouldn't have put a smiley face there!" The more students practice self-assessing around clear learning targets, the more realistic they become about the learning process.

What the Research Says

Self-assessment has been shown to raise students' achievement significantly (Chappuis & Stiggins, 2002; Frederiksen & White, 1998; Rolheiser & Ross, 2001). In 2000, cognitive scientists and cognitive psychologists combined their knowledge in the book *How People Learn: Brain, Mind, Experience, and School* (Bransford et al., 2000). A key finding in their research is that "a 'metacognitive' approach to instruction can help students learn to take control of their own learning by defining learning goals and monitoring their progress in achieving them" (Bransford et al., 2000, p. 18). The implication of this research is that teaching metacognitive skills "should be consciously incorporated into curricula across disciplines and age levels" (Bransford et al., 2000, p. 21). Self-assessment is a key component for student self-regulation. A self-regulated learner is metacognitive, or able to coordinate cognitive resources, emotions, and actions in the service of his or her learning goals (Boekaerts & Cascallar, 2006). If we want students to self-regulate, they must be aware of their mindsets as well as their skill sets. They need to able to monitor and adjust what's working for them, what's not working, and what other strategies will help them achieve understanding and success. Metacognition and self-assessment are the keys to growing self-resilient learners.

While many of us can define *metacognition* as thinking about thinking, we must ask ourselves if we have consciously integrated teaching students to be metacognitive consistently into our teaching practices. Mindsets and metacognition go hand in hand in helping students to develop an internal locus of control, thus becoming more responsible and accountable for their own learning.

When you begin having students self-assess, you may find that students rate themselves higher or lower than your own assessments. For example, young students (grades K–5) may overestimate "because they lack the cognitive skills to integrate information about their abilities and are more vulnerable to wishful thinking" (Ross, 2006, p. 3). Inflation is more likely to occur for older students (grades 6–12) if they believe that the self-assessments will directly affect their grades (see Dunning, Heath, & Suls, 2004).

So self-assessment is a skill that students need to develop. If we teach students to self-assess in age-appropriate ways from the time they enter our schools, they stand a much better chance of building their emotional, cultural, and academic mindsets and skill sets and becoming self-regulated, metacognitive learners.

Classroom Practices for Student Self-Assessment

In this section, we offer teaching practices to help students effectively learn how to assess themselves. As with all the techniques we are sharing, these must be taught intentionally and transparently through modeling and scaffolding and deliberate practice.

Help Students Self-Assess Accurately

The following list provides steps for helping students become accurate self-assessors.

- Intentionally teach students how to self-assess using clear criteria they helped define. First, determine an area of learning you want students self-assessing. Students can self-assess their knowledge and understanding of the learning objectives, their mindsets and effort, their behavior, or their learning styles. If you see that students aren't showing ownership of some aspect of their learning, it's a perfect time to create a self-assessment. For example, if students aren't using their mathematics time wisely, have them brainstorm ideas about what a good mathematics learner would look like, and then synthesize their criteria into a self-assessment rubric (see the following explanation for developing rubrics) that they then use for a few days or weeks to improve their use of mathematics work time.

- Involve students in constructing rubrics so that they may deepen their understanding of the criteria they are using to self-assess. Once you have constructed a rubric or self-reflection form (see examples of self-assessments later in this chapter), model how you would think to fill out the rubric or form.

- Provide many opportunities to practice, practice, practice self-reflection.

- Ensure that students understand that self-assessments are not evaluative, they are formative, designed to help them build growth mindsets and improve their overall performance.

- Create opportunities for learners to compare their self-assessments to those of their peers and teachers so they can monitor and adjust their self-assessments more effectively.

- Collect self-assessments at various times (in other words, not always immediately following instruction), and provide feedback from your perspective.

You can learn a lot from student self-assessments, so be sure to examine student self-assessments and use that information to help you help your students. For example, Clare, a mathematics teacher from Watertown, New York, had her students self-assess how they liked working in small groups to check their mathematics work, rather than her just giving answers. She wanted to see what students thought about this new collaborative technique she was trying. She found that most students really liked working in groups and felt they learned better correcting work this way. However, one student said he didn't like the technique because he didn't understand how to do the work when he got his answer wrong. What Clare (personal communication, April 2015) realized from his self-reflection was that this student didn't have the academic language skills to articulate his mathematics thinking, so she needed to model and help him practice how to explain his mathematics thinking.

Develop Student Awareness of Metacognitive Processes

If our students are going to self-regulate and become effective metacognitive learners, we need to explicitly teach them how to do that. The following are ideas and practices for helping your students become aware of their own metacognitive processes.

- Have students share think-alouds on what they've done that helped them be successful so they can learn from each other's self-assessments and strategies.

  - "To do the math problem, I broke it down into steps and did each step, and then I checked my answer to see if the steps led me to the correct answer. When I take the time to break it down and check like this, I am doing better in my math work."

  - "When I practiced my spelling by skipping around the room while I spelled the words, it really helped me remember them."

  - "When I don't want to do my homework, I set a timer for how long I think I can work, and when it goes off, I get to take a five-minute break to check my phone. When I give myself short breaks like that, it helps me tackle the stuff I don't feel like doing."

  - "When I'm mad, my mom taught me to take some deep breaths before I say or do something mean."

- As students begin to develop metacognitive strategies that work, post their strategies that effective learners use on anchor charts around the room. You can add strategies that you teach them as well. When students are self-assessing, they can use these learning strategies and start to self-assess whether or not they are using them effectively or using them at all (see figure 8.1). We have found that students love it if you add their name or initials on the chart next to the strategy they shared.

Reading Strategies List

What effective readers do when reading
and interacting with text

* Look for context clues (connect the dots). —Wenting G.

* Ask questions. —Jack N.

* Write in margins.

* Connect to prior knowledge.

* Develop an educated guess or hypothesis.

* Read line by line.

* Infer (read between the lines).

* Reread. —Bernadette P.

* Paraphrase (put it in your own words).

* Give an opinion.

* Ask why.

* Look for literary elements (metaphors, alliteration, and so on).

* Predict. —Joy S.

* Underline parts that jump out.

* Skip irrelevant hard words.

* Sound out important hard words.

* Look for prefixes, suffixes, and roots in hard words.

* Ask someone else. —Tulio O.

* Look up hard words as a last resort. —Bettina M.

* Use a word you know for one you don't know. —Richard K.

Figure 8.1: Reading strategies anchor chart.

- Have students create metacognition books or blogs so they can keep a personal record of strategies they are learning as well as self-reflections about what they are learning about themselves as learners.

- Have students self-assess weekly on their mindsets and use of metacognitive strategies. (See the effort rubric in figure 8.2.)

- Get paint color palettes from home-improvement stores, one for each student. Students keep the cards on top of their desks. Once you have taught a chunk of new information, you can ask students to self-assess by putting their finger on the color that describes their current understanding. The lightest color means "This information is crystal clear to me." The middle color means "I think I get it." The darkest color means "I am in a fog and don't get it at all."

4 (Growth mindset)		I worked on the tasks until they were finished. I saw difficulties as opportunities to strengthen my understanding.
3 (Fairly growth mindset)		I worked on the tasks until they were finished. I tried even when it was difficult.
2 (Somewhat fixed mindset)		I put some effort into tasks, but I stopped working when it became difficult.
1 (Fixed mindset)		I did not try.

Figure 8.2: Effort rubric.

*Visit **go.solution-tree.com/instruction** for a reproducible version of this figure.*

Build In Checkpoints During Instruction

As students practice becoming self-reflective (metacognitive), it will be important for them and for you to stop and check along the way so they can see how they are doing and monitor and adjust their course of action if need be. The following are teaching techniques you can use to reflect during the learning process.

Plan-Do-Review

This is a technique to help young learners (preK–2) start to build their self-reflection skills while they are working in learning centers. Learning centers are stations that are set up around the room for students to work in and practice learning skills. Centers can be designed for practicing reading, mathematics, or strategies such as sorting and matching. You can even have play or imagination centers. Before students start to work in their centers, they have to plan which center they want to work in during center time.

- **Plan:** Students say their plan or sign up (name on whiteboard) for their plan for during center time. For example, "I plan to work in the Sequencing Center today."

- **Do:** Students work in the centers for an allotted amount of time.

- **Review:** Students come together in a circle. After reviewing what they did during their circle time, they share three-finger self-assessments around a clear target—for example, "I used my time wisely. I cooperated. I cleaned up my space." Three fingers means excellent. Two fingers means good. One finger means try harder next time.

Admission and Exit Cards

These cards are an easy, helpful way for students to communicate with you about how things are going. (See examples in figure 8.3 and figures 8.4 and 8.5, page 108.) Admission cards are collected at the beginning of class as admission into the room that day. Exit cards are collected at the end of the class period as students exit the room. These cards are short writings or drawings that students can do before (to preassess) and during (to formatively assess) learning. This helps students, and teachers, to know where they are going and how well they are doing on the journey. Information from admission and exit cards allows teachers to make adjustments in content or methodology that will better meet student or group needs. These cards also make sure all students are sharing information about themselves and their learning process. Admission and exit cards need to be simple and designed around a clear learning target that you want students to assess either at the beginning of a lesson or unit or as a formative checkpoint along the way. You will find reproducible exit card templates in the appendix (pages 175–176).

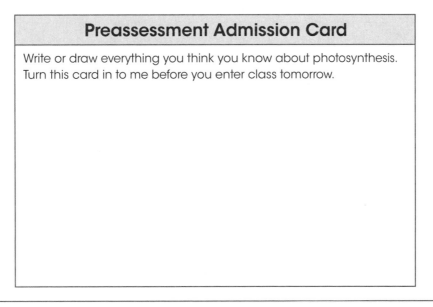

Preassessment Admission Card

Write or draw everything you think you know about photosynthesis. Turn this card in to me before you enter class tomorrow.

Figure 8.3: Preassessment admission card example.

*Visit **go.solution-tree.com/instruction** for a reproducible version of this figure.*

Preassessment Exit Card
Write or draw everything you think you know about time. Turn this card in to me before you leave class today.

Figure 8.4: Preassessment exit card example.

*Visit **go.solution-tree.com/instruction** for a reproducible version of this figure.*

Vocabulary Stations Self-Assessment Exit Card					
Name:	Low				High
1. I used my time wisely and had a good attitude.	1	2	3	4	5
2. I completed work at each station.	1	2	3	4	5
3. I understand the key terms better now.	1	2	3	4	5
I learn vocabulary words best this way:					
Here's how I plan to study for my test based on what I know about myself as a learner.					

Figure 8.5: Formative assessment exit card example.

*Visit **go.solution-tree.com/instruction** for a reproducible version of this figure.*

Here are some variations on the exit card concept. In the Note to a Friend activity, pass out sheets of paper at the end of an explanation or lesson, and ask each student to write a note to a friend explaining the concept the class just learned. In the My Questions activity, hand out paper, and ask the students to jot down two questions or wonderings they have about what they learned before they leave. This reinforces the notion that we are never finished learning, and it gives you a sense of what they are confused about or what they want to know more about.

The following are examples of prompts you could use for exit cards for formative assessment.

- "What did you hear, feel, or experience today that affirmed your thinking?"
- "What questions or thoughts are you left with today?"
- "If you understood today's lesson well, would you be able to help others?"
- "Write one thing you learned today."
- "What area gave you the most difficulty today?"
- "Something that really helped me in my learning today was . . ."
- "What connection did you make today that made you say 'Aha! I get it?'"
- "Describe how you solved a problem today."
- "What strategy did you use when you got stuck today?"
- "Did you have a fixed or growth mindset as you worked today?"

Traffic-Light Self-Assessment

There are many ways to use traffic-light colors to help students self-assess, but the essential idea is that the three colors of the light mean the following. (See the traffic-light reproducible in the appendix, page 177.)

- **G (green light):** I understand this very well, or I am happy with my work.
- **Y (yellow light):** I need a bit of support but understand the basics, or I'm not quite sure.
- **R (red light):** Help, I don't understand, or I'm stuck!

See an example in figure 8.6.

I don't get this. I need more explanation.

I am starting to get it, but I don't think I could explain it to someone else.

I get it, and I could easily explain it to someone else.

Figure 8.6: Traffic-light self-assessment example.

Students can assess by putting a check mark in or drawing and coloring in the appropriate light. You can use colored drinking cups that the students keep on the table in front of them. This is good for students working individually or in groups. They put up a green cup if they are working fine, a yellow cup if they are doing OK but could use a check-in from you, and a red cup if they are stuck.

Use the traffic-light system to have students assess how they are doing on a project, understanding a key learning objective, working together, and so on. The traffic-light system can also help you target students far more effectively for small, flexible groups. If students get it, they can be in a group that receives enrichment, and if they are struggling, they can be grouped together for more support.

Group Self-Assessment

When students start working in groups, it's really helpful to have them self-assess how their groups are working together.

- Have students brainstorm a list of criteria for what it looks like and sounds like when a group is working well together. Jot down all their ideas on chart paper.

- Take all your students' or classes' ideas, and categorize them by two to five criteria for effective group work. (For example, criteria for working well in a group might include "We all work hard," "We are cooperative," "We use our time wisely," and "We all know the information.") Because the students create the criteria with you, they will feel ownership about the criteria, and it will be age appropriate.

- Create a simple rubric (see examples in figures 8.7 and 8.8) for students to use when self-assessing their groups. The recorder in the group fills in the two to five criteria that the class selected.

- Assign a group leader to guide students through each of the criteria, determining how well students feel they did. (This can be on a scale of 1 to 5 or with smiley and frowny faces.)

- Once groups are done, the leader lets you know they are ready. You evaluate each group's assessment, giving your feedback as to how it did based on your expert observation.

How Our Group Did	🙂	😐	🙁
We helped each other.			
We all worked.			

Figure 8.7: Elementary group self-assessment chart.

Visit **go.solution-tree.com/instruction** *for a reproducible version of this figure.*

Rate your group from 1 to 5 for each group expectation (1 is the lowest, and 5 is the highest).					
Group Expectations **The Group Is ...**	**Date:**	**Date:**	**Date:**	**Date:**	**Date:**
Being on task					
Cooperating					
Sharing information (Everybody in the group is informed.)					
Respecting others in the room					

Figure 8.8: Secondary group self-assessment chart.

*Visit **go.solution-tree.com/instruction** for a reproducible version of this figure.*

Create Rubrics With Students

The more students are involved in creating and self-assessing the rubric with you, the more invested they are in the outcomes of their learning. The following are steps and suggestions for developing rubrics. Rubrics can be done individually or in groups.

- Begin with a clear learning target. As much as possible, involve students in helping you write learning targets. Part of the learning target will come from your standards and benchmarks, so inform students that the state determined this standard to be something they need to know or be able to do. Have students help you define other parts of the rubric, creating items like quality work and effort on the rubric.

- Depending on students' grade level, you can use either words or pictures to note whether students have been successful (*excellent*) or not so successful (*not so good*). Students should see the rubric as they begin to work on their projects. You can give students a copy of the rubric, show it to them on the overhead, or make a wall chart of it. Explain what's expected of them as you walk through the rubric. That way, they are clear about expectations all along as they work on their projects.

- After students have shared their projects, have them use the rubric to self-assess by placing check marks in the boxes of how they think they performed. (To keep things simple, avoid having them assign themselves points.) They complete the self-assessment by responding to the prompts: "What we did that was quality work was . . ." or "What I did that I was proud of was . . ." and "What we would do differently next time is . . ." Then they turn in the rubric.

- You then assess the students' work on the same rubric, adding the points and the grade along with specific comments before returning the rubric.

- Connect self-assessment in school to the type of reflective self-assessing they will need to do as they enter the work world. Explain to students that they need to do quality work and be able to know when they are doing quality work. As they get better at self-assessing, they should find the scores they give themselves on the rubric become very close to the teacher's scores.

- If you are giving grades, explain to students that the grade you give is the final grade because you are the professional, coach, and guide for their learning. You know what it looks like when they get it.

Self-assessment is metacognition; it's how we become more effective at self-regulating our behaviors and our learning actions. As you work with your students to help them grow their self-assessment skills, you will be delighted to see how much more accountable for their own learning they become. This is a powerful foundation to build for helping you to teach smarter, not harder. The long-term benefit is that you will send students out into their future with a more realistic ability to self-reflect and become more responsible citizens.

In the next chapter, you will learn about the benefits of teaching mindfulness in your classroom. This valuable foundation will help ground your students and help them create the calm mind and space they need to become effective self-assessors.

chapter *Nine*

Learning Foundation Six: Mindfulness

Feelings come and go like clouds in a windy sky. Conscious breathing is my anchor.

—Thích Nhất Hạnh

Batman goes to his cave, Superman goes to his Fortress of Solitude, and Iron Man goes to his mansion. We all need a place of retreat—time to regroup and recuperate. Mindfulness can be done anywhere and bring us the same benefits. You and your students can also learn to create your own sacred place to be still. Educators often ask if there is some way, magic trick, or tool that could address students who:

- Can't focus on the lesson or their work

- Are impatient

- Have no impulse control

- Get extremely anxious before they take a test

- Don't know how to get along with their classmates

- Give up when learning gets challenging

- Come in with so much stress from home

Yes! A very powerful tool you can teach students is mindfulness. Mindfulness is not new. It's a part of what makes us human—the capacity of being fully conscious and aware. Mindfulness is a tool and technique that has been around for centuries and is now being introduced and used as a teaching practice to achieve student success in and out of the classroom.

What It Means

Mindfulness is cultivating attention and awareness. It is the practice of being present and aware of things happening in the current moment:

> [Mindfulness] is a way of paying attention that originated in Eastern meditation practices. It has been described as "bringing one's complete attention to the present experience on a moment-to-moment basis" (Marlatt & Kristeller, 1999, p. 68) and as "paying attention in a particular way: on purpose, in the present moment, and nonjudgmentally" (Kabat-Zinn, 1994, p. 4). (as cited in Baer, 2003, p. 125)

Teaching mindfulness in the classroom helps students pay attention, it contributes to acceptance of differences, and it promotes students' growth as human beings and as learners. Using mindful teaching practices in the classroom has double benefits: while these practices nurture a safe, calm learning community where students can flourish emotionally, socially, culturally, and academically, the practices also allow teachers to thrive professionally and personally.

What the Research Says

The research on the benefits of using mindfulness practices in the classroom is overwhelmingly positive:

> Studies of mindfulness programs in schools have found that regular practice—even just a few minutes per day—improves students' self-control and increases their classroom participation, respect for others, happiness, optimism, and self-acceptance levels. It can help reduce absenteeism and suspensions as well. A mindfulness practice helps reduce activity in the amygdala, the brain's emotional center responsible for fear and stress reactions. (Schwartz, 2014)

Experience has shown that spending a few minutes on mindfulness training with students greatly reduces the time spent on interruptions from misbehavior.

There are many benefits of mindfulness. In addition to the following list, the brain actually begins to function differently, enabling the mindful thinker to respond more consciously. It changes the brain as it changes the behaviors (Hawn Foundation, 2011) and:

- Improves executive-functioning skills
- Supports readiness to learn
- Promotes academic performance
- Strengthens attention and concentration
- Reduces anxiety before testing
- Promotes self-reflection and self-calming
- Improves classroom participation by supporting impulse control

- Provides tools to reduce stress

- Enhances social and emotional learning

- Fosters positive social skills, such as empathy, compassion, patience, and generosity

- Improves students' self-control and self-regulation skills

- Strengthens students' resiliency and decision making

- Increases empathy and understanding

Why It Works

Mindfulness increases the strength and sensitivity of our awareness. Have you ever started eating a snack, taken a couple of bites, and then noticed all you had left was an empty packet in your hand? Or have you ever been driving somewhere and arrived at your destination only to realize you remember nothing about your journey? These are common examples of mindlessness or going on automatic pilot. In our busy lives, we constantly try to multitask; therefore, we are not fully aware of what's happening to us, in us, and around us from moment to moment. We often fail to notice the good things about our lives, fail to hear what our bodies are telling us, or hurt ourselves with self-criticism.

Our minds are easily distracted, always examining past events and trying to anticipate the future. Becoming more aware of our thoughts, feelings, and sensations may not sound like a helpful thing to do, but learning to do this in a way that suspends judgment and self-criticism can have an incredibly positive impact on both our students and ourselves.

Mindfulness is a way of paying attention to and seeing clearly whatever is happening in our lives. It will not eliminate life's pressures, but it can help us respond to them in a calmer manner that benefits our heart, head, and body. It helps us recognize and step away from habitual, often unconscious emotional and physiological reactions to everyday events. It provides us with a scientifically researched approach to cultivating clarity, insight, and understanding. Practicing mindfulness allows us to be fully present in our life and work and improve our quality of life.

The changes brought on through a mindfulness practice do not happen overnight, nor do they last without continuous practice. Mindfulness is like going to the gym—you have to keep practicing to enjoy the benefits. When you first practice mindfulness, it might seem as if nothing is changing, but eventually, the benefits will reveal themselves. If we understand it takes time and practice before our inner voice begins to quiet, we will be more apt to continue and not give up after a few attempts that don't seem to be working.

Let's take a look at how mindfulness benefits students emotionally, culturally, and academically.

Socially and Emotionally

Socially and emotionally, students benefit from learning mindfulness because it gives them a tool to use when they feel angry, stressed, anxious, depressed, or overwhelmed. According to the Hawn Foundation (2011), "Mindful attention centers on conscious awareness of the present moment: by focusing our attention and controlling our breath, we can learn to reduce stress and optimize the learning capacity of the brain" (p. 8). Additionally, it leads students to "self-regulation of their behavior" (Hawn Foundation, 2011, p. 6).

Mindfulness creates a space for changing impulsive reactions to thoughtful responses. Many of our students go from a stimulus to a quick, impulsive reaction. Students who only know this impulsive response to emotional triggers continue to be reactive, and oftentimes, their behaviors will escalate with more and more intensity. Certain stimuli or triggers will act like the push of a snowball down a slope of emotional impulsivity, picking up momentum and getting bigger and more out of control. Mindfulness practice gives students awareness of their behaviors and then tools to slow down the momentum of their reactions. "The child who learns to monitor his or her senses and feelings becomes more aware and better understands how to respond to the world *reflectively* instead of *reflexively*" (Hawn Foundation, 2011, p. 6). A calmer, happier brain means more control of emotion and better choices.

Culturally

According to Colleen Ricci (2015):

> Mindfulness meditation—the practice of quietening the mind to bring awareness and attention to the present moment—is increasingly being used in schools around the world as a tool to improve student wellbeing and enhance academic performance. Although originating in Buddhist religious tradition, it is a secular form of the practice that has become popular in classrooms and workplaces.

The concept of mindfulness originated in Eastern cultures and focuses on cultivating awareness, attention, compassion, and acceptance. Wouldn't we want to cultivate those traits in all our students? With a growing number of doctors, therapists, and neuropsychologists studying the benefits of mindfulness, the definition of mindfulness has broadened, and it is becoming a widely accepted practice in schools around the world.

As American culture moves faster and faster, a culturally significant reason for bringing mindfulness practices into U.S. schools is that it can help overbusy, overstimulated, and overanxious American students develop tools to slow down their bodies and their minds. Students from Latin America, southern Europe, Asia, and Slavic countries are more likely than Americans to culturally value the ability to accept situations and one's given position in life. They have a fatalistic worldview. ("Whatever happens, happens, and I have no control over my life.") Students from these cultures need to understand that mindfulness is a way they can control their reaction to life's circumstances and that they can change the way they perceive the world (UGA Beyond the Arch, 2012).

Thus, students from both cultural perspectives will benefit from intentional and transparent instruction on mindfulness practices. They need to understand how mindfulness practices can shape the neural pathways in their brains. They need to know the benefits that mindfulness can have on their emotional well-being. We need to model and scaffold mindfulness techniques and deliberately practice, practice, practice throughout the school year.

Academically

The deleterious effect of stress on the brain not only causes students to act inappropriately but can also actually prevent them from learning. In their research, van der Kolk, McFarlane, and Weisaeth (2007) found that stress can physically change children's brains. Too much stress can shrink part of the brain (the hippocampus) that stores and retrieves memories (van der Kolk et al., 2007). When learners are stressed, their brains are not in optimal condition for taking in new information. A calm, safe brain is optimal for learning (Sousa, 2010). A learner who has the ability to notice and suspend judgment while collecting information has a calmer mind that allows information to travel past the fight-or-flight part of the brain (the amygdala) to the prefrontal cortex for processing. The mindful thinker has better access to the hippocampus for memory storage, thus helping students learn better and resolve conflicts more effectively.

Classroom Practices for Mindfulness

Here are some activities for teachers who want to teach mindfulness or to incorporate mindfulness into the school day.

Teach About the Mindful Brain

Introduce the three key parts of the brain involved in thinking and learning: (1) the amygdala, (2) the prefrontal cortex, and (3) the hippocampus. This will help students understand how their feelings arise and that they have the ability to change what they do in response. This will also lay the groundwork for them to self-regulate their behavior and will assist them in how to approach difficult assignments.

1. **Amygdala:** Its job is to keep you safe. It regulates and blocks information from entering the prefrontal cortex so you can react quickly.

2. **Prefrontal cortex:** This is the learning, reasoning, and thinking center of the brain. It uses important information to focus, compute, decide, analyze, and reason.

3. **Hippocampus:** It stores and processes all our important facts, memories, and learned information.

There are many books and YouTube videos that will assist you in teaching mindfulness and the brain at various grade levels. One of our favorite programs is MindUP (http://thehawnfoundation.org/mindup) from the Hawn Foundation.

MindUP combines neuroscience, cognitive psychology, and educational methods to help educators create and maintain environments where a student's ability to succeed both academically and personally is directly linked to his or her overall state of well-being. MindUP is a curriculum that includes activities and exercises for maintaining a calm and positive atmosphere. It covers topics including brain function, mindfulness listening, seeing, smelling, tasting and movement, choosing optimism, expressing gratitude, and performing acts of kindness.

Another great technique is STOP, which helps students slow their brain when taking tests or dealing with strong emotions. Try the following activity with your students.

- **S:** Stop what you are doing; put things down for a minute.

- **T:** Take a breath. Breathe normally and naturally, and follow your breath coming in and out of your nose. You can even say to yourself "in" as you're breathing in and "out" as you're breathing out if that helps with concentration.

- **O:** Observe your thoughts, feelings, and emotions. You can reflect about what is on your mind and also notice that thoughts are not facts and they are not permanent. If the thought arises that you are inadequate, just notice the thought, let it be, and continue. Notice any emotions that are there, and name them. In her book *Uncovering Happiness: Overcoming Depression With Mindfulness and Self-Compassion*, Elisha Goldstein (2015) describes how just naming your emotions can have a calming effect. Then, she says, notice your body. Are you standing or sitting? How is your posture? Any aches and pains?

- **P:** Proceed with something that will support you in the moment, whether that is talking to a friend or just rubbing your shoulders.

Teach About the Here and Now

Teach mindful awareness, which is attending to the here and now. Have students close their eyes and listen very carefully for all the sounds they can hear around them in the classroom, in the hallways, and outside. After thirty seconds, ask the students to open their eyes and list everything they heard. Now challenge them to try the exercise again to see if there were any sounds they didn't hear the first time. Add those sounds to the list.

A continuation to the previous STOP exercise is to change the focus each time. For example:

- Ask students to pay attention to smells (perfume, lunch being cooked down the hall, flowers, and so on).

- Ask students to pay attention to sensations of their body (tightness in their neck, an itch on their nose, or the breeze on their skin).

- Use a percussion instrument like a triangle or chime to make a simple reverberating sound or ring. Everyone listens to the sound until it diminishes. Have students stay focused only on the sound. Repeat this a number of times.

Focus on Breathing

Have students find a comfortable seated position.

- Sitting on the floor cross-legged

- Sitting in a circle facing inward or outward

- Sitting at their desk

It is important that students and adults are comfortable in order to be able to relax and focus. Next, have students follow the step-by-step instructions for breathing mindfully.

1. Ask them to either close their eyes or look down at one point on the floor.

2. Tell them to start by listening to a sound until it softens into silence. (Use a sound such as a chime or soft music. Use the same sound as a cue to gently transition back to full awareness of the classroom.)

3. Encourage them to then switch their attention to notice their breathing.

4. Ask them to breathe normally, paying attention to the feeling of the breath as it fills their lungs and then flows up and then back out the same way.

5. Tell them to pay attention to when they lose awareness of breath and start thinking about something else, daydreaming, worrying, or sleeping. Ask them to simply say to themselves "thinking" and then bring their attention back to the breath.

6. Next, encourage them to find an anchor spot. An anchor spot is a place to look that helps keep students' attention while breathing. Have them breathe in and out and rest one of their hands on their stomach to feel the air go in and out, one hand on their chest to feel the rising and falling or in front of their nose to feel their warm breath. They will pick the place where they can feel movement and feel most comfortable.

Use Focus Words

For some students, it is easier to give them a word to repeat to help maintain focus on the breath.

- Counting—1 on inhale, 2 on exhale

- Silently saying "inhale, exhale" or "in, out" each time

- Repeating a nonword over and over—"oooommmmm" or "ahhhhhhhh"

Students' minds are busy, and their attention will wander just as ours does. Remind them, perhaps in intervals, to refocus on their word or breath to help them develop mindfulness skills. By practicing focusing and refocusing their attention, they'll internalize the process of noticing when they become distracted and then remembering to re-engage. When students can recognize that they are not focused on their breathing, it is a huge step toward them recognizing when they are not focused on their work.

Everyone has thoughts; they are always running through our mind. Thoughts are what keep us out of the present moment. We just need to notice them and not fight them, and when we notice them, we can bring our attention back to the present.

Use Monkey Mind

Monkey mind is a phrase that means the busy, random, and reactive state of mind that happens when we are not practicing mindfulness. Teaching the phrase to students can give them empowerment for just noticing when their mind is moving away from mindfulness and into monkey mind. Young students can learn the "Crazy Monkey" song (Kidding Around Yoga, n.d.). This song not only teaches what monkey mind is but also allows for movement before students pause to breathe mindfully.

Older students can conjure up the phrase *monkey mind* when they notice thoughts arising during their mindfulness practice. Simply naming it allows us to build our skills of noticing and move back to a calmer state of staying in the present moment. The following are additional activities to practice mindfulness.

- **Funhouse mirrors:** Students pair up. One student slowly moves his or her body, and the other student mirrors the movements. This practice helps students listen, focus, stay present in the moment, and maintain eye contact.

- **Kindness practice:** Young students can sit with a special toy or item from home placed against their stomach and practice deep breathing into their belly where the item rests. Just being present for a few breaths with an item that they feel gratitude for having is a great start. Eventually, they can send friendly wishes to their item and then to themselves. Older students can begin to conceptualize what they are grateful for and visualize it being held while breathing and eventually send friendly wishes to themselves and other students or people in their lives. This practice helps students become aware of their breathing and also cultivates a kindness practice.

Create Pause Moments

Hitting the pause button is a way to give your students a time-in, which is a simple way to allow them to check in with themselves to refocus their awareness and attention. Here are a few suggestions on how to create pause moments in the classroom.

- Have students do one minute of mindful listening and one minute of mindful breathing.

- Tell students, "Please get into your mindful bodies—still and quiet, sitting upright, eyes closed," and then set the timer for one minute.

- Ring a mindfulness chime, or have a student ring the chime. Use a chime with a sustained sound or a rain stick to encourage mindful listening.

- You can help students stay focused during the breathing with reminders like, "Just breathing in . . . just breathing out . . ."

- Ask for thirty seconds of silence in the middle of class, during which students stop reading, put down their pens, and simply take a break. Then continue with the lesson.

- Ask students to focus their attention on the experience of opening and closing their hands. Encourage them to give themselves a brief hand massage and feel the sensation in their hands.

- Have the class focus its attention on a peaceful picture or poster in the room and take a moment just to look at it.

- Play a one-minute clip of music—something calming or inspiring—and then ask students to take a moment to simply listen with their eyes closed.

Teach the Art of Being Grateful

Gratitude is a feeling of thankfulness and joy we feel in response to something or someone for some act we received or noticed. A number of studies have shown that even a small dose of daily gratitude can increase optimism, decrease negative feelings, enhance school connectedness, and improve overall attitudes toward school and learning. Alex Korb (2012), in his article "The Grateful Brain," also argues that practicing gratitude increases activity in the hypothalamus, the part of the brain that controls hunger, sleep, metabolic processes, and stress. A regular gratitude practice also increases dopamine, the neurotransmitter responsible for happiness and joy, which is why people who regularly practice gratitude often report greater levels of happiness (Korb, 2012).

Each day, ask students to focus for one minute on three things for which they are grateful. Encourage them to select new and different things each day. Some students may be worried that they will run out of things for which to be grateful. However, it is a common experience that the more you look for opportunities to be grateful for, the more you find.

Following are more examples of ways students can show gratitude.

- Create a gratitude tree. Create a paper tree on a bulletin board. Make leaf-shaped cutouts using craft paper. Ask your students each day or week to draw or write about things they are thankful for. Paste them to the branches on the tree.

- Keep a gratitude journal. This helps students make a special effort to find and focus on times when they have felt appreciative or thankful for a person, a situation, or new things they learned or did.

- Make a collage of things they are thankful for in nature, at school, or at home.

- Send a kind letter or email to a classmate or family member.

- Cheer up someone who needs it.

- Have lunch with someone who is sitting alone.

- Volunteer.

- Perform a random act of kindness. (See the Random Acts of Kindness Foundation's website, www.randomactsofkindness.org, for ideas.) Random acts of kindness are when a person makes a deliberate attempt to cheer up another individual by doing something thoughtful and caring. Try simple actions such as letting someone in front of you in the lunch line or grocery line, writing a note of thanks and leaving it on a student's desk or in your spouse's car, or smiling when you say hello to people in the hallway. Kindness toward others is an essential part of a healthy community.

Mindfulness will give you and your students better focus, better decision-making skills, the ability to respond rather than react, and better retention of new knowledge. However, one of the most important reasons for mindfulness is that it gives students hope. Once hope is gone, hopelessness replaces it. Students without hope won't take action. "Hope changes brain chemistry, which influences the decisions we make and the actions we take. Hopefulness must be pervasive, and every single student should be able to feel it, see it, and hear it daily" (Jensen, 2009, pp. 112–113). Hope is not an emotion; it is a way of thinking. It is a thought process. Mindfulness helps with this thought process. If you want to give students help, give them hope.

chapter Ten

Teaching With the Social-Emotional Self in Mind

For many people, one of the most frustrating aspects of life is not being able to understand other people's behavior.

—Johann Wolfgang von Goethe

Martin Luther King Jr. and Mother Teresa were superheroes even though they didn't have superpowers. They changed the world by uniting people using love, compassion, and determination around a common cause. They led from their heart and soul, and people followed.

We think it is important as educators to have a tool belt filled with a variety of effective strategies to address students with emotional needs. We all know that saying "If you only have a hammer, everything looks like a nail." This book and the other resources found in the appendix are intended to help you fill your tool belt with many effective strategies to deal with kids' social-emotional needs. Our goal for this chapter is to help see student behavior differently and to offer an appropriate tool to help you help your students.

What You Need to Know

If we could give you one big idea for understanding and effectively dealing with student behavior, it would be "Don't take behavior personally; respond with skills rather than react with emotions!"

The biggest classroom struggles happen when teachers take students' behavior personally. As a behavior specialist, one of MaryAnn's favorite quotes from *The Godfather* is "It's not personal, Sonny; it's strictly business" (Coppola, 1972). Granted, not taking something personally is so much easier said than done. The moment a student is behaving in a disrespectful way, you may feel that it is personal because you feel his or her behavior is aimed at you. You are interacting with the student, and as a result, you are the one receiving the behavior.

However, what you want to keep in mind is the student may be acting out the culmination of a long morning of pain, days of unexpected stress, or years of all the past hurts and who knows how many unmet needs. Her behavior may be for no other reason except that you are *there* and she needs to vent. Have you ever heard the story about the man whose boss yells at him, who spills lunch on his suit before a big meeting, and who gets stuck in hours of frustrating traffic all in one day? When the man arrives at home, his dog greets him at the door with a wagging tail. Annoyed and overwhelmed by the events of the day, the man kicks the dog!

What did the dog do to deserve this? Is it personal? Like the dog in this story, sometimes teachers are simply a safe target for a student to release his or her frustration. So it may hurt. It may feel unfair. But it helps us to *not* take it personally if we are aware that we were not the ones who created frustration, hurt, or pain in the misbehaving student. (Although, take note: Be aware that if you find yourself having frequent power struggles with students, it really might be you and how you are relating with students. Refer to your self-reflection from chapter 1 [figure 1.1, page 11] and see what might be causing you to create power struggles.)

What you don't want to do is get involved in a power struggle with the student. A power struggle happens when both parties fight for control. When a student and teacher engage in a power struggle, the student in stress is expressing anger, frustration, helplessness, or insecurity toward the adult. This, in turn, causes the adult to behave in a counteraggressive, impulsive, or rejecting way. The adult begins to mirror the student's aggression or inability to control behavior. A power struggle creates a no-win situation. When you take disrespectful behavior personally, three things are likely to happen.

1. You will want to get even to show your student who is boss.

2. You will be inclined to scold, lecture, or react harshly.

3. You will back down and allow the student to win. (As soon as your other students see this happen, it will weaken your ability to manage your classroom.)

The bottom line is that if you take students' misbehavior personally, you send the message that they can push your buttons and disrupt your day if they choose. They win. You lose.

Three Important Understandings About Behavior

So the key is to learn to go *against* our most natural reactions and responses and, at all costs, stay out of the power struggle. It is challenging but critical to stop using counteraggression. It doesn't work. The only way to stop using counteraggression is to have a growth mindset and practice, practice, practice using the new strategies. Remember that challenging students offer us great opportunities to grow on our teacher hero journey. To help you grow your skills, consider some of the following concepts.

Misbehavior Has an Underlying Cause

No misbehavior happens without a cause. In his book *Lost at School*, author Ross Greene's (2008) philosophy is "Kids do well if they can," as opposed to "Kids do well *if they want to*" (p. 10). That means if the student is displaying problematic, maladaptive behavior, it is a symptom of an underdeveloped skill. If there was nothing wrong, the student would not be acting out or withdrawing. Therefore, what might seem like out-of-the-blue behaviors—throwing a chair, dancing around the room, calling out, having an off-topic conversation, singing while drumming with a pencil, or walking out of the classroom—are cries for help.

Nicholas J. Long, Mary Wood, and Frank Fecser (2001), authors of *Life Space Crisis Intervention*, state, "The stress and problems kids create are an attempt to gain safety and comfort. It is their attempt to establish a sense of control. They act up and act out due to fear of losing something" (p. 37). So when students have a fear of losing safety, dignity, self-control, control over environment, or property, misbehaviors will play out in your classroom. Other behaviorists, such as Lee Canter and Fred Jones, add that unmet needs for attention or power can lead to misbehaviors. Some specialists believe behavior problems are a need to escape a task due to feeling inadequate, and yet others add that they can be a sensory issue that causes the misbehavior. A dear colleague, Mary Beth Hewitt (personal communication, July 15, 1999), says, "Behavior is a song kids sing, and it is our job to name the tune." .

Behavior Is Communication

People understand that behaviors like crying or tantrums are ways babies and toddlers communicate when they are frustrated. While we don't like these behaviors in young children, we understand that they are doing their best to communicate something to us. However, once students are older and can speak, we are less empathetic when they use inappropriate ways to communicate. We need to keep in mind that these students don't have the skills to communicate effectively.

The more upset a student is (inwardly or outwardly), the more likely he or she is to use behavior rather than words to show how he or she feels. When a student becomes agitated, he or she is irrational and less able to demonstrate the higher-level brain processing necessary for achieving perspective and thinking about future consequences of his or her behavior.

Even though students' behavior can look bizarre or disruptive, their actions are purposeful and are their attempt to solve a problem. It is critical to step back and try to decipher what the student is trying to communicate and the intent of the behavior. With practice, teachers can learn to stop and listen to the message the behavior is conveying, "Name that tune," and then respond in more productive ways.

Behavior is not random or aimless. Individuals would not repeat a behavior unless they were getting something out of it. Perhaps they are seeking a response from other people or looking for a way to escape an uncomfortable situation. For example:

- A student may whine to get a teacher's attention.

- A student may swear to get kicked out of class.

- If a student repeatedly has tantrums and then gets to leave a classroom, he or she has learned that tantrums further his or her desire to escape.

- A student may make fun of you or challenge you in front of the entire class to gain power.

As we figure out what the student is communicating with the inappropriate behavior, we can find different ways to respond so as not to inadvertently reinforce the behavior but rather teach an appropriate way to communicate his or her need.

Behaviors are rarely random, and they can be predictable. Look for repetitive patterns in student behaviors. Time patterns or activities to find clues about why the behavior is occurring. For example:

- He always asks to go to the nurse when mathematics starts.

- She gets more work done when the assistant is in the room.

- He has a rough day every Monday and Friday.

- When it is time to read orally, she suddenly behaves in a mean and almost violent way, disrupting the whole class.

Once you discover the pattern, the behavior's intent will often reveal itself, and then you might see possible solutions.

Another pattern to note is that students will tend to use the same behavior when stressed. A bully will bully, an angry student will hit or swear, and an anxious student will cry or shut down. When you identify the recurring type of behavior, you can begin to be prepared for it on another day. Discuss options before the next incident with other staff members who have been successful with that type of behavior, and make a plan for how you will respond the next time. (Include the student in making the plan.)

Teachers Can Only Control Their Own Behavior

This is the bottom line regarding behavior: the only behavior we can control is our own. We have this false belief that because we are the adults, we can make our students do what we ask. This is simply not true. Even though administrators may keep this myth alive by stating, "You better get control of your class!" the truth is you can't. You can't make a student pick up his or her pencil and do the work, stop talking, or stop arguing. However, you do have control over your own behavior. How you make the request and how you choose to respond will influence how the student responds. "Pick up the pencil now, or you are out of here" will generate a different response than "How can I help you get started on this right now?" When we realize and accept that the only person we can control is ourself, then we are in a place where we can begin to develop new skills to help us respond in more effective ways.

Strategies for Responding With Skills Instead of Reacting With Emotions

When we are stressed, we often react to misbehavior with emotional behavior, such as yelling, punitive punishments, or saying disrespectful comments we later regret. This can often escalate a situation. When we are able to keep our emotions in check, we are more able to recall and respond with the skills needed to handle the situation.

Practice Mindfulness

In chapter 9, we described learning foundation six—mindfulness. Keep in mind that the brain does not make good choices when it is in a stressed state. In the middle of a student's misbehavior, you can train yourself to hit the pause button. Take a minute to breathe before responding. Ask yourself, "What does this student need from me right now to feel safe to make a better choice?" Remind yourself, "Don't take this behavior personally; respond with skills rather than react with emotions." When *you* are mindful, you will also be able to recall and put into practice more of the strategies you learned in this chapter.

Do Not Create a Situation You Cannot Handle

This usually occurs because we angrily and hastily address the student in front of the whole class. For example, we may feel we are losing classroom control, so we ask a student to leave the class, and he or she refuses! Now you have backed yourself into a corner, created a situation you cannot handle, and are in a power struggle with the student.

Remember, you don't have to give a consequence right away. Wait—time is on your side. It is better to wait until you are calm and have thought things through and to give a consequence when there is no audience for the student to impress.

So how do you buy time to calm down before you deal with the behavior that's occurring? If you are able to talk without sounding too upset, one option would be to say something like this to the student: "This behavior is not appropriate. We will talk about it later." (This could make the student sweat, much like her mom saying, "Wait until your father comes home.")

Use Planned Ignoring

The planned ignoring technique is a conscious decision not to attend to the behavior at the time it occurs. Let your students know at the beginning of the year that when you notice misbehaviors that are not danger-ous, you may choose to do what's called *planned ignoring*. It doesn't mean the rules have changed, but when you are busy with the important job of teaching your lesson, you may ignore the immediate behavior, and it will be dealt with when the time is right. Then students know that you know, and there will be consequences given at a later time.

Offer Choices

We often offer students two choices: either (1) do your work or (2) go to the office. However, neither choice is desirable to the student; therefore, he or she doesn't choose, and this can lead to a power struggle.

It is helpful to defuse power struggles by offering three choices, making one of the choices neutral and presenting them all in a nonthreatening tone: "You have a few different choices; you may do your work now, do it after school, or pick another area in the classroom to work. [This is the neutral choice.] You decide what will work best for you at this time." Then be sure to walk away and give the student some time to make the decision without you standing over him. Once the student has made a good choice, don't rush in with praise: "Oh, Billy, you did such a good job." Do say, "I am happy to see you found a place that works for you." See page 178 in the appendix for language for framing student choices.

Write Notes

Keep a supply of prewritten reminders (or pictures for nonreaders) on a clipboard. If a disruption occurs while you are teaching, walk toward the disruptive student, and without interrupting instruction, place the message on his or her desk. (See figure 10.1, for example.) This helps to avoid a verbal interaction or escalation. This also helps you to remain calm while dealing internally with your own counteraggression. It keeps your angry and frustrated tone out of the message and keeps the rest of the class on task. While this does not guarantee compliance, it is another way to communicate what you want from the student without getting into a power struggle.

Figure 10.1: An example of a prewritten reminder.

Don't Take the Bait; Switch the Focus

Sometimes students can be like fishermen: they try to hook and reel you into a confrontation. They will intentionally do things they know will get a charge or a rise out of you. If you respond emotionally to these actions, you will lose. It's best to find ways to switch the focus and defuse the situation in a way that disarms the student or students. Following are some techniques you can use to switch the focus.

Use Humor

Humor can be a great way to break up a tense situation. Teacher heroes who have a sense of humor can use this gift in certain situations. Here is a great example of using humor to defuse a situation.

The student says, "This is boring."

The teacher responds, ringing a bell and saying, "Yay, you are the hundredth person to say that today!" The teacher gives the student a raffle ticket. The ticket might say something like, "The more that you read, the more things you will know. The more that you learn, the more places you'll go" (Dr. Seuss, 1990, p. 10).

Be very careful not to confuse humor with sarcasm. Sarcasm has no place in the classroom. Sarcasm is anger in humorous disguise: anger + humor = sarcasm. Don't fool yourself. It's not funny. Sarcastic remarks create an unsafe learning environment and can further escalate the stress response from the student. In order to use humor without sarcasm, you have to check yourself. If you are really angry, it might not be the time to try humor. If you are unsure if your comments or pet names for students are funny versus sarcastic, ask a respected colleague or a student. (For example, if you call an unmotivated student *broccoli* because he's in a vegetative coma in your class, it may be funny to you and the other students, but it is cruel and unkind to the student.) If you can laugh at the situation or yourself, not the student, then humor might be just what you need.

If you are not a naturally funny person, you can still use humor as a strategy. Often students use the same handful of behaviors and comments. Once you notice this, seek out the funniest person in your building, and get some ideas from him or her on funny ways to respond.

Use the Unexpected

Do something silly to interrupt the behavior and break the tension: skip, jump, sing, recite a poem, dance, and then without any comment about what you did, pick up the lesson where you left off.

If a student says, "I hate this class!" your random response could be one of the following.

- Sing, "Oh, say can you see . . ."
- Say, "A man landed on the moon in . . ."
- Say, "I heard mice in the attic last night . . ."
- Sing and dance, "I love the nightlife; I got to boogie . . ."

Weird? Yes. But it works!

The idea you are communicating when you do something unexpected is to not react to a misbehavior and also to clearly communicate, "I am not going to take the bait!" Your actions are saying to the student, "You are not going to hook me or engage me in a confrontation!"

Walk Away

Humor and silly songs aren't for everyone. Another strategy is to respond in a calm and matter-of-fact tone, then walk away.

For example, when you ask a student to open her book and she shouts back, "No, you can't make me!" the student and the entire class are waiting for your response. You feel the pressure to control the situation. Keep in mind that you cannot control anyone except yourself. A good response might be to state calmly, "You are absolutely right; I can't make you. I hope you make a good choice for yourself." Then walk away. You have made your point. You aren't taking the bait. Do not engage.

Put the Game on the Table

The purpose of this powerful technique is to bring an unconscious behavior to a conscious level and create a win-win solution—a solution that works for both the student and the teacher. Putting the game on the table helps us discover what the student is thinking, feeling, and needing. The more you understand the reasons behind the behavior, the better you can find ways to support the student and enlist the student in working to change his or her own behaviors.

This strategy offers a respectful way to create a mutual plan to support the student in changing his or her behavior. Think of this strategy as an intentional and transparent conversation you have with a student to help both of you. This conversation often results in the teacher feeling empathy and compassion instead of anger and judgment. Our goal is not to manipulate or set up a coercive behavior plan: "If you do this, I will give you that." Instead, you come to a mutual understanding while the student gets a need met and some new life skills, rather than a piece of candy or a token.

This is a technique to use with those few students who exhibit very persistent problems. This is not a technique to use for a student with minor or occasional problems. It is best to find time to have a private conversation with the student. You will need between ten and twenty minutes to do this most effectively, so you may need to find someone to cover your class or plan to meet before or after school, at lunchtime, or during your prep time. Believe us, when it works, it's time well spent. Following are thirteen steps to put the game on the table.

1. Establish your goal for the conference. What is the concern or issue that needs attention?

2. Focus on only one specific behavior. Start with either the behavior that predominantly interferes with the student's success in school or the behavior the student is most able and motivated to change. Do not overwhelm the student with all his or her negative behaviors. Some questions to help you establish a behavior to focus on include:

   - "Which behavior is dangerous or most getting in the way of success in school?"

   - "Which behavior is most irritating to the other students?"

   - "Which behavior is interfering with the feeling of community in the classroom?"

   - "Which behavior, if left unaddressed, might become habitual?"

   - "Which behavior is the student able and motivated to change?"

3. Set a time to meet, and if possible, select a place that would be free from interruptions and distractions.

   - Prior to scheduling the conference, be sure to choose a time the student is willing to meet with you (lunchtime versus recess time).

4. At the meeting, begin by reaffirming the teacher-student rapport.

   - Begin by chatting about a topic that interests the student. It is important to discuss your faith in the student's ability to succeed in school by pointing out his or her positive behaviors.

   - Most importantly, be truthful. Do not stretch the truth about the unacceptable behavior to be complimentary. The goal here is to remind the student of the genuine relationship you share by enforcing the fact that he or she is noticed and valued but that this behavior is hurting him or her, classmates, and you as well.

5. State the behavior of concern in a nonjudgmental manner using a matter-of-fact tone: "Here is what I am noticing . . ." A neutral tone not only makes the difference between success and failure but implies that everyone struggles with issues now and then and just needs reassurance or to be noticed and valued.

6. Get the student's input on your observations and statements. For example, "Have you noticed this also? What are your thoughts about this? What have you noticed?"

7. Explore the causes of the problem. Find out the student's underlying need or message. Simply asking students, "Why do you do this behavior?" often results in a shrug or an "I don't know" type of response. Prompting them with possible explanations is helpful, such as, "I am wondering why you rush to finish your work. Could it be you are afraid you will miss recess?" Suggestions for prompts include:

   - "Might it be . . . ?"
   - "Could it be . . . ?"
   - "Why do you suppose . . . ?"
   - "For some kids, it's because _____. Do you think it is that way for you?"

8. Give the behavior a name, and say why it is a concern for you or the class.

9. Invite the student to work together with you on the area of concern. For example, "Would you be willing to work with me to come up with solutions that would create a win-win environment?" It is best to teach the win-win concept to the entire class at the start of the year. (Explain that *win-win* means we all have needs, and ask how you can work together to meet everyone's needs so that you can teach and all students in class can learn.)

10. Once you have agreed, work together to design a clear and specific goal.

11. Work together to generate solutions. It is helpful to be ready to suggest some potential solutions in case the student cannot think of any. For example, "I am going to throw out some ideas. One might sound right to you. If not, I can also share what some other students in a similar situation have tried."

    It is important to be ready to switch to a whole new set of suggestions if the cause of the problem turns out to be something other than what you had anticipated.

12. Set a weekly time to observe how the plan is working (check-in) and where it might need to be modified. For problem solving to be successful, we need to schedule regular check-ins to monitor progress toward the goal. Note that a check-in does not sound like this: "Did you do your work today? Why not?" It sounds more like, "How do you feel the plan is working? Do you feel your needs are being met? What do you think is getting in the way of this plan being successful?" Some strategies are effective immediately, while other strategies are effective only for a short time. Occasionally, a strategy fails to work at all. This is why the follow-up check-in conferences are so crucial. They provide a time to discuss why a particular strategy isn't working and how to create a different approach. Even if the strategy is working, still have a check-in conference to acknowledge the student's effort.

13. If the student does not own the behavior, he or she cannot change the behavior. If this is the case, do not continue with the problem-solving conference. Instead, suggest proceeding using the diminishing quota strategy. (See Brittingham [2003] for details.) The purpose of the diminishing quota strategy is to make the student aware of his or her behavior at the moment it occurs while giving the least amount of attention to the student. This visually demonstrates for the student how often the behavior occurs. The goal is then to decrease the number of times the behavior occurs and increase the number of times the correct behavior occurs. The strategy involves a card with two columns. The left column is labeled with "Remember to do the behavior" and a plus sign and the right column with "Forget to do the behavior" and a minus sign. The card is labeled with the days of the week down the left side. This card should be used for two weeks. The first week, the teacher fills it out with the student watching, adding a check mark in the appropriate row and column for each time the student remembers or forgets to do the behavior. The second week, the student and teacher have their own cards to keep track of the behavior. (Tape it onto the student's desk, if age appropriate.) At the end of every day or period, compare the results. There is no reward or consequence. The main purpose is to bring the behavior to the student's conscious awareness because one cannot change a behavior until he or she is aware of the behavior.

While this strategy takes time, it's well worth making time for it since it creates a mutual plan students can honor and self-regulate. You can also work with students to have them do a behavioral self-assessment. Once a student has calmed down from a behavioral incident, the student can fill out the form alone or with the teacher. (See the appendix, page 179, for a student self-reflection form.) With all we have on our plates to do in a day, it may seem impossible to find time to have this conversation with students. We can't afford not to find the time. If we exchange the time we spend lecturing, writing students up, disciplining students, making calls, and having parent-administrator meetings to have a put-the-game-on-the-table conversation, we may find there is enough time.

Habits Are a Process, Not an Event

Changing your response to student behaviors takes patience, courage, and vulnerability for both you and your students. We all have behaviors we would like to change. As teachers, we may make some progress with changing how we respond to students, and then we have a bad day and take some steps backward. Don't beat yourself up when that happens. You are in the process of training your brain to respond in new ways. Sometimes, we completely fail because we are overwhelmed with other things happening in our life, so re-evaluate, recharge, and try again in a few days. We know there are some changes in life that take many attempts.

It's important to remember this same advice when thinking compassionately about our students. Don't immediately abandon an idea that doesn't change the student's behavior the first time or the first week. Remember that the behavior didn't develop overnight and it will most likely not go away overnight.

It takes time to change habits. We would like to remind you that the popular knowledge that it takes twenty-one days to change a habit is actually a myth. The idea of changing your life in just three weeks is very appealing. It is short enough to feel doable yet long enough to be believable. Phillippa Lally, a health psychology researcher at University College London who published a study in the *European Journal of Social Psychology*, finds it takes anywhere from two months to eight months to truly build a new behavior into your life, the average being sixty-six days to change a habit (Lally, van Jaarsveld, Potts, & Wardle, 2010). It is critical to keep in mind for ourselves and our students that the time it takes to build a new habit can vary widely depending on the behavior, person, and circumstances.

Persistence, flexibility, and positive expectations can affect changes in the strongest of human defenses. Rather than setting yourself up for failure or believing your students can make instant changes, remember that habits are a process, not an event. Having expectations focused on small, incremental goals will help you manage your expectations and remain committed to your goals and committed to trying again, for yourself and your students. Finally, remember this André Gide quote: "Man cannot discover new oceans unless he has the courage to lose sight of the shore."

chapter Eleven

Teaching With the Cultural Self in Mind

A nation's culture resides in the hearts and in the soul of its people.

—Mahatma Gandhi

In our global 21st century world, heroes will reach us across cultures and show us the way. Malala Yousafzai, seventeen-year-old Nobel Peace Prize winner, touched all our lives from Pakistan with her courage and convictions. "Let us pick up our books and our pens, they are the most powerful weapons. One child, one teacher, one book, and one pen can change the world" (Yousafzai, 2013).

What You Need to Know

In chapter 1, we shared that, even though we thought we were quite culturally aware and responsive, the three of us discovered our own misunderstandings around cultural differences. We realized we had much to learn about teaching students from cultures that were different from our own worldview. Our students from varied cultures need us to recognize their cultural experience, to not assume that we all share the same cultural norms, and to not expect them to follow all our cultural norms.

Ignoring or not understanding culture can be detrimental when it comes to student success. Research reveals that culture can have a stronger impact on student achievement than socioeconomic status:

> On average, minority students—with the exception of Asian Americans—are doing worse than their white counterparts on standardized tests. . . . The achievement gap transcends social class. Even within the same schools, middle-class

black students tend to score lower on achievement tests than whites. (Manning
& Kovach, 2003, p. 27)

Many of us have the perceived notion that poverty is the most dominating factor in students' academic struggles; however, JoAnn Manning and John Kovach's (2003) research indicates something else is at play other than socioeconomics. This forces us to ask the question, "If poverty is the great divide, why are poor white students outperforming middle-class black students?" The fact is culture trumps poverty when it comes to student success. Poverty presents a compounded challenge for students who are also from the nondominant culture. If poor white kids outperform middle-class black kids, then being both poor and from a minority culture will present two barriers for these students to overcome. Differences in cultural values impact minority students' access to education, interpersonal relationships, and deep issues of identity. So we need to gain insight into cultural differences so we can nurture students from varied cultures who come into our classrooms.

With this in mind, the big idea regarding culture we'd like to share with you that will most significantly impact your teaching is to understand the individualist-collectivist continuum of cultural values and how it impacts learners. Different cultures adopt specific values, thoughts, or ideas that they view as important. Values play a central role in determining if a culture is individualist or collectivist.

An *individualistic society* depends on the values of freedom and independence for the individual, while a *collectivistic society* depends on group harmony and consensus. The values in each society influence how our students learn in our classrooms. It is important to keep in mind that these are cultural variations, not to be confused with ethnic variations. For example, a person who emigrates from Japan to Brazil will adopt Brazilian cultural values as he or she is raised within that culture, but he or she is still ethnically Japanese. Likewise, the United States, Australia, Canada, and several other countries are comprised of people from various ethnic backgrounds who are culturally Americans, Australians, and Canadians. The first culture will highly influence family members when they initially emigrate; then as children are raised in their new cultural surroundings, they begin to take on the cultural values of the culture that they are exposed to. As you can imagine, one family may have varying degrees of cultural orientations based on how influenced family members have been by their cultural surroundings. Table 11.1 defines the individualist and collectivist cultural values and describes their attributes and how those might play out in the classroom. See the Volunteer Alberta website (http://volunteeralberta.ab.ca/intersections/staff/building-cultural-knowledge/cultural-values) for a chart of cultural orientations scaled for the most individualist to the most collectivist cultures to help you understand your students and your own culture more deeply. As we can see, what a person values drives his or her behaviors. If we understand what values our students come from, we will understand their behaviors better and, more important, we can proactively plan to teach them more effectively.

In an individualist value system, the emphasis is placed on the needs, ideas, and development of the individual. It indicates that a person's actions and his or her own choices are based on personal concern, and when interacting in a group, people do so as individuals. The United States has one of the world's strongest individualist value systems. These individualistic values are reflected in the way American schools operate from instruction to grading to student behavioral expectations. Poor white children are acculturated into an individualist cultural value system while most minorities are left out of the unspoken rules of values, expectations, and measures of success of U.S. culture.

Table 11.1: Individualist Society Versus Collectivist Society Values

Culture	Who	Values	Value Attributes	How It Plays Out
Individualist	The strongest individualist value systems are found among Northern Europeans, Americans, Canadians, and Australians (Triandis, 1988).	Control	Social power, wealth, authority, social recognition, and preservation of one's public image	• Encourages independence, values, and achievement • Views intelligence as competitive and assertive • Regards physical objects as objects to construct knowledge and become competent (for example, cubes help babies learn about spatial relationships) • Includes distal modes of communication, such as reading and writing • Defines children's early development in terms of knowledge and language (substance first, relationship second)
		Accomplishment	Ambition, success, capabilities, intelligence, and influence	
		New experiences equal the good life	Pleasure, fun, enjoyment, varied experiences, and an exciting or daring life	
		Self-direction	Creativity, the ability to choose one's own goal, freedom, curiosity, independence, and self-respect	
Collectivist	Native Americans, Native Hawaiians, Native Alaskans, Latin Americans, Africans, Asians, and Arabs (Triandis, 1988)	Goodwill Conduct equals a life well lived	Helpfulness, respect for tradition, acceptance of social hierarchy, devoutness, humbleness, and modesty	• Emphasizes interdependence • Preserves relationships structured around the hierarchy of family or community roles • Regards physical objects as objects to construct relationships because they can be shared with someone else (for example, cubes can be shared and build relationships of giving) • Includes proximal modes of communication, such as touching and communicating with body language • Promotes social intelligence and emphasizes personal relationship skills, respect, responsibility, and cooperation (relationship first, substance second)
		Traditions	Obedience, self-discipline, politeness, respect for elders, and maintenance of social order	

Sources: Adapted from Ambady & Adams, 2011; Chiao, 2009; Fantino, 2006; Hofstede, 2001; Laroche & Rutherford, 2007; Rule, Freeman, & Ambady, 2011; Storti, 1999; Tileston & Darling, 2008; Triandis, 1988, 1995.

Nearly all minority cultures come from a collectivist value system. Collectivism is a value system that views groups as the primary entity; choices are made with consideration of the group, and interactions are interdependent based on the role a person plays in the group. Individuals are seen as a part of the collective.

Cultural values become essential when we look at the disconnect between some cultures that have a high regard for individualism as opposed to most other cultures, including cultures of Asia, Latin America, Africa, and parts of Europe, that have varying degrees of a collectivist value system (Hofstede, Hofstede, & Minkov, 2010; Nelson & Fivush, 2004; Triandis, 1993, 1995). Said in another way, unless students in your classroom are from the American majority culture, they most likely have a more collectivist values orientation.

There are elements of both individualism and collectivism in any culture (Trumbull, Rothstein-Fisch, Greenfield, & Quiroz, 2001), and students will be on a continuum of values depending on such factors as how closely they identify with traditional culture, their level of education, the ethnic mix of their community, and their individual personality. This awareness can help us teach in a way that is responsive to cultural values.

How Cultural Values Play Out in the Classroom

The effects of these cultural differences in the classroom can be confusing if we are unaware of how a different value system will drive different student behaviors. While we may encourage students to be independent and work in isolation, this will be uncomfortable for our students from collectivist cultures who are raised to work collaboratively toward the greater good of a group. What Americans may perceive as cheating is the way work is done in many other cultures. When we ask students to speak up, to think independently, or to voice their opinion, we may be asking them to perform the same behaviors that they are punished for at home.

You may also see these differences emerge in the way that students communicate. With an orientation of achievement and goal attainment, individualists communicate in a direct communication style. This means communication is primarily focused on the exchange of information, facts, and reasoning. It is the *speaker's* responsibility to make herself and her message clear. However, students from a collectivist culture are more prone to use an indirect communication style. They will rely on the listener to be sensitive to the information that is and is *not* shared as well as the style in which the communication takes place. The purpose of communication is to maintain positive relationships.

Consider this culture clash in interactions:

> A kindergarten teacher was showing her class an actual chicken egg that would be hatching soon. She was explaining the physical properties of the egg, and she asked the children to describe eggs by thinking about the times they had cooked and eaten eggs. One of the children tried three times to talk about how she cooked eggs with her grandmother, but the teacher disregarded these comments in favor of a child who explained how eggs look white and yellow when they are cracked. (Greenfield, Raeff, & Quiroz, 1996, p. 44)

Without an understanding of communication differences, the teacher may only hear that the student is not answering the question in a structured way that would indicate she understood, and so she eventually moves on to elicit answers from other students. The student, not understanding expectations for different structures in communication, feels that her answer is not honored, so she feels confused and rejected. In these intercultural communications, the individualist is thinking, "Get to the point!" Conversely, a person from a collectivist culture will perceive the direct communicator as inappropriate and rude. This might lead to feelings of tension and possibly harm their relationship. In this scenario, the student is obviously not aware of the unspoken rules of communication, and the teacher, unaware of strategies for culturally responsive listening, doesn't have the tools to listen accurately to the student responsively. Table 11.2 shows common feelings and approaches in direct and indirect communication styles (Joyce, 2012).

Table 11.2: Direct Versus Indirect Communication

Direct Communication	Indirect Communication
Speak from facts.	Tell someone what you think he or she wants to hear.
Tell it like it is.	If you don't have anything nice to say, don't say anything.
Get respect from expressing individual achievements.	Get rejection from expressing individual achievements.
Be honest.	Be polite—it's more valuable than being honest.
Know it's OK to say no.	Say "maybe" or "possibly"—even if you mean no; it's rude to say no.
Don't beat around the bush—the truth is more important than sparing someone's feelings.	If the truth might hurt, soften it.
Say what you mean, and mean what you say.	Read between the lines.
Take communication at face value.	Handle communication to save face.
Get to the point—time is money.	Have small talk before business to build relationships.
Stand up to a person of authority.	Don't criticize others, especially people with more authority, or carefully veil criticism.

Source: Adapted from Joyce, 2012.

Individualist and collectivist cultures also differ in the internal goals that drive success and motivation to do well. While people from each cultural value system will work diligently to succeed, the underlying drive for success and the relative outcome of the achievement can vary greatly. Competition and a drive to do better than others are shared practices in American individualistic culture. Americans are often perceived as being too competitive and too focused on material rewards (Kohn, 1992). Collectivists have a stronger sense of group goals, group victories, and group success whether at the level of family business or national sports. Members of successful groups take pride in what the groups have accomplished (Black, Mrasek, & Ballinger, 2003).

An underlying drive in a typical individualistic American student is to want to improve his or her success for individual growth, superiority, and status, which culturally are all held in high regard and given much respect. The collectivists will also strive to succeed, but it will be in light of how the group members are affected by the individual's success (Markus & Kitayama, 1991). Pressures can result for students from a collectivist value system. In addition to their own performance, they have additional expectations because of the reliance of the group on their performance. While we may think this added expectation may drive some students to try to achieve at the top of the class, that isn't necessarily the case. Americans strive to be the best, which satisfies their need for individualism. Rather than stand out and be superior, collectivists tend to be driven by the need to save face in light of the group by not falling behind or being a shameful burden. Gold stars, rewards, and ranking students just don't appeal to all cultures in the same way!

Teach to All Cultural Values

With these new understandings, it is possible to have greater insight when working with students who have different cultural values. We are not advocating that you teach individualistically for the individualist and teach collectively for the collectivist. The truth is students need them both. Collectivists will still have preferences for some individualistic values, and some students will fall in the center of the continuum. What is important for teachers to know is that deep cultural preferences are sometimes so pervasive that students cannot explain why school just doesn't feel comfortable to them. (See the "Individualist Versus Collectivist" survey in the appendix, page 180, to see how your students score.) It is important that teachers are able to recognize the learning preferences students bring to the class and to balance their teaching style along the continuum as well. Students need both collectivist skills for working in groups toward group goals and the ability to complete tasks independently. The following are some ideas and strategies to support your students both individually and collectively.

Teach Students to Honor Both Cultures

Begin your school year by explaining to your students (in age-appropriate ways) that some cultures are individualistic and value the individual while others are collectivist and value the group. Explain that, in reality, both values are important in school and in life, so the classroom will balance group and individual expectations.

With lower-elementary students, simply begin by building their awareness of cultural preferences for grouping and completing work. Have them reflect on their own preferences for independent work, small-group work, or whole-class work and build respect for those who are different. (See the "How I Like to Learn Survey" reproducible in the appendix, page 183.) You can open class by explaining to students what type of groups they will be working in and why it's important. Likewise, you can close class by having students reflect on their preferences for different work configurations. It might sound something like this: "Today, we worked in several different groupings. We worked as a large group to learn new information. You practiced in your core groups, and then eventually, you worked independently to practice your skills. How many of you prefer to learn in a larger group? Who enjoys working through their learning with a group? Is there anyone who prefers to practice independently the best?"

For upper-elementary, middle, and high school students, give a survey to see what cultural values students feel most inclined toward. (See the reproducible "Individualist Versus Collectivist," page 180, for a student survey on learning preferences.) From the survey, you can then begin to talk to students about cultural values and the continuum of preferences that exists. Having awareness of these preferences will help students develop their own skills for working in culturally diverse settings in the future.

The key to remember is that students need both sets of skills. They need to know how to be responsible to a group, work in collaborative pairs, and be able to self-regulate as independent learners. It is important to teach them that while we may have differences, at the core, we all have common needs. See the student-needs chart in table 11.3 as a reference for teaching to differences and core needs.

Table 11.3: Teaching Individualists, Collectivists, and All Learners

Individualists as Learners	Collectivists as Learners	All Learners
Are more task oriented	Are more relationship oriented	Want to feel appreciated
Focus efforts on individual accomplishments	Focus efforts on group accomplishments and harmony	Want to have efforts recognized
Enjoy competition	Enjoy cooperating	Want to feel valued
Value independence	Value helpfulness, sociality, and interdependence	Want to feel accepted
Highly value success in school or in their career	Highly value duty to family	Want to feel successful
Use direct messages in explicit communication	Use nonverbal communication	Want to feel understood when communicating
Show emotional honesty	Use emotional control to maintain harmony	Want their emotions to be understood
View time as firm	View time as flexible	Want to understand what is expected and when

Use Strategies for Collectivist Learners

In chapter 3, we examined *how* to teach new skills to students. We looked at the important four steps of modeling and scaffolding: I Do It, We Do It, You Do It Together, and You Do It Alone. When we use this effective way of supporting learners' acquisition of new skills, we will also be teaching to the needs of both the collectivist and individualist cultural variations in our class. Here are six other ways to intentionally balance your instruction to meet learners' needs.

1. **Core workgroups:** At the beginning of the year, randomly assign students to groups. Then assign the group members jobs, such as leader, recorder, teacher getter (the only one in the group who goes to the teacher when the core group is stuck), timekeeper, life coach, organizer, and so on. Groups can then give themselves a name, a silent signal, or a symbol. Then have groups do fun community-building activities, such as building the tallest tower from straws and tape—but without talking! The groups stay together for a marking period, a semester, or a school year. If anyone from the core group is absent, he or she gets the make-up work and assignment from the core group members. (This buys you valuable teaching time and builds responsibility.) You can always call the core group together at the beginning or end of class to plan, reflect, review, and so on.

2. **Call and response:** Many collectivist cultures employ call and response as a way for leaders to get attention or share important information. Call and response also contributes to a sense of connectivity through establishing a group identity. When you say, "Class!" the class responds with "Yes!" in the same tone and rhythm. You can also use lines from famous books or popular songs. Younger students enjoy connected call and response, such as, "When I say peanut butter, you say jelly" as a way to bring the class together. Older students can use call and response based on current or popular songs.

3. **Learning circles:** A learning circle is a group of students who have similar interests or needs and pursue learning together. They may form a literature-focused circle to read the same text in a small group based on interest. The circle can follow a discussion guide to help focus discourse on characters, the author's craft, or personal experiences related to the story. Students can form learning circles based on a mathematical concept that they are struggling with. There may be a learning circle in social studies based on a historical event that a group would like to dig deeper into to build depth of knowledge. Younger students can form these same learning circles around common book titles, concepts they want to relearn together, or ideas they want to delve deeper into.

4. **Choral speaking or chanting:** When students are encouraged to answer collectively, it creates a safe place for students to participate without being isolated or feeling they have to stand out. Choral speaking can be done with a simple short answer or a longer passage read in unison. To make choral speaking engaging and interesting, you can switch between girls and boys or have students use various types of voices, such as, "Let's read that like a witch," "Let's all say that in a whisper," and, a favorite of students', "Let's repeat that like a rock star!" At the secondary level, have students chant and repeat the definitions of key terms or formulas you want them to recall.

5. **Shared or community resources:** You may have noticed that some students have a desire to share resources. For example, in an after-school program for language minorities that Alicia supervised, it was common for students to save half their snack to take home to share with siblings. Goods are not seen as personal possessions in collectivist cultures; they are viewed for their abilities to be shared and to build community and relationships. The need to share can be quite intrinsic for students from collectivist cultures because community is a core value. Having shared resources in the class is a way to encourage building relationships.

6. **Invited stories:** Keep in mind that collectivist cultures use small talk about relationships or people to build a connection with the listener. Be patient with students from various cultural backgrounds. Understand that through group identity and shared group experiences, students are telling us how they experience their lives when they are allowed to bring their stories into the classroom. Instead of assuming a student misunderstands a question because he is not direct with communication, listen to the student's story, and see if he is helping share his world, how he learns, and his experiences that lead to him to understand what you are asking of him.

Use Strategies for Individualist Learners

Think again about how we teach students using gradual release of responsibility. As we move closer to the scaffolded stage of You Do It Alone, we are moving toward students working in a more individualist way. Keep in mind, if we are already working in schools with a highly individualist cultural orientation, many of our daily instructional practices are already oriented for students to do work independently because that's the culture of the school. However, here are a few suggestions that you can be intentional about in planning to ensure students have experience working on their own.

Common practices in individualist classrooms include:

- Students do homework alone.

- Students practice in class quietly and individually.

- Students test alone.

- Students do individual projects and performances.

- Students take notes individually.

- Students perform writing tasks individually.

- Students read alone.

- Students complete worksheets alone.

- Students read directions for assignments individually.

If you work in a classroom that is oriented to a highly individualist culture, you may recognize that these practices are very culturally bound by an individualistic nature. You can add to those practices and help collectivist students gain more independent skills by implementing the following two practices.

1. **Self-monitoring tracking sheet or checklist:** The following is a sample list of skills that can be explicitly taught so students can self-monitor their learning while being independent, which appeals to individualist learners. Remember to not assume students understand what each skill looks like or sounds like. To avoid *assumicide*, make sure to teach each skill using apprenticeship learning (be intentional and transparent, model and scaffold, and use deliberate repeated practice).

   Students can assess themselves using the following criteria on a tracking sheet or checklist.

   - I have the materials I need.

   - I know how long I have to get my work done.

   - I got my mindset ready before I started working.

   - I understand the directions.

   - I picked a strategy to help me complete this task.

   - I use self-talk to follow a procedure for completing this task.

   - I monitored my time.

- I asked questions if I was uncertain.
- I reviewed my work to see if it made sense.

2. **Self-assessment of learning preferences:** Helping students become aware of their preferences for learning will build their cultural proficiency by not only allowing them to recognize their own cultural preferences and personal preferences for learning but also allowing them to see that there are many variations to learning preferences and none is "right." They are all to be honored and valued. Having students reflect and share their responses to the following questions can help build that empowering awareness.

   - How did we learn today?
   - What did you like?
   - Did you like to compete or cooperate?
   - Did you prefer to work in groups, with partners, or alone?
   - Did you prefer to work to help yourself or work to help others?

Honor Cultural Needs

When we are intentional and transparent about why we are learning in different grouping configurations, we help students understand themselves and their cultural needs as learners as well as honor those who have different needs than they do. When we model and scaffold our instruction as we teach students to work independently and in groups, we give our learners many opportunities to use their cultural selves to aid in their learning. When we practice, practice, practice, we give students the skill sets to manage through the cultural diversity of various school settings and within their community. Cultural knowledge that our students gain about themselves and others will not only build stronger classroom communities, it will help your students navigate cultural diversity with a deeper understanding in the future.

chapter *Twelve*

Teaching With the Academic Self in Mind

Chunk, chew, and check—that's how the brain learns best!
—Kathleen Kryza, Alicia Duncan, and S. Joy Stephens

At his speech for the opening of the Nelson Mandela Foundation in Africa on July 16, 2003, Nelson Mandela (2003) said, "Education is the most powerful weapon which you can use to change the world." True heroes like Mandela know that in order to make sense of the world around them, they have to stop, process, and interpret the multitude of new information they take in along their journey. Judy Willis (2007), neurologist and brain-based instructor, says:

> We can identify the practices that benefit all learners by looking at the skills most heavily emphasized in special education classes: time management, studying, organization, judgment, prioritization, and decision making. Now that the brain imaging research supports the theory that students process these activities in their executive function brain regions, it appears that brain-compatible strategies targeting these skills will benefit all students. (pp. 6–7)

What You Need to Know

Educators have so much information about the learning brain that we can no longer ignore using evidence-based strategies that we know work. However, we also need doable ways to implement the strategies because the more intentional and transparent we are as we teach them, the more our students develop and own the skills they need to succeed.

There are so many books and ideas about best teaching practices we could share in this chapter. Some of our favorites are listed in the "Resources for the Teacher Hero" reproducible in the appendix (page 185). But the big idea that will give you the biggest bang for your teaching buck in meeting the academic needs of all learners is a simple, yet powerful, teaching framework that we teach all our teachers and students.

Here's the key phrase to remember: chunk, chew, and check. It's how the brain learns best.

The Chunk, Chew, Check Framework

The chunk, chew, check (CCC) framework offers a simple and doable way to design lessons that are meaningful and engaging for all learners. These terms are defined in figures 12.1–12.3 (Kryza et al., 2010).

The brain learns best when it receives new information in small chunks. Because each brain perceives incoming information differently, we need to vary how we offer chunks of new learning.

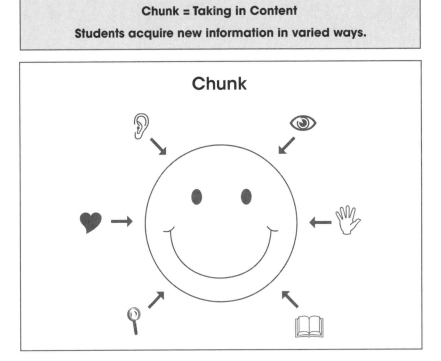

Source: Reprinted with permission from Kryza, K., Duncan, A., & Stephens, S. J. (2010). Differentiation for real classrooms: Making it simple, making it work. *Thousand Oaks, CA: Corwin Press.*

Figure 12.1: Chunk—One learning target with different ways to input new information into a learning brain.

All brains have a unique way of connecting new information to what they already know. Therefore, we need to offer students a variety of ways to chew on new information we have presented to them.

We know that individuals possess unique talents and therefore demonstrate understanding in their own way. We need to balance the ways we formatively and summatively *check* for student understanding.

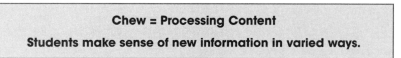

Source: Reprinted with permission from Kryza, K., Duncan, A., & Stephens, S. J. (2010). Differentiation for real classrooms: Making it simple, making it work. Thousand Oaks, CA: Corwin Press.

Figure 12.2: Chew—One learning target with different ways for a learner to process the new information.

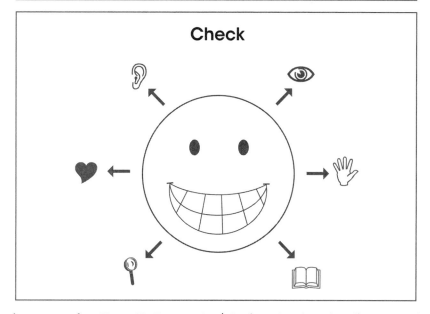

Source: Reprinted with permission from Kryza, K., Duncan, A., & Stephens, S. J. (2010). Differentiation for real classrooms: Making it simple, making it work. Thousand Oaks, CA: Corwin Press.

Figure 12.3: Check—One learning target with different ways for a learner to show what he or she has learned.

Varying these three steps of CCC in your lesson design allows you to thoughtfully respond to how well all your students (1) gain access to content, (2) process and make sense out of what you have taught, and (3) produce ways to show they have mastered outcomes.

Designing your lessons with the CCC framework in place will help you more carefully monitor where learning, or the demonstration of learning, is successful or where learning breaks down for the learner. For example, if Juanita doesn't speak English well or Robert has a learning disability and can't read the assigned book, we need to find another way for them to access the text (chunk), such as books on tape, leveled text, a reader, and so on. If Stefano and Emily are struggling to process how to do mathematics problems (chew), we can't keep re-explaining slower and louder the same way. We may need to try different learning modalities for chewing on those new ideas (draw it, move it, or chant it), or we may need to do more modeling of the steps for processing the problem. And if Jack and Bernadette don't do well on tests and quizzes (check), we need to support them by teaching them test-taking strategies and balancing traditional kinds of checks with more performance-based assessments that allow them to show what they know in ways that work better for them. Gifted learners may need more of a challenge at the chunk, chew, or check part of your lesson.

The CCC framework gives students access to content while allowing teachers to see how well students respond to instructional interventions, thus moving all learners toward the same learning outcomes. As we design our lessons, the CCC framework helps us be thoughtful about what's working and not working in our lesson design. The more thoughtful we are in our lesson planning, the more we create joyful, successful, and meaningful opportunities for learning to occur in our classrooms. Remember, the best tool for managing student behavior is a great lesson!

All kids will find learning a richer and more rewarding experience when they understand where they are going, what's working or not working, and what they can do to get unstuck; therefore, it's important that we are intentional and transparent about the CCC process with our students. We use this terminology with our students to explain how the learning process works; we named the steps *chunk*, *chew*, and *check* because those terms stick with kids and with adults too.

We know the terms stick with kids because they tell us so. Kathleen was modeling a lesson on growth mindsets in a third-grade classroom in Michigan. One of the students approached her after class and asked, "Are you the lady who taught our teacher about chunk, chew, and check? We like that!" CCC is sticky, and if we want learning to stick, we have to teach in ways that make it sticky!

CCC also helps students become better self-assessors. A student can say, "Am I able to take in a new piece of information? Am I locking it in so that it sticks? Am I able to show that I got it?" When we teach students about the CCC framework, it gives them a common language to help them advocate for themselves: "Ms. Douglas, can we chew on that a bit more, because I didn't quite get it," or "Mr. Otero, I don't get that chunk you just taught. Help!"

CCC empowers students to become lifelong learners. Outside of class and outside of school for the rest of their lives, students will know how their own brain works best and have the tools they need to help themselves learn something new. Once you know the CCC framework, you'll see that any strategy you learn at any workshop will fit into one of the parts, and you'll know how to use it more effectively. Any new technology you use in your classroom will fit into the CCC steps. Technology is a tool, so it's up to you to decide where in your lesson design it makes the most sense to use the tool.

Ask yourself:

- "Is this a tool that can help me teach the chunk more powerfully?"
- "Does this technology allow students to chew on the new learning?"
- "Which new technologies will best help me check for student understanding?"

When you implement interventions or individualized education program (IEP) goals, you can determine if the intervention or accommodation is needed at the chunk, chew, or check part of the lesson. If you are co-teaching, you can decide who's going to lead teach the chunk, chew, or check part of the lesson. In the appendix, you will find a lesson-planning reproducible ("Basic Differentiated Lesson Plan," page 186) as well as a list of ideas for chunking, chewing, and checking ("CCC Ideas," page 188) in varied learning modalities and also some great technology that can be used to chunk, chew, and check in your classroom ("Chunk, Chew, and Check Tech," page 196).

As you grow your skills at using the CCC framework, you can look back over a week or two of your lesson plans and see clear delineations among chunk, chew, and check. As you get better at identifying the CCC of your lessons, you will notice that sometimes the chunk and chew blend (in a jigsaw, for example), or it may happen that one project is both a chew and check. No matter how we mix it up, the intent is to vary the ways in which we have our students input, process, and output new learning. If we design the chunk, chew, or check in the same way day after day (read the book, answer the text questions, and take the test, for example), we are not differentiating our instruction.

Keeping the CCC framework in mind as you design lessons allows you to thoughtfully respond to how well your learners gain access to content, process it, and own what they've been taught and demonstrate mastery of outcomes. CCC helps you vary your teaching and offer better access to learning for all students in your classroom. Every day during every lesson, we can begin to think this way: "Chunk, chew, and check. It's how the brain learns best!"

The CCC Framework in Action

When you are teaching using the CCC framework, it would sound like this in your classroom: "While I teach you science this year, I am going to implement a way of teaching that works best for the learning brain. As a rule, I will teach you chunks or have you read chunks of new information for about ten minutes because the brain can only take in so many new ideas. Once you learn a chunk of new information, then you will have time to chew on it or make sense out of it in a variety of ways. The goal is for you to start to self-assess what way of chewing on new ideas and information in science works best for you. Some of you make sense of information by writing, some by drawing, and some by moving. We will do a lot of thinking with talk partners in this class because sharing ideas with another person is a great strategy for chewing and deepening our science reasoning. After you've had time to chunk and chew on the new ideas, I will let you know that it's time to check your progress. Most checks will be quick checks for understanding, perhaps a quiz or a drawing or a homework assignment that will not be graded. There are two reasons for these minichecks. The first reason is for me to see how you are doing so I can support you or challenge you as needed. Second, and most important, these checks are for you to self-assess how well you are getting it as we move toward the final checks or assessments that will count as a large part of your final grade. Being self-reflective is an essential life skill that successful people of all ages do to make sure they are on track, because, let's face it, when you are an adult, you often don't have a boss telling you what to do minute to minute. You have to start thinking, 'Do I know what I need to know?' and, if not, 'How do I make a plan for what to do if I need help?' So, throughout the year, we will be chunking, chewing, and checking because that's how the brain learns best!"

Figure 12.4 shows an example of a chart you could make to post on the classroom wall to remind students of the CCC process.

Figure 12.4: Sample classroom CCC chart.

The focus of the rest of this chapter will be on the importance of building time to chew because it is the most effective way to keep all learners engaged in your instruction. The phrase we teach our teachers to remember is this: "For every ten minutes you teach something new, the brain needs one or two minutes to chew." Then we shorten it to "Ten and two, chunk and chew!" to make it stick. Figure 12.5 is an example of a poster to hang in the classroom to remind students that chewing is where learning happens.

Figure 12.5: Sample poster for "Chewing is where learning happens!"

Input-Output Learning

On our hero's journey, it's important to self-reflect on our own instruction. How often are we approaching teaching and learning like this?

- Students learn a body of facts.
- They do graded homework.
- They take the test on Friday.
- They dump the information from their memory over the weekend.
- You repeat this again the next week.

We call this *input-output learning*: learn it one day, and forget it the next. Notice that in this kind of instruction, there is an absence of time to chew or process learning. Chewing is where the learning happens. According to Eric Jensen (n.d.):

New evidence suggests the value of teaching content in even smaller chunk sizes. Why? The old thinking was that students could hold seven plus or minus chunks in the head as capacity for working memory. But that science is outdated. The new research says two to four chunks are more realistic. In addition to this shorter capacity for working memory, our mid-term 'holding tank' for content, the hippocampus, has a limitation on how much it can hold. It is overloaded quickly, based partly on learner background and subject complexity. There are other reasons our students get overloaded quickly with content. Learning and memory consume physical resources such as glucose and our brain uses this quickly with more intense learning. Teachers should teach in small chunks, process the learning, and then rest the brain. Too much content taught in too small of a time span means the brain cannot process it, so we simply don't learn it.

So the brain needs valuable time to process and make sense of incoming information if it's going to lock it into long-term memory. When we fail to give students that time to process what they are learning, it's no wonder our students repeatedly ask us, "Why do we have to learn this?" This lack of processing time and meaningful connection in our lessons not only creates apathy in our students but also, for many, prohibits them from retaining the information.

Just because we are teaching, it doesn't mean students are learning. Processing or connecting to new learning in meaningful ways is essential if we are going to help students to store the new learning in their long-term memory. Brain researcher and author David Sousa (2006) tells us, "Information is often taught in such a way that it lacks meaning for the student. . . . Yet the brain needs to attach significance to information in order to store it in long-term memory" (p. 42). A student may practice a task repeatedly with success, but if he or she has not found meaning after practicing, there is little likelihood that the learning will move into long-term memory (Sousa, 2006). Input-output learning is not what the brain needs.

What *does* the brain need in order to store new learning into long-term memory? In a word—*transfer* (Sousa, 2006). The concept of transfer is not new. Lev Vygotsky (1978) points out that the central role to learning should be making meaning. It is the processing of information that essentially enables students to transfer learning into long-term memory and causes a cognitive transformation for the student (Vygotsky, 1978). Vygotsky calls it *transfer*. Sousa calls it *processing*. We call it chewing—because it's sticky!

During the chew part of the lesson, we are emphasizing that teaching kids *how* to learn is as important as teaching them *what* to learn. The importance of processing and connecting to new learning in meaningful ways is vital, yet this step is often left out of our lessons as we go from input to output with little time to process (chew) and make sense out of what we just learned. We often move from chunk to check without time to chew in order to save time or cover more content. But if we only value the final outcome (check) and not what it takes to get there (chew), we can send the false message that learning should happen easily and without effort. Carol Dweck (2006) might call this fixed mindset teaching: when we teach it to you, then you spit it out, and it's either right or wrong, and we move on. Chewing on new learning in a lesson is the step that allows students to really dig in and work hard to make sense and to lock in their learning. This is growth mindset learning, where we value the struggle that comes with truly learning new ideas and skills.

Students need many opportunities to deepen their learning by chewing on new information in varied ways. It's our job to build strategies for chewing and processing into our lesson plans and to plan to intentionally vary the ways students process new information so they understand how they learn best and so the learning transfers from the classroom into their lives. In the appendix, you will find a learning style survey (page 199) and a multiple intelligence survey (page 202), along with a scoring rubric that you can give your students at the beginning of the school year (either one or both) so that they, and you, can start to reflect on ways they learn best. As students are working to make sense of new learning through processing, they should be asking themselves the following kinds of questions.

- "What's my mindset about doing this processing activity (chewing)? Do I have a growth mindset, or am I quitting before I even tried? What am I saying to myself? I can't, or I can't *yet*?"

- "What do I need to do to make sense of this new information?"

- "What's working or not working for me?"

- "What are my learning style strengths? How should I put that to work in helping me make sense of this?"

- "Do I need to ask for help? Try another way? Practice some more?"

Top Strategies for Chewing

This section features some of our favorite ways to help students process information in the classroom. When kids are looking at us all hazy-eyed, we will switch to one of these tried-and-true techniques. Note that these techniques are in varied learning modalities. Many teachers we work with make a list of their top strategies for chewing in the classroom as a way to remind themselves and their students of how important it is to process new learning.

Turn and Talk

This is a great strategy to lead students to deeper academic talk as they regularly practice chewing in short-term talk partnerships.

- Give students a prompt on the board, on the overhead, or on a PowerPoint.

- Students turn and talk to a partner who is near them and easily accessible to talk to. (You can call them "chat chums" or "elbow partners.")

- Students have two to three minutes to talk and share. While they are talking, the teacher is floating around the room listening for quality talk.

- The whole class processes the talk, with the teacher noting quality talk that he or she heard while walking around the room.

Clock Partners

This activity works well to get students talking and keeps them talking.

- Give students a blank clockface with blank lines at four specific times (twelve, three, six, and nine; see "Clock Partners Clockface" in the appendix, page 205).

- Students have two minutes to go around the room and "make a date" with four people who will be their clock partners, one at each time slot. Students write their names in the blanks of times they have agreed to meet with the owner of the clock.

- Throughout the class period, or over the day or week, you can have students meet with their partners to share: "Meet with your three o'clock partner, and complete practice number five together." Or "Meet with your twelve o'clock partner, and talk about who the outcomes of this decision will affect."

- You could also intentionally assign some of their clock partners by readiness or learning style.

- You can adapt this activity so that, instead of clock partners, students have north, south, east, and west partners or green, yellow, blue, and red partners. Get creative, and name them whatever works for you.

Stand and Share

This activity works well for discussions that involve several responses or for reviews.

- Ask the whole class to stand, and then pose a question. Then ask for volunteers to share their ideas.

- Once a student shares, he or she gets to sit down, and all students who had the same idea and nothing further to share sit down as well.

- The teacher calls on students until all ideas have been presented and all students are sitting.

- Call on the shy or more struggling learners first so they have the opportunity to contribute. Save the gifted students or more vocal students for last, as they will still have ideas to contribute.

Stop and Draw

This activity works well for representing the meaning of vocabulary words and for visually capturing big ideas.

- After you have taught students a key concept or key term, give them two minutes to stop and sketch their visual representation of that idea. Tell them you are looking for very simple drawings, as they would do if playing the game Pictionary.

- After students do their sketches, have them share what they've drawn with their table mates or talk partners.

- Float around the room, and look for quality and unique visuals to share with the whole class.

- For deeper visual processing, you can use Robert J. Marzano's strategy of discussing similarities and differences between each other's drawings (Marzano et al., 2001).

Total Physical Response

Movement cements learning in the brain (Sousa, 2006), so having the teacher or students create movements to help recall important ideas about what they're learning is powerful and great for kinesthetic learners. For example, make up movements for the following.

- **Rise over run for finding slope in mathematics:** Students raise their hands, lifting them over an imagined slope, and then run in place.

- **Longitude and latitude in geography:** Students stand up straight with arms overhead for longitude and rotate their hips in a horizontal circle for latitude. (This is silly and very memorable.)

- **Prepositions in language arts:** Students move their hands and bodies to demonstrate placement of prepositions (for example, around, behind, over, and so on).

- **The parts of a plant:** Students show their feet as roots, their bodies as stems, their arms as leaves, and their fingers as flowers.

Tips to Help Students Chew Effectively

To help your students effectively process new information, consider the following.

- Be transparent; tell students *why* these chew strategies help everyone be more successful— that chewing is where learning happens.

- Model strategies and the kind of talking and thinking you expect students to use. Many students don't know how to talk about mathematics, science, and so on. They need to hear and see examples.

- Practice, practice, practice. Students will get better at thinking, sharing, and learning together if you keep doing them. If you only pull these out once in a while, they are not as powerful.

For more information on learning to chunk, chew, and check your instruction, see Kathleen and Alicia's book *Differentiation for Real Classrooms* (Kryza et al., 2010).

Tips to Help Teachers Chew

Let's look at the way teachers process new information when they are learning together. Imagine a collaborative team in a PLC is focusing on increasing the amount of homework. The meeting starts with the team leader describing the problem. From there, groups turn to talk about possible strategies for getting more students to complete homework. The groups create and share charts listing the reasons they feel homework is not being done, and the team leader shares an article about increasing the rate of homework completion. The teams read the article, return to their lists of possible problems, and begin to correlate their ideas with those from the article.

The teachers in these working groups are processing information together in varied ways to connect new information with what they already know in order to take their understanding deeper and to build new, more effective skills. The leader intentionally designed opportunities for the teachers to do what teachers love to do the most: gather, talk, share, and learn from one another.

Leaving a Hero's Legacy: The Choice Is Yours

*We are all caught in an inescapable network of mutuality, tied in
a single garment of destiny. Whatever affects one directly, affects all
indirectly. For some strange reason I can never be what I ought to be
until you are what you ought to be. And you can never be what you
ought to be until I am what I ought to be.*

—Martin Luther King Jr.

At the end of the hero's journey, the newly transformed hero returns to her community with new insights and understandings and begins to transform the community. The hero lives on in the legacy and future lives of the people and the community she has served. At the end of *The Lord of the Rings*, good prevails, and life in the community will be better as a result of the courage of a hero and the hero's brave companions. The courageous decisions of real-life heroes—such as Malala Yousafzai, Nelson Mandela, and Martin Luther King Jr.—forever change our world in positive ways.

So do we, as teacher heroes, leave a legacy each time we wrap up a school year and say good-bye to the students we have served (and learned from) throughout the year. A part of us lives on in these young people as they leave our classrooms on that final day. We must never lose sight of how our teaching impacts the future in ways we may never see.

It will always be our choice—the kind of legacy we leave our students. What will you choose? What legacy do you envision for yourself? Have you asked yourself, "When I close that classroom door, what do I want remembered about my life's work? Do I want my students to remember me because I impacted their learning lives in powerful ways, because I instilled a passion for learning in them that they can take with them forever? Or am I really just here for the paycheck and summers off?" How you choose to teach and reach kids *will* become a part of their lives and impact how they go out into the greater world. What life lessons will you have etched into the hearts and minds of your students? The choice will always be yours.

It is our hope that as you've traveled through this book, you've discovered some new insights and strategies to support you on your journey. We have unveiled why we must all find the courage to embrace and enjoy the journey. We have asked you to go within and know why it is important to understand your own as well as your students' strengths and needs. We've unpacked the essential hows, the methodology that the best teachers use to apprentice all their students into learning lifelong skills. Lastly, we offered you a powerful toolkit of whats—rich foundational strategies that will ground your classroom and help you teach and unite all your students within an emotionally, culturally, and academically responsive learning community. All students will benefit when we teach this way. Those kids whose needs may not have been understood or met in the past can now hope to *survive and thrive* in your classroom.

Combine this new learning with the skills you have now, and you will create a legacy of caring, compassion, and growth that will support your students as they head out on their own life journeys. You will close that classroom door for the last time knowing that you chose to do your small part to make a meaningful difference in the world. As Margaret Mead said, "Never doubt that a small group of thoughtful, committed citizens can change the world; indeed, it's the only thing that ever has."

Finally, we'd like to remind you that as you move forward on this new day of your hero's journey, remember to be gentle with yourself. Teachers can be very hard on themselves, and this harshness toward ourselves can lead to being judgmental and harsh with others. The more we love and honor our own imperfections, the more we can be compassionate with ourselves. When we treat ourselves with loving kindness, we will naturally be more inclined to be patient and kind with our students. Honor yourself. Honor your students. Change the world.

For the teacher hero, working with those kids is not a job—it is a life mission. The best teacher heroes really *want* kids to succeed. Our primary goal is not simply imparting curriculum; we believe in teaching the whole student. Our passion is people, not subjects. To teach from this place, we must be willing to self-reflect and be brave enough to study our own journey.

The powers of teacher heroes are not magical; they are thoughtful by intention. Teacher heroes work hard internally to develop boundless patience and creativity. We *grow* the patience to reteach a concept in yet another way for the fifteenth time to find new ways to work with the challenges presented to us each day.

Teacher heroes strive not to judge, ridicule, or punish. Instead, we work to accept, guide, care for, and encourage all our students. Teacher heroes see the fear behind a student's belligerence, and instead of fighting back with our own fear, we seek to connect with love, honesty, and vulnerability.

Teacher heroes see past their own protective walls through to students' walls of protection. We learn to observe the fear, see the hurt, and notice the embarrassment around feeling inadequate or being misunderstood. We see the whole student and work to make him or her feel whole. Instead of standing at the end of the forest shining a light, saying, "Come this way if you want to get out of the woods," teacher heroes go to the thick of the woods, stand beside students, and take them by the hand. They lead students out of the dark and into the light, *and* they are brave enough to admit that they are afraid of the dark too.

Thank you for joining us on this journey. Thank you for being real heroes who make a real difference for kids. Never doubt that you can and do impact lives every day!

It is not the critic who counts; not the man who points out how the strong man stumbles, or where the doer of deeds could have done them better. The credit belongs to the man who is actually in the arena, whose face is marred by dust and sweat and blood; who strives valiantly; who errs, who comes short again and again, because there is no effort without error and shortcoming; but who does actually strive to do the deeds; who knows great enthusiasms, the great devotions; who spends himself in a worthy cause; who at the best knows in the end the triumph of high achievement, and who at the worst, if he fails, at least fails while daring greatly, so that his place shall never be with those cold and timid souls who neither know victory nor defeat.

—Theodore Roosevelt

APPENDIX

Teacher Hero Self-Reflection Journal

As noted in chapter 1, we invite and encourage you to take time to stop and reflect on your life journey and how it impacted you academically, culturally, and emotionally. We have created the following questions to guide you through what we have found to be a profound self-reflection experience. The first questions in each section ask you to write about and reflect on your experiences, successful and challenging, in your early years of schooling and through college. Then the questions go deeper, asking you to explore how those past experiences impacted the kind of teacher you've become. If it would be helpful to see examples, get some ideas from chapter 1, or visit **go.solution-tree.com/instruction** to find more detailed examples from Kathleen, MaryAnn, and Alicia. We found that in really taking the time to do this self-reflection deeply and then talking together about how our past impacted our present work, we have new insights to help grow ourselves and our work within schools, with teachers, and with students.

My Academic Self

When you were in school (K–12), what was your academic learning experience like? Did learning come easily for you, or did you have challenges? As you reflect, think about how you interacted with your teachers and peers in the area of academics.

My History

How academically successful were you in school? Did this change during your experience in college?

How hard did you work in school?

Did you enjoy the academic or social aspect of school?

Were you motivated by grades or learning even if you had to struggle?

Effects of My Academic Profile

What are some positive outcomes from your academic experiences, and how have they impacted your teaching and the students you teach?

What are some negative or challenging experiences or outcomes from your academic experiences, and how have they impacted your teaching and the students you teach?

How could your past academic experiences impact how you respond to students you teach who have special academic needs?

Have you gained any insights into how you need to shape your teaching mindset and skill set in reaching the students you struggle to teach?

My Cultural Self

When you were in school (K–12), what was your cultural experience like? Did you fit into the majority culture of your school, or were you different? As you reflect, think about how you interacted with your teachers and peers in the area of culture.

My History

Describe your cultural self.

Describe the majority culture of the schools you attended.

page 2 of 4

Was your school culture similar to or different from your cultural identity? How? If you were the person from a different culture, how did you feel?

Was your understanding of your school culture at the surface level or at a deep cultural level?

How did you feel when you were with a person from a different culture?

Effects of My Cultural Profile

What are the positive outcomes from your experiences and their impact on the students you teach?

What are the negative outcomes from your experiences and their impact on the students you teach?

What could you do to reach the students you struggle to teach?

What do you know now about what makes culture different and causes culture clashes?

My Social-Emotional Self

When you were in school (K–12), how did you fit in socially? What was your predominant emotional state? As you reflect, think about how you interacted socially and emotionally with your teachers and peers.

My History

Describe what was happening socially and emotionally at home when you were growing up.

Describe what was happening socially and emotionally at school.

How did you respond socially and emotionally in each situation?

What are your current triggers when working with students that are related to your social-emotional experiences?

Effects of My Social-Emotional Profile

What are some positive outcomes from your experiences and their impact on the students you teach?

What are some negative outcomes from your experiences and their impact on the students you teach?

What could you do to reach the students you struggle with and reduce your triggers in order to be more healed and helpful to your students?

Cultural Iceberg

Surface Culture

Explicitly spoken differences

Low emotional load

Food, dress, music, visual arts, drama, crafts, dance, and literature celebrations

Visible culture is above the surface. You can see the differences, but these differences are just the tip of what is really core to a cultural difference. Like an iceberg, there is more below the surface than what you can see.

Deep Culture Unspoken Rules

High emotional load

Courtesy, concepts of time, personal space, facial expressions, nonverbal communication, notions of modesty, relationships with animals, and concepts of leadership

Deep culture is below the surface. The differences aren't readily apparent, but it is the core of human perceptions and values that will drive behaviors and create the deepest cultural conflicts and misunderstandings.

Deep Culture Unconscious Rules

Intense emotional load

Ideals of child rearing, rates of social interaction, notions of friendship, notions of adolescence, tolerance of physical pain, a preference of competition or cooperation, concepts of past and future, the definition of obscenity, attitudes toward dependents, and problem-solving roles in groups according to gender, age, occupation, kinship, and so on

Like an iceberg, what lies below the surface is the part that can cause the most problems.

Sources: Adapted from French & Bell, 1995; Hall, 1976; Selfridge & Sokolik, 1975; Weaver, 1986.

Intentional and Transparent Learning Target

Talk Frameworks

We have found that using this framework helps us design our lessons with the why in mind and be completely transparent with our students.

Framework for Explaining the What, Why, and How Learning Targets

"Today, we are learning _____." (What)

"This is important to know because _____." (Why)

"You will know you got it when _____." (How)

Framework for Explaining the How and With Learning Process

"To learn this important concept or idea, we are going to _____ _____." (How—the kind of learning activity or learning modality; with—the types of groupings: whole group, small group, pair, or independent).

Planner for Gradual Release of Responsibility

Use this gradual release of responsibility planner to help you map out steps and lessons for apprenticing students into learning a new skill that they need to develop. Chapter 3 offers details and examples of what this would look like in the classroom.

Steps of Gradual Release	Teacher and Student Actions
"I do."	How will you model, demonstrate, and think aloud?
"We do." (Whole class)	How will the class share, process, respond, and ask questions?
"You do." (Small group)	How will students work in small groups to deepen their thinking by sharing, processing, responding, and answering questions?
"You do." (Independent)	How will students self-regulate and self-assess to complete independent tasks?

Fair Versus Equal Books

Teaching Peace: Preparing for Differentiation and Diversity in Today's Classroom

Children's Books

123: A Family Counting Book by Bobbie Combs

ABC: A Family Alphabet Book by Bobbie Combs

Angel Child, Dragon Child by Michele Maria Surat

A Bad Case of Stripes by David Shannon

The Big Orange Splot by Daniel Manus Pinkwater

The Crayon Box That Talked by Shane DeRolf

Free to Be . . . You and Me by Marlo Thomas and Friends

Giraffes Can't Dance by Giles Andreae

Heartbeat by Sharon Creech

Hey, Little Ant by Phillip Hoose and Hannah Hoose

I'm Gonna Like Me: Letting Off a Little Self-Esteem by Jamie Lee Curtis

It's Okay to Be Different by Todd Parr

Leo the Late Bloomer by Robert Kraus

Listen to the Wind: The Story of Dr. Greg and Three Cups of Tea by Greg Mortenson and Susan L. Roth

Marianthe's Story: Painted Words and Spoken Memories by Aliki

The Morning Chair by Barbara M. Joosse

Mrs. Spitzer's Garden by Edith Pattou

My Name Is Yoon by Helen Recorvits

The Name Jar by Yangsook Choi

One by Kathryn Otoshi

The Other Side by Jacqueline Woodson

Pa Lia's First Day by Michelle Edwards

The Peace Book by Todd Parr

Whoever You Are by Mem Fox

You Are Special by Max Lucado

Young Adult Books

Angus, Thongs and Full-Frontal Snogging: Confessions of Georgia Nicolson by Louise Rennison

"Change My Life Forever": Giving Voice to English-Language Learners by Maureen Barbieri

Define "Normal" by Julie Anne Peters

Freak the Mighty by Rodman Philbrick

Hard Love by Ellen Wittlinger

"Harrison Bergeron" short story from *Welcome to the Monkey House* by Kurt Vonnegut

Loser by Jerry Spinelli

Love That Dog by Sharon Creech

The Moves Make the Man by Bruce Brooks

My Thirteenth Winter: A Memoir by Samantha Abeel

Reach for the Moon by Samantha Abeel

The Report Card by Andrew Clements

Seedfolks by Paul Fleischman

The Silent Boy by Lois Lowry

Stargirl by Jerry Spinelli

Surviving the Applewhites by Stephanie S. Tolan

The Wave: The Classroom Experiment That Went Too Far by Todd Strasser

Fair Versus Equal Sayings

After teaching, reading stories, or discussing fair versus equal, hang the following sayings around the room as a reminder for both you and your students.

Fair Versus Equal

* **Equal** means the **same**.

* I **will not** be treating each student **exactly the same** way.

I will always be **fair, not equal**.

* Being **fair** means I will do my best to give **each student** what he or she **needs** to be **successful**.

* What **you** need and what **someone else** needs may be **very different**.

Save the Last Word for Me Bookmarks

Secondary Example

Save the Last Word for Me!	
Step 1	Reread the text, and find five passages you like.
Step 2	Record your five passages and the location of the text on an index card or in your reader's notebook.
Step 3	On the back of the card, write why you chose each of your five passages. • Why did the passage appeal to you? • What did it make you think? • How would you extend the idea presented in your passage?
Step 4	In your core groups, share each passage one by one. • The reader listens to all other thoughts about his or her passages. • When all others have shared their thoughts, the reader shares his or her thoughts at the end.
The reader of the passage always gets to "save the last word for me."	

Elementary Example

Save the Last Word for Me!		
Step 1	Find 5!	👍 I like!
Step 2	Jot 5	✏️ Jot
Step 3	Why?	❓ Why? 💡 What does it make you think? 📎 What does it make you think?
Step 4	Share	⭕ One by one 👂 Listen 💬 Talk about each person's text selection.
The reader of the passage always gets to "save the last word for me."		

Levels of Talk Processing Guide and Prompts

As noted in chapter 7, these prompts should be used as talk stems for students to use as they are learning to deepen their level of talk. The prompts can be posted on an anchor chart or used as a handout for students to refer to and practice with as they enter into conversations with their classmates.

Level of Discourse	Discourse Prompts
Any Comment Any experience, any thought, any comment—say it out loud.	"I noticed . . ." "I like . . ." or "I don't like . . ." "I feel . . ." "I thought . . ." "I wonder . . ."
Connected Comment (Information) Say something meaningful about the book or information, and then connect it to the ongoing conversation. (People) Respond to what others have said. Add on to, agree with, or disagree with what's already been said.	"This makes me think of . . ." "This reminds me of . . ." "I agree (or disagree) with _____ because . . ." "I'm thinking about what _____ said, and I would like to add . . ." "What _____ said makes me think of . . ." "I'd like to piggyback on what _____ said and say . . ."
Clarifying Comment Find words, and explain what you mean when others are confused. Stretch it out, explain your thinking, and tell us what you meant. Express your ideas more articulately. Speak clearly and thoughtfully.	"What I really meant was . . ." "What I'm trying to say is . . ." "Let me add that . . ." "An example might be . . ."
Extending Comment Lengthen your ideas; use more words to describe your thinking.	"I want to tell you more about . . ." "Let me explain more."
Processing Comment How do you see it now? What have you learned? How has your thinking changed? What helped you make connections?	"Before I thought _____, but now I think . . ." "My thinking has changed . . ." "Thinking about what _____ said, now I'm thinking . . ."
Stimulating Comment Invite others to discuss, ask for ideas, encourage a new idea, or ask for a perspective.	"What was your thinking?" "I wonder why . . ." "Why do you think . . .?" "How would you . . .?"

Source: Adapted from Kryza et al., 2009.

Self-Assessment Exit Card Template

During Assessment Exit Card

On a scale of 1 (low) to 5 (high), how well do you . . .

Understand the following:

_____

1   2   3   4   5

_____

1   2   3   4   5

_____

1   2   3   4   5

_____

1   2   3   4   5

_____

1   2   3   4   5

Write down anything we learned today that was confusing to you.

Aha moments:

Questions:

Quick Write Exit Card Template

Preassessment Exit Card

Write or draw everything you think you know about _____.
Turn this card in to me before you leave class today.

Traffic Light

As noted in chapter 8, the traffic light is used as a visual tool to have students self-assess where they are in their learning. Green means they are good to go, yellow means they may have some challenges but they are able to work through them, and red means they are stuck and need help.

Directions: Write a check mark on the line under the description that is closest to your understanding.

Language for Framing Student Choices

Use these sentence stems to help you help explain when you are giving students a choice or setting a choice expectation.

- "Either _____ or _____—you decide. I'll respect your decision."

- "Would you rather _____ or _____?"

- "Would it be better for you to _____ or _____?"

- "When _____, then _____."

- "I'd prefer _____, but maybe there is a better choice for you. Let me know."

- "Feel free to _____ or _____."

- "You have a choice: do _____ or _____. It's your choice."

- "You are welcome to _____ or _____."

- "We'll try again later."

- "You can solve this problem on your own, or I can solve it for you. Which would you prefer?"

- "That doesn't work for me. You need to come up with a solution that works for both of us."

- "We'll try again tomorrow."

- "Leave a note."

Student Self-Reflection

Use this form once a student has calmed down from a behavioral incident. The student can fill out the form alone or with the teacher.

Name: _____ Date: _____

This self-reflection sheet is a way to help you learn from your mistakes in order to be more successful.

1. Who is responsible for your behavior? _____

2. What did you do?

   _____

   _____

   _____

   _____

3. Did you have a better choice? Describe it.

   _____

   _____

   _____

   _____

4. Is this behavior helping you? _____ Is it helping anyone? _____

5. What can you do to correct this situation?

   _____

   _____

   _____

   _____

6. What can you do about your behavior to keep this from happening again when you are in a similar situation? How can teachers support you with this?

   _____

   _____

   _____

   _____

Individualist Versus Collectivist

Directions: This survey will help you know if you are more of an individualistic or collectivist person. Read each sentence. Decide how strongly you disagree or agree with each statement. Put a check mark in the column that correlates with the way you feel about each statement.

Statement	Strongly Disagree Nope! (1)	Not a Lot (2)	Kind Of or Sometimes (3)	Sure (4)	Strongly Agree Oh, Yeah! (5)
1. My happiness depends very much on the happiness of those around me.					
2. Winning is everything!					
3. I usually give up my own self-interests for the benefit of my group.					
4. It annoys me when other people per-form better than I do.					
5. It is impor-tant for me to maintain har-mony within my group.					
6. It is important to me that I do my job better than others.					
7. I like sharing little things and time with my neighbors.					

8. I enjoy competitions and challenges against others.					
9. The well-being, health, and happiness of other students (not just my friends) are important to me.					
10. I often do my own thing regardless of what the group says, thinks, or wants to do.					
11. If one of my family members needed money, I would help with my own money.					
12. It is up to people or family to take care of themselves with their own money.					
13. If a friend gets a prize, I would feel proud of him or her.					
14. Being a unique individual is important to me.					
15. To me, pleasure is spending time with others.					

	Strongly Disagree				Strongly Agree
Statement	Nope! (1)	Not a Lot (2)	Kind Of or Sometimes (3)	Sure (4)	Oh, Yeah! (5)
16. When another person does better than I do, I get tense and a little upset.					
17. Children should be taught to take care of duties and jobs before pleasure and fun.					
18. Competition is what makes our society improve and get better.					
19. I feel good when I cooperate and work in groups with others.					
20. Performing better than others makes me feel really proud and accomplished!					

Now add up the totals for all your answers to the **odd** statements: _____

Then add up the totals for all your answers to the **even** statements: _____

Odd numbers correspond with **collectivist** values. How strong are your collectivist values? What is your total for odd answers? [   ]

Even numbers correspond with **individualist** values. How strong are your individualist values? What is your total for even answers? [   ]

page 3 of 3

How I Like to Learn Survey

Give this survey to your students at the beginning of the year as a great way to start to learn about their academic strengths and challenges or to see if they have any knowledge about who they are as learners.

Name: _____ Date: _____

1. What is your favorite subject to learn about in school? (Check all that apply.)

☐	Reading and literature	☐	Music
☐	Writing	☐	Mathematics
☐	Science	☐	Computers
☐	Art	☐	Physical education
☐	Geography	☐	History
☐	History	☐	Other: _____

2. What do you enjoy the most about school? What do you enjoy the least about school?

   _____

   _____

   _____

   _____

3. How do you prefer to work? (Circle one.)

   a. Alone   b. In groups   c. Both

4. What hobbies and special interests do you have (such as sports, clubs, collections, or activities)? Be specific.

   _____

   _____

   _____

   _____

5. What do you like to do when you have free time?

   _____

   _____

   _____

   _____

page 1 of 2

6. How much time do you spend watching TV each week? _____ What do you watch?

_____

_____

_____

_____

7. How much time do you spend on the computer each week? _____ What do you like to do on the computer?

_____

_____

_____

_____

8. What types of music do you listen to?

_____

_____

_____

_____

9. What should a teacher know about you that will help you learn best in school?

_____

_____

_____

_____

10. What is the most important thing to you in your life? What are your future goals?

_____

_____

_____

_____

11. What should a teacher know about you that will help you do your best in school?

_____

_____

_____

_____

page 2 of 2

Resources for the Teacher Hero

Becoming a Reflective Teacher by Robert J. Marzano

Better Learning Through Structured Teaching: A Framework for the Gradual Release of Responsibility (2nd ed.) by Douglas Fisher and Nancy Frey

Brain Rules: 12 Principles for Surviving and Thriving at Work, Home, and School by John Medina

Breaking the Poverty Barrier: Changing Student Lives With Passion, Perseverance, and Performance by Ricardo LeBlanc-Esparza and William S. Roulston

Choice Words: How Our Language Affects Children's Learning by Peter H. Johnston

Classroom Instruction That Works: Research-Based Strategies for Increasing Student Achievement by Robert J. Marzano, Debra J. Pickering, and Jane E. Pollock

Cultural Literacy for the Common Core: Six Steps to Powerful, Practical Instruction for All Learners by Bonnie M. Davis

Different Brains, Different Learners: How to Reach the Hard to Reach by Eric Jensen

Differentiation for Real Classrooms: Making It Simple, Making It Work by Kathleen Kryza, Alicia Duncan, and S. Joy Stephens

Helping Children Learn: Intervention Handouts for Use in School and at Home (2nd ed.) by Jack A. Naglieri and Eric B. Pickering

Inspiring Elementary Learners: Nurturing the Whole Child in a Differentiated Classroom by Kathleen Kryza, Alicia Duncan, and S. Joy Stephens

Inspiring Middle and Secondary Learners: Honoring Differences and Creating Community Through Differentiating Instructional Practices by Kathleen Kryza, S. Joy Stephens, and Alicia Duncan

Lost at School: Why Our Kids With Behavioral Challenges Are Falling Through the Cracks and How We Can Help Them by Ross W. Greene

Mindful Teaching and Teaching Mindfulness: A Guide for Anyone Who Teaches Anything by Deborah Schoeberlein

Mindset: The New Psychology of Success by Carol S. Dweck

Motivating the Unmotivated by MaryAnn Brittingham

Positive Discipline by Jane Nelsen

Respectful Discipline: Your Guide to Effective Classroom Management by MaryAnn Brittingham

Shrinkin' Stinkin' Thinkin': A Guide to Raising Children's Self-Esteem by MaryAnn Brittingham

Spark: The Revolutionary New Science of Exercise and the Brain by John J. Ratey

Spirit Whisperers: Teachers Who Nourish a Child's Spirit by Chick Moorman

Start With Why: How Great Leaders Inspire Everyone to Take Action by Simon Sinek

The Talent Code: Greatness Isn't Born. It's Grown. Here's How. by Daniel Coyle

Basic Differentiated Lesson Plan

This is a simple planner designed to help you follow the steps for lesson planning with chunk, chew, and check in mind. Starting with a clear learning objective, first plan your lesson, and then plan for formative assessments and summative assessments that match your learning objectives. Once you have the end in mind, plan to teach the lesson in short chunks of instruction, and then make sure you build in activities for students to chew on the new learning in between your chunks of teaching.

Date: _____   Content Area: _____

Standard Addressed: _____

Lesson Objective

Understand (Why is this important?) _____

Know (What are the important facts?) _____

Be able to do (What are the skills?) _____

Prime: How will I connect this concept to students' lives or to other content they have learned?		
Series of chunks (inputs) and chews (processes)—think ten and two.		

page 1 of 2

Formative check: How will I assess or have students self-assess during learning?

Summative check: What will my final assessment look like?

Routines and procedures:

Am I differentiating this lesson by:

- Varying the learning styles

- Offering choices or using stations

- Meeting the needs of my high-, middle-, and low-level learners

What will I do when the data inform me that kids aren't getting it or need more of a challenge?

CCC Ideas

The following are lists of ideas for chunking, chewing, and checking in varied ways, offering many possibilities for keeping your lessons engaging and meaningful for your students.

Chunk = Taking in Content

Students acquire new information in varied ways.

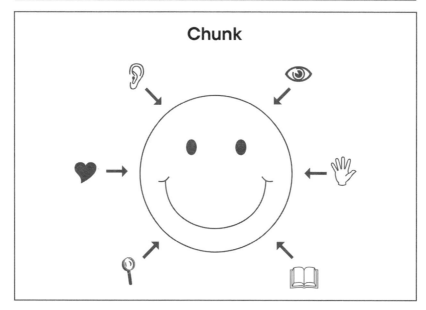

Chunk

Source: Reprinted with permission from Kryza, K., Duncan, A., & Stephens, S. J. (2010). Differentiation for real classrooms: Making it simple, making it work. Thousand Oaks, CA: Corwin Press.

Chunk Ideas

Ask yourself . . .

What are some other ways I can help students acquire new knowledge?

Visual: Can I . . .

- Show a movie or clip from a movie; demonstrate from a chart or graph; watch a United Stream or TeacherTube video; share a blog, Wikipedia entry, WebQuest, or PowerPoint; use graphics, pictures, graphic organizers, conceptual organizers, articles, magazines, or books; give a presentation or demonstration; use technology or media; or read in various structures (small groups, aloud, jigsaws, paired readings, and reading centers)

Auditory: Can I . . .

- Say it, have students say it to each other (repeat information they have learned and need to recall to each other), play a song, listen to a speech, encourage them to talk to each other, listen to a speaker, listen to music, play recorded lectures, or use audiobooks

page 1 of 8

Kinesthetic: Can I . . .

- Role-play; demonstrate; have students demonstrate; rotate students through stations set up to teach content; encourage movement, touch, building, drawing, and taking apart; play charades; create a group tableau; or conduct a lab experiment

Social: Can I . . .

- Encourage talking, listening, or telling others; use brainstorming; have students share experiences; use predicting or hypothesizing; do a role play; play a game; or have a class discussion

Activities

- **Event cards:** Groups of students sort events from a story in order to build anticipation.

- **Visual literacy:** Students use images to chunk new information.

- **Gallery walk:** Students view photos in carousel style and then engage in a chew activity to process what they have taken in.

- **Expert groups:** Students become experts in an area, topic, or subset of information and continue to share information throughout a unit.

Chew Ideas

Ask yourself . . .
How can I vary the ways I help students process new knowledge?

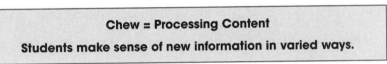

Source: Reprinted with permission from Kryza, K., Duncan, A., & Stephens, S. J. (2010). Differentiation for real classrooms: Making it simple, making it work. Thousand Oaks, CA: Corwin Press.

page 2 of 8

Ways to Collaborate to Chew

1. Jigsaw

    a. Each student receives a portion of the materials to be introduced.

    b. Students leave their home groups and meet in expert groups.

    c. Expert groups discuss the material and brainstorm ways in which to present their understandings to the other members of their home groups.

    d. The experts return to their home groups to teach their portion of the materials and to learn from the other members of their home groups.

    Note: You can also jigsaw poetry, text, and vocabulary.

2. Numbered heads together

    a. Number students from 1 to 4 within their groups.

    b. Call out a question or problem (for example, "Where do plants get their energy?").

    c. In teams, students put their heads together to discuss the answer. They must make sure everyone on the team knows the answer.

    d. Randomly call a number from 1 to 4 (use a spinner, draw Popsicle sticks out of a cup, roll a die, and so on).

    e. On each team, the student whose number was called says or writes the answer. He or she may not receive any help from his or her team at this point!

3. Turn and talk / walk and talk

    a. Give students a prompt on the board, on the overhead, or on a PowerPoint.

    b. Students turn and talk to a partner or stand up and walk (five giant steps) and find a talk partner.

    c. Students have two to three minutes to talk and share. While they are talking, the teacher is floating around the room listening for quality talk.

    d. The whole class processes the talk, with the teacher noting quality talk that he or she heard while going around the room.

4. Core workgroups

    a. At the beginning of the year, students are randomly assigned to groups.

    b. The group members are assigned jobs, such as leader, recorder, teacher getter, timekeeper, life coach, organizer, and so on.

    c. Groups then give themselves a name, a silent signal, or a symbol.

    d. The groups do fun community-building activities, such as building the tallest tower from straws and tape, all without talking!

    e. The groups stay together for a marking period, a semester, or a school year.

page 3 of 8

f. The core group responsibilities are as follows.

- If anyone from the core group is absent, he or she gets the make-up work and the assignment from the core group members. (This buys the teacher valuable teaching time and builds responsibility.)

- The teacher can always call the core group together at the beginning or end of class to plan, reflect, review, and so on.

Ways to Move to Chew

- **Classification cruise:** When teaching information that falls into natural categories (or could be sequenced), create cards that have all the components of the categories (for example, parts of the body systems or categories of rocks and their features). Pass out a card to each student, and then students have to categorize themselves with others who have similar cards (such as types of exercises, states of matter, or parts of government). Once students have categorized themselves, you can all discuss if they are placed in the correct categories. This is a great way to formatively assess for learning.

- **Charades:** Students act out what they have learned, and other students have to guess what they are acting out about the learning.

- **Moving mathematics:** The following mathematics strategies help students move and chew.

  - Use mathematics manipulatives.

  - Have students become mathematics numbers and build mathematics problems. (For example, they can make arrays by arranging themselves into six groups of four, then four groups of six.)

  - Play "What time is it?"

    a. Make a clockface on a sheet of paper.

    b. Line students up with partners around the clock so they can see the clock.

    c. Give each pair a time on an index card.

    d. When it is the pair's turn, have the two students make the time on their card with their bodies. (The student acting as the minute hand must bring his or her knees up.)

    e. The rest of the class says the time.

    f. The pairs can then make up their own times and have other students guess.

- **Building sentences:** Give each student a card that is part of a sentence. Students must move into the correct order to make the sentence make sense. The rest of the class reads the sentence and agrees or disagrees.

Ways to Talk to Chew

- **Act it out:** Become a person, place, or thing you are studying, and act out who, what, or where you are. For example, students could act out how chemical bonds happen or become the characters in a novel and act out how one character is impacted by another character.

page 4 of 8

- **Think-pair-share:** Students are given a question or prompt to think about in their head for one minute. They then pair up with a partner and discuss their thoughts or answers. Then the teacher leads a whole-class share by drawing names randomly and asking those students to share.

Ways to Write to Chew

- **Learning logs and journals:** Students use writing logs for processing learning in their own words.

- **Note-taking strategies:** Students use note-taking techniques for gathering facts, summarizing information, and processing with the teacher model note-taking techniques.

- *TV Guide* **summaries:** Students write a summary like a *TV Guide* synopsis.

- **Blogs:** Students keep a blog of their thinking, like a journal only using technology.

Ways to Draw and Design to Chew

- **Comic strips:** Students create comic strips that summarize new learning.

- **Vocabulary pictures:** Students draw pictures to show the meaning of words.

- **Graphic organizers:** Students design their own organizers to process new learning.

- **Doodle notes:** As students are reading or listening to the teacher, they doodle or sketch ideas, thoughts, and so on.

Other Ways Students Can Process New Learning

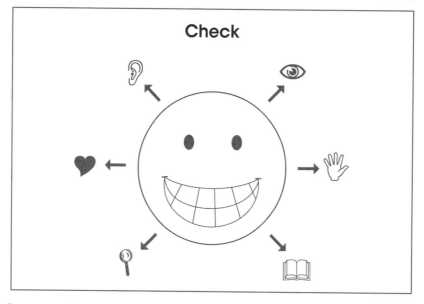

Source: Reprinted with permission from Kryza, K., Duncan, A., & Stephens, S. J. (2010). Differentiation for real classrooms: Making it simple, making it work. Thousand Oaks, CA: Corwin Press.

Ask yourself . . .

How can I vary the ways students show me what they know (outputs)?

Ways to Check for Understanding

- Explanation (provide through supported facts and data)

  - Show and say.

  - Describe.

  - Construct.

  - Write.

  - Provide conceptual clarification.

  - Reveal patterns.

  - Clarify.

  - Link.

- Interpretation (offer good translations)

  - Report on the meaning.

  - Develop an oral history.

  - Write on the meaning of the results.

  - Draft a decision.

  - Do trend analysis.

  - Represent a concept through dance or art.

  - Conduct research on a question.

  - Write a narrative that provides meaning.

- Application (effectively use and adapt what we know in diverse contexts)

  - Design a product.

  - Create a game.

  - Make a tape.

  - Develop an analysis.

  - Make an accurate projection.

  - Perform.

  - Use knowledge in a new situation.

  - Create a plan.

- Perspective (see and hear points of view through critical eyes and ears)

  - Compare and contrast.

  - Research the impact.

  - Recognize fallacies.

  - Argue for and against.

  - Analyze assumptions.

  - Write a critical review.

  - Conduct thought experiments.

  - Self-assess your writing as someone else.

- Empathy (find value in what others might perceive)

  - Take on a persona.

  - Imagine from another viewpoint.

  - Speak to others' needs or feelings.

  - Role-play a meeting of minds.

  - Write about a social issue or people in need.

- Self-knowledge (awareness of what shapes and impedes your thinking)

  - Keep a log reacting to your learning.

  - Self-assess your participation.

  - Develop a résumé of strengths and weaknesses.

  - Revise, edit, and self-assess your writing.

  - Reflect.

Source: Ways to Check Understanding section adapted from Wiggins & McTighe, 1998.

Ways to Check for Understanding Using Multiple Intelligences

Interpersonal	Intrapersonal
Teach peers.	Design a one-man show.
Do a group project.	Keep a journal.
Create and present a play.	Do a monologue.
Create and play a game.	Do a soliloquy.
Empathize.	Present observations.
Lead a group.	Demonstrate personal imaginings.
Imagine.	
Musical	**Bodily Kinesthetic**
Match feelings to rhythms.	Play a game.
Sing or rap.	Use body language.
Move to music.	Dance.
Rewrite song lyrics.	Act or mime.
Create musical mnemonics.	Build a model or replica.
Linguistic	**Logical-Mathematical**
Write in a favorite genre.	Demonstrate practical applications.
Tell stories.	Analyze and offer solutions.
Create a word game.	Develop questions and answers.
Explain in words.	Construct diagrams.
Give a speech.	Create strategy games.
Debate.	Show connections to things.
	Make a graph or chart.
Naturalist	**Spatial**
Demonstrate connections.	Make a photo journal.
Present observations.	Make storyboards.
Notice relationships.	Make a comic strip.
Create a collection.	Design.
Categorize and chart.	Reconstruct.
Create a new way to see things.	Create three-dimensional models.

Chunk, Chew, and Check Tech

Lesson planning with chunk, chew, and check in mind will help you easily know where to weave technology into your lessons. The following list offers some great technology tools and sites to use to chunk, chew, and check in your lessons.

Subject Areas	Grade Levels	Name of Site	Web Address	Description	Chunk	Chew	Check
All subject areas	K–12	Wikispaces	www.wikispaces.com	A wiki is a space on the web where you can share work and ideas, pictures and links, videos and media, and more. Wikispaces is special because it gives you a visual editor and a bunch of other tools to make sharing all kinds of content as easy for students as it is for their teachers. Create student portfolios. Create presentations.		X	X
All subject areas	1–12	Google Maps or Google Earth	https://maps.google.com or www.google.com/earth/index.html	Google Maps and Google Earth can both be used to create a multimedia story. Try having your students write the biography of a famous person by plotting points on a map and adding text, images, and videos about that person to each placemark. Visit Jerome Burg's Google Lit Trips to learn more about using Google Earth in a literature course: www.speedofcreativity.org/2010/11/18/google-lit-trips-by-jerome-burg-microsoft-education-award-laureate-gct Visit Tom Barrett's Maths Maps to get ideas for using maps in mathematics lessons: http://edte.ch/blog/maths-maps		X	X
Foreign language, language arts, and others	2–12	Aviary Myna	http://advanced.aviary.com	Students can record their own voices to practice a foreign language, practice reading fluency, or share a lesson with a friend.	X	X	X

Subject Areas	Grade Levels	Name of Site	Web Address	Description	Chunk	Chew	Check
Mathematics and ELA	K–12	BrainNook	www.brainnook.com /Educators.php	BrainNook helps your students build mathematics and language skills while playing a fun game with their classmates, and it gives you powerful tools to customize and accelerate your students' learning.		X	X
Writing	2–12	TikaTok	www.tikatok.com /classroom	TikaTok is an award-winning site endorsed by educators and an interactive platform where students have fun creating and publishing their own books. This innovative platform is an excellent cross-curricular tool for writing, reading, mathematics, science, social studies, art, and more. Students publish their writing as real books, building confidence and motivation in writing and reading.		X	X
Writing	4–12	Showbeyond	http://showbeyond .com/show/home	Showbeyond is a multimedia slidecast creator, online publishing platform, and story-sharing community. With Showbeyond, you can easily grab your images, then add your sound and text to create multimedia stories. You can share your stories with friends or post to blogs and social-networking sites.		X	X
Social studies	9–12	PBS Online	www.pbs.org /americanrootsmusic /pbs_arm_into_the _classroom.html	The resources offered are designed to help you use the PBS American Roots Music video series and companion website in middle school and high school social studies and history classes.	X		
Writing	2–12	Figment	http://figment.com	This website is like Facebook for aspiring writers. Students can share their work with readers around the world. After creating a free Figment profile, students can post original short stories, poems, and novels for their classmates and others to read and review. Figment also has excerpts from new books, interviews with authors, writing contests, and discussions.		X	
All subject areas	3–12	BrainPOP	www.brainpop.com	This website requires a subscription. It has a variety of short cartoon videos that teach ELA, science, mathematics, and social science standards. There are also activities for students and a multiple-choice quiz with each lesson.	X	X	X

Continued →

Subject Areas	Grade Levels	Name of Site	Web Address	Description	Chunk	Chew	Check
Mathematics	3–9	LearnZillion	www.learnzillion.com	This website is a learning platform that combines video lessons, activities, assessments, and progress reporting using the Common Core mathematics standards.	X	X	X
Mathematics	2–12	GeoGebra	www.geogebra.org /cms	GeoGebra provides free software that supports student learning in geometry, algebra, and calculus, all the way from elementary school to college. The software can be used to design dynamic worksheets that let students explore mathematical concepts.	X	X	X
Mathematics	K–12	National Library of Virtual Ma-nipulatives	http://nlvm.usu.edu	This website provides a collection of virtual manipulatives—interactive, web-based, visual representations of mathematics concepts. The library is organized by strand (geometry, algebra, measurement, data analysis and probability, and number and operations) and grade level.		X	
Science	K–12	The GLOBE Program	www.globe.gov	The GLOBE Program is a worldwide hands-on, primary and secondary school–based science and education program.	X	X	X
Science	8–12	Sumanas	www.sumanasinc .com/webcontent /animation.html	Sumanas develops animated tutorials in a variety of formats for many scientific disciplines. Its public gallery of animations is divided into ten categories dealing with various topics in biology, chemistry, earth science, and statistics.	X		
Science (astronomy)	1–12	Celestia	www .celestiamotherlode.net	Celestia is a free, interactive, real-time, 3-D astronomy program. It doesn't just show you the sky as it can be seen from Earth, as most planetarium software does, but instead allows you to move to and view the universe from any point among the planets and the stars.	X	X	

Learning Styles Inventory

There are six basic learning styles: (1) reading, (2) writing, (3) listening, (4) speaking, (5) visualizing, and (6) manipulating. You probably use a combination of several learning styles as you go about your work. The Learning Styles Inventory is designed to point out your *strongest* learning styles. Put a check mark next to each sentence that describes you. Then count how many checks you have in each group, and note that number on the line at the end of each group.

Group 1

_____ 1. I like to read when I have free time.

_____ 2. I like to read a report rather than be told what's in it.

_____ 3. I understand something best when I read it.

_____ 4. I remember what I read better than I remember what I hear.

_____ 5. I would rather read a newspaper than watch the news on TV.

_____ Total number of check marks in group 1.

Group 2

_____ 1. I take notes when I read to better understand the material.

_____ 2. I take lecture notes to help me remember the material.

_____ 3. I like to recopy my lecture notes as a way of better understanding the material.

_____ 4. I make fewer mistakes when I write than when I speak.

_____ 5. I find the best way to keep track of my schedule is to write it down.

_____ Total number of check marks in group 2.

Group 3

_____ 1. I like to listen to people discuss things.

_____ 2. I learn more when I watch the news than when I read about it.

_____ 3. I usually remember what I hear.

_____ 4. I would rather watch a TV show or movie based on a book than read the book.

_____ 5. I learn better by listening to a lecture than by taking notes from a textbook on the same subject.

_____ Total number of check marks in group 3.

page 1 of 3

Group 4

____   1.   I remember things better when I say them out loud.

____   2.   I talk to myself when I try to solve problems.

____   3.   I communicate better on the telephone than I do in writing.

____   4.   I learn best when I study with other people.

____   5.   I understand material better when I read it out loud.

____   Total number of check marks in group 4.

Group 5

____   1.   I can see words in my mind when I need to spell them.

____   2.   I picture what I read.

____   3.   I can remember something by seeing it in my mind.

____   4.   I remember what the pages look like in books I've read.

____   5.   I remember people's faces better than I remember their names.

____   Total number of check marks in group 5.

Group 6

____   1.   I like to make models of things.

____   2.   I would rather do experiments than read about them.

____   3.   I learn better by handling objects.

____   4.   I find it hard to sit still when I study.

____   5.   I pace and move around a lot when I'm trying to think through a problem.

____   Total number of check marks in group 6.

Interpreting the Inventory

Look over the inventory you took. In which groups do you have the most check marks?

If you have three or more check marks in group 1, *reading* is one of your preferred learning styles. You find it easier to learn information by reading printed words.

If you have three or more check marks in group 2, *writing* is one of your preferred learning styles. You learn information more easily when you express it in written form.

If you have three or more check marks in group 3, *listening* is one of your preferred learning styles. You find it easy to learn information that you hear.

If you have three or more check marks in group 4, *speaking* is one of your preferred learning styles. You are best able to learn when you express yourself out loud.

If you have three or more check marks in group 5, *visualizing* is one of your preferred learning styles. Your mind's eye is a very powerful learning tool for you. You learn well when you use your brain to "photograph" information.

If you have three or more check marks in group 6, *manipulating* is one of your preferred learning styles. You learn well when you are able to handle objects you're learning about. Manipulating situations by changing your location, moving around, and so on also help you learn.

Source: Sonbuchner, 1991. Reprinted with permission.

How Are You Smart? Multiple Intelligences Survey

Directions: The following tables list eight types of intelligence and activities that relate to each. Read the descriptions, and check the ones that describe you. Go with your first instinct. Then total the number you checked at the bottom of each intelligence section. At the end, transfer each total to the Multiple Intelligence Scoring Rubric, and see what your strongest intelligences are. Remember most people are strong in more than one intelligence. Have fun!

Intelligence 1

_____ I can hear or see words in my head before I speak, read, or write them.

_____ I like games such as Scrabble, Jeopardy, Trivial Pursuit, word searches, crossword puzzles, and so on.

_____ I enjoy writing and have received praise or recognition for my writing talents.

_____ I often talk about things that I have read or heard.

_____ I love to read books, magazines, or anything!

_____ I am good with words. I learn and use new words in creative or funny ways regularly.

_____ When I am in a classroom, I pay attention to all the written posters and the writing on the board.

_____ I have a very good memory for hearing and seeing words.

Total _____

Intelligence 2

_____ I enjoy activities like dancing, swimming, biking, and skating.

_____ I play a sport or do a physical activity regularly.

_____ I need to do things with my hands or by moving in order to learn them best.

_____ I am good at imitating others and like drama and acting.

_____ I use my hands and body when I am talking with someone.

_____ I need to move around a lot and change positions often when sitting.

_____ I need to touch things to learn about them.

Total _____

Intelligence 3

_____ I like to draw and doodle.

_____ I am good at finding my way around places I don't know well.

_____ I can easily see in my head how furniture would fit in a room. I am also good at jigsaw puzzles.

_____ I remember things better if I can draw or create an image of them.

_____ When I look at paintings or pictures, I really notice the colors and shapes and how objects are spaced.

_____ I prefer learning from pictures.

_____ I picture things in my mind.

Total _____

Intelligence 4

_____ I listen to music or have music playing in my head most of the time.

_____ I play a musical instrument or have a good singing voice.

_____ I can easily pick up rhythms and can move to them or tap them out.

_____ I can easily remember or create songs.

_____ I often make tapping sounds or sing while working or studying.

_____ I can remember things better if I put them in a song.

_____ I can hear all the parts when I listen to music.

Total _____

page 1 of 3

Intelligence 5

_____ Mathematics is one of my favorite subjects.

_____ I like to play games such as chess, Clue, and Stratego.

_____ I like to do scientific experiments.

_____ I like to calculate, measure, and figure things out.

_____ I enjoy solving brain teasers and puzzles.

_____ Using a computer comes easily to me. I understand how they work and can spend time learning about them.

_____ I see patterns in things.

Total _____

Intelligence 6

_____ I understand and can express my feelings.

_____ I enjoy spending time by myself.

_____ I like to work alone.

_____ I am comfortable having ideas and opinions that are not the same as others.

_____ I feel good about who I am most of the time.

_____ I have a realistic view of my strengths and weaknesses.

_____ I enjoy playing games and doing activities that I can do by myself.

Total _____

Intelligence 7

_____ I have many friends.

_____ I enjoy playing group games and group sports.

_____ I enjoy working in groups and tend to be the leader in the group.

_____ I really care about others and try to understand how others feel and think.

_____ I feel comfortable being in the middle of groups or crowds.

_____ I enjoy teaching another person or group of people something that I know how to do well.

_____ I like to get involved in social activities in school, church, or the community.

Total _____

Intelligence 8

_____ I like to watch and observe what is going on around me.

_____ I think about the environment a lot and want to make sure that we don't pollute our planet.

_____ I like to collect rocks, leaves, or other nature items.

_____ I feel best when I am out in nature.

_____ I understand how different plants and animals are connected to each other.

_____ I can easily get used to being in new places.

_____ I like to organize things and put them in categories.

Total _____

Source: Reprinted with permission from Kryza, K., Duncan, A., & Stephens, S. J. (2010). Differentiation for real classrooms: Making it simple, making it work. _Thousand Oaks, CA: Corwin Press._

Multiple Intelligence Scoring Rubric

Directions: Circle the number that you scored in each section of the survey. If you scored five to seven points in any areas, those are your areas of strength as a learner.

	Weak						Strong
Intelligence 1: Word smart (linguistic)	1	2	3	4	5	6	7
Intelligence 2: Body smart (bodily kinesthetic)	1	2	3	4	5	6	7
Intelligence 3: Art smart (spatial)	1	2	3	4	5	6	7
Intelligence 4: Music smart (musical)	1	2	3	4	5	6	7
Intelligence 5: Mathematics smart (logical)	1	2	3	4	5	6	7
Intelligence 6: Self smart (intrapersonal)	1	2	3	4	5	6	7
Intelligence 7: People smart (interpersonal)	1	2	3	4	5	6	7
Intelligence 8: Nature smart (naturalistic)	1	2	3	4	5	6	7

My strongest areas of intelligence are:

_____

_____

_____

_____

_____

_____

_____

I need to build my strengths in these areas:

_____

_____

_____

_____

_____

_____

_____

_____

Source: Reprinted with permission from Kryza, K., Duncan, A., & Stephens, S. J. (2010). Differentiation for real classrooms: Making it simple, making it work. *Thousand Oaks, CA: Corwin Press.*

Clock Partners Clockface

My Partners

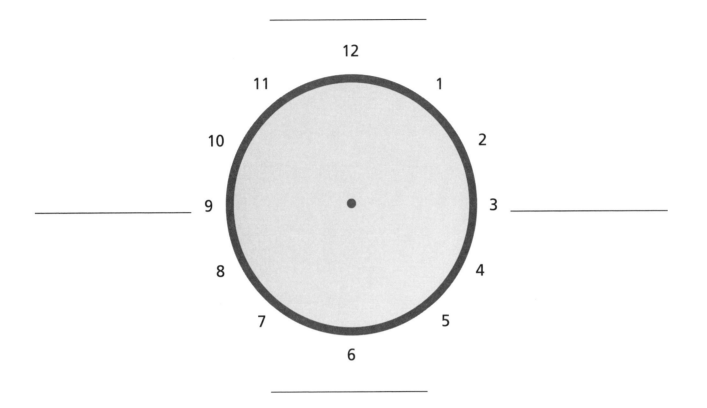

REFERENCES AND RESOURCES

American Psychiatric Association. (2013). *Diagnostic and statistical manual of mental disorders* (5th ed.): Arlington, VA: Author.

Ambady, N., & Adams, R. B., Jr. (2011). Us versus them: The social neuroscience of perceiving out-groups. In A. Todorov, S. T. Fiske, & D. A. Prentice (Eds.), *Social neuroscience: Toward understanding the underpinnings of the social mind* (pp. 135–143). New York: Oxford University Press.

Añez, L. M., Silva, M. A., Paris, M., Jr., & Bedregal, L. E. (2008). Engaging Latinos through the integration of cultural values and motivational interviewing principles. *Professional Psychology: Research and Practice*, 39(2), 153–159.

Baer, R. A. (2003). Mindfulness training as a clinical intervention: A conceptual and empirical review. *Clinical Psychology: Science and Practice*, 10(2), 125–143.

Black, R. S., Mrasek, K. D., & Ballinger, R. (2003). Individualist and collectivist values in transition planning for culturally diverse students with special needs. *Journal for Vocational Special Needs Education*, 25(2–3), 20–29.

Bloom, B. S. (Ed.) (1956). *Taxonomy of educational objectives, handbook I: Cognitive domain*. New York: McKay.

Bluestein, J. (2001). *Creating emotionally safe schools: A guide for educators and parents*. Deerfield Beach, FL: Health Communications.

Boekaerts, M. (1993). Being concerned with well-being and with learning. *Educational Psychologist*, 28(2), 149–167.

Boekaerts, M., & Cascallar, E. (2006). How far have we moved toward the integration of theory and practice in self-regulation? *Educational Psychology Review*, 18(3), 199–210.

Boykin, A. W. (1994). Afrocultural expression and its implications for schooling. In E. R. Hollins, J. E. King, & W. C. Haymen (Eds.), *Teaching diverse populations* (pp. 243–256). Albany: State University of New York Press.

Bransford, J. D., Brown, A. L., & Cocking, R. R. (Eds.). (2000). *How people learn: Brain, mind, experience, and school* (Expanded ed.). Washington, DC: National Academies Press.

Brittingham, M. A. (2003). *Respectful discipline: Your guide to effective classroom management*. Pine Bush, NY: Author.

Brophy, J. E., & Evertson, C. M. (1976). *Learning from teaching: A developmental perspective.* Boston: Allyn & Bacon.

Brown, B. (2007). *I thought it was just me: Women reclaiming power and courage in a culture of shame.* New York: Gotham Books.

Brown, B. (2010a). *The gifts of imperfection: Let go of who you think you're supposed to be and embrace who you are.* Center City, MN: Hazelden.

Brown, B. (2010b, June). *The power of vulnerability* [Video file]. Accessed at www.ted.com/talks /brene _brown_on_vulnerability on February 12, 2015.

Brown, B. (2012). *Daring greatly: How the courage to be vulnerable transforms the way we live, love, parent, and lead.* New York: Gotham Books.

Buehl, D. (2005, September 27). *Scaffolding.* Accessed at http://weac.org/articles/readingroom_scaffolding on February 12, 2015.

Buehl, D. (2014). *Classroom strategies for interactive learning* (4th ed.). Newark, DE: International Reading Association.

Bunn, S. (2000, May). *Keeping kids connected: How schools and teachers can help all students feel good about school . . . and why that matters.* Salem, OR: Office of Curriculum, Instruction, and Field Services, Oregon Department of Education.

Campbell, J. (1968). *The hero with a thousand faces.* Princeton, NJ: Princeton University Press.

Canter, L. (2010). *Assertive discipline: Positive behavior management for today's classroom* (4th ed.). Bloomington, IN: Solution Tree Press.

Centers for Disease Control and Prevention. (2015). *Autism Spectrum Disorder.* Accessed at www.cdc.gov /ncbddd/autism/index.html on February 26, 2015.

Chappuis, J., Stiggins, R. J., Chappuis, S., & Arter, J. (2011). *Classroom assessment for student learning: Doing it right—using it well* (2nd ed.). New York: Pearson.

Chappuis, S., & Stiggins, R. J. (2002). Classroom assessment for learning. *Educational Leadership, 60*(1), 40–43.

Chiao, J. (Ed.). (2009). Cultural neuroscience: cultural influences on brain function. *Progress in Brain Research*, Vol. 178. New York: Elsevier.

Coppola, F. F. (Director) (1972). *The godfather* [Motion picture]. Los Angeles, CA: Paramount Pictures.

College Board. (1999). *Reaching the top: A report of the National Task Force on Minority High Achievement.* New York: Author.

Cortiella, C., & Horowitz, S. H. (2014). *The state of learning disabilities: Facts, trends and emerging issues* (3rd ed.). New York: National Center for Learning Disabilities.

Crouch, R. (2012). *The United States of education: The changing demographics of the United States and their schools.* Alexandria, VA: Center for Public Education.

Darling-Hammond, L., Orcutt, S., Strobel, K., Kirsch, E., Lit, I., & Martin, D. (2003). *Session 5—Feelings count: Emotions and learning.* St. Louis, MO: Annenberg Learner.

Davis, D. M., & Hayes, J. A. (2011). What are the benefits of mindfulness?: A practice review of psychotherapy-related research. *Psychotherapy, 48*(2), 198–208.

Diz, S. (2009, March). *The individualism/collectivism dichotomy: Argument in favor of the theoretical construct in cross-cultural research.* Accessed at www.academia.edu/3089521/The_Individualism_Collectivism _Dichotomy on February 5, 2015.

Dr. Seuss. (1978). *I can read with my eyes shut!* New York: Random House.

Dr. Seuss. (1990). *Oh, the places you'll go!* New York: Random House.

Dunning, D., Heath, C., & Suls, J. M. (2004). Flawed self-assessment: Implications for health, education, and the workplace. *Psychological Science in the Public Interest, 5*(3), 69–106.

Dweck, C. S. (2006). *Mindset: The new psychology of success.* New York: Ballantine Books.

Ericsson, K. A., Krampe, R. T., & Tesch-Römer, C. (1993). The role of deliberate practice in the acquisition of expert performance. *Psychological Review, 100*(3), 363–406.

Fantino, A. M. (2006). *Cultures at work: Intercultural communication in the Canadian workplace.* Edmonton, Alberta, Canada: Muttart Foundation.

Fisher, D., & Frey, N. (2003). Writing instruction for struggling adolescent readers: A gradual release model. *Journal of Adolescent and Adult Literacy, 46*(5), 396–405.

Fisher, D., & Frey, N. (2008). *Better learning through structured teaching: A framework for the gradual release of responsibility.* Alexandria, VA: Association for Supervision and Curriculum Development.

Fisher, D., Frey, N., & Rothenberg, C. (2008). *Content-area conversations: How to plan discussion-based lessons for diverse language learners.* Alexandria, VA: Association for Supervision and Curriculum Development.

Flanders, N. A. (1970). *Analyzing teaching behavior.* Reading, MA: Addison-Wesley.

Frederiksen, J. R., & White, B. Y. (1998). Teaching and learning generic modeling and reasoning skills. *Journal of Interactive Learning Environments, 5*(1), 33–51.

French, W. L., & Bell, C. H., Jr. (1995). *Organization development* (5th ed.). Englewood Cliffs, NJ: Prentice Hall.

Fuligni, A. J., & Tseng, V. (1999). Family obligation and the academic motivation of adolescents from immigrant and American-born families. In T. C. Urdan (Ed.), Advances in motivation and achievement: *The role of context* (Vol. 11, pp. 159–184). Bingley, West Yorkshire, England: Emerald Group.

Gay, G. (2000). *Culturally responsive teaching: Theory, research, and practice.* New York: Teachers College Press.

Ghonim, W. (2011, March). *Inside the Egyptian revolution* [Video file]. Accessed at www.ted.com/talks /wael_ghonim_inside_the_egyptian_revolution on February 12, 2015.

Gladwell, M. (2008). *Outliers: The story of success*. New York: Little, Brown.

Goldstein, E. (2015). *Uncovering happiness: Overcoming depression with mindfulness and self-compassion*. New York: Atria Books.

Greene, R. W. (2008). *Lost at school: Why our kids with behavioral challenges are falling through the cracks and how we can help them*. New York: Scribner.

Greenfield, P. M., Quiroz, B., & Raeff, C. (1996). Cross-cultural conflict and harmony in the social construction of the child. *New Directions for Child and Adolescent Development, 2000*(87), 93–108.

Greenfield, P. M., Raeff, C., & Quiroz, B. (1995). Cultural values in learning and education. In B. Williams (Ed.), *Closing the achievement gap: A vision for changing beliefs and practices* (pp. 37–55). Alexandria, VA: Association for Supervision and Curriculum Development.

Greiner, A. (2012). *The write tools*. Centennial, CO: Write Tools LLC.

Guess, C. D. (2004). Decision making in individualistic and collectivistic cultures. *Online Readings in Psychology and Culture, 4*(1). Accessed at http://scholarworks.gvsu.edu/cgi/viewcontent.cgi?article=1032&context=orpc on February 9, 2015.

Hall, E. T. (1976). *Beyond culture*. New York: Anchor Books.

Hattie, J. (2012). *Visible learning for teachers: Maximizing impact on learning*. New York: Routledge.

Hawn Foundation. (2011). *The MindUP curriculum, grades 6–8: Brain-focused strategies for learning—and living*. New York: Scholastic.

Healy, J. M. (1999). *Endangered minds: Why children don't think—and what we can do about it*. New York: Touchstone.

Hofstede, G. (1980). *Culture's consequences: International differences in work-related values*. Newbury Park, CA: SAGE.

Hofstede, G. (2001). *Culture's consequences: Comparing values, behaviors, institutions, and organizations across nations* (2nd ed.). Thousand Oaks, CA: SAGE.

Hofstede, G., Hofstede, G. J., & Minkov, M. (2010). *Cultures and organizations: Software of the mind* (3rd ed.). New York: McGraw-Hill.

Hofstede Centre. (n.d.). *Welcome to the Hofstede Centre*. Accessed at www.geert-hofstede.com on June 6, 2015.

Individuals With Disabilities Education Act, 20 U.S.C. 1400 (2004). Accessed at http://idea.ed.gov/download/statute.html on June 3, 2015.

Jensen, E. (n.d.). *What is brain-based learning?* Accessed at https://feaweb.org/brain-based-learning-strategies on June 4, 2015.

Jensen, E. (1998). *Teaching with the brain in mind*. Alexandria, VA: Association for Supervision and Curriculum Development.

Jensen, E. (2009). *Teaching with poverty in mind: What being poor does to kids' brains and what schools can do about it*. Alexandria, VA: Association for Supervision and Curriculum Development.

Johnston, P. H. (2004). *Choice words: How our language affects children's learning.* Portland, ME: Stenhouse.

Joyce, C. (2012). The impact of direct and indirect communication. *Independent Voice.* Accessed at www .ombudsassociation.org/Resources/IOA-Publications/The-Independent-Voice/November-2012/The -Impact-of-Direct-and-Indirect-Communication.aspx on August 1, 2015.

Kalyanpur, M. (2003). A challenge to professionals: Developing cultural reciprocity with culturally diverse families. *Focal Point, 17*(1), 1–6.

Kidding Around Yoga. (n.d.). *Crazy Monkey.* Accessed at http://kiddingaroundyoga.com/buy-songs/using -our-music/crazy-monkey on February 12, 2015.

Kohn, A. (1992). *No contest: The case against competition* (Revised ed.). New York: Houghton Mifflin.

Kong, A., & Pearson, P. D. (2003). The road to participation: The construction of a literacy practice in a learning community of linguistically diverse learners. *Research in the Teaching of English, 38*(1), 85–124.

Korb, A. (2012, November 20). The grateful brain: The neuroscience of giving thanks. [Blog post] *Psychology Today.* Accessed at www.psychologytoday.com/blog/prefrontal-nudity/201211/the-grateful -brain on February 5, 2015.

Kryza, K., Duncan, A., & Stephens, S. J. (2007). *Inspiring middle and secondary learners: Honoring differences and creating community through differentiating instructional practices.* Thousand Oaks, CA: Corwin Press.

Kryza, K., Duncan, A., & Stephens, S. J. (2009). *Inspiring elementary learners: Nurturing the whole child in a differentiated classroom.* Thousand Oaks, CA: Corwin Press.

Kryza, K., Duncan, A., & Stephens, S. J. (2010). *Differentiation for real classrooms: Making it simple, making it work.* Thousand Oaks, CA: Corwin Press.

Kryza, K., Stephens, S. J., & Duncan, A. (2011). *Developing growth mindsets in the inspiring classroom.* Ann Arbor, MI: Inspiring Learners.

Lally, P., van Jaarsveld, C. H. M., Potts, H. W. W., & Wardle, J. (2010). How are habits formed: Modelling habit formation in the real world. *European Journal of Social Psychology, 40*(6), 998–1009.

Laroche, L., & Rutherford, D. (2007). *Recruiting, retaining, and promoting culturally different employees.* New York: Routledge.

Lloyd, S. L. (2004). Using comprehension strategies as a springboard for student talk. *Journal of Adolescent and Adult Literacy, 48*(2), 114–124.

Long, N. J., Wood, M. M., & Fecser, F. A. (2001). *Life space crisis intervention: Talking with students in conflict* (2nd ed.). Austin, TX: Pro-Ed.

Mandela, N. (2003, July 16). *Lighting your way to a better future.* Speech delivered at the launch of the Mindset Network, University of the Witwatersrand, Johannesburg, South Africa.

Manning, J. B., & Kovach, J. A. (2003). The continuing challenges of excellence and equity. In B. Williams (Ed.), *Closing the achievement gap: A vision for changing beliefs and practices* (2nd ed., pp. 25–47). Alexandria, VA: Association for Supervision and Curriculum Development.

Markus, H. R., & Kitayama, S. (1991). Culture and the self: Implications for cognition, emotion, and motivation. *Psychological Review, 98*(2), 224–253.

Marlatt, G. A., & Kristeller, J. L. (1999). Mindfulness and meditation. In W. R. Miller (Ed.), *Integrating spirituality into treatment* (pp. 67–84). Washington, DC: American Psychological Association.

Marzano, R. J., Pickering, D. J., & Pollock, J. E. (2001). *Classroom instruction that works: Research-based strategies for increasing student achievement.* Alexandria, VA: Association for Supervision and Curriculum Development.

Maslow, A. H. (1943). A theory of human motivation. *Psychological Review, 50*(4), 370–396.

McLeod, S. (2014). *Maslow's hierarchy of needs.* Accessed at www.simplypsychology.org/maslow.html on February 5, 2015.

Meloth, M. S., & Deering, P. D. (1999). The role of the teacher in promoting cognitive processing during collaborative learning. In A. M. O'Donnell & A. King (Eds.), *Cognitive perspectives on peer learning* (pp. 235–255). Mahwah, NJ: Erlbaum.

Ministry of Education of Ontario. (2004). *Think literacy: Subject-specific examples language/English, grades 7–9.* Toronto, Ontario, Canada: Author.

Miriam-Webster dictionary. (2015). *Definition of* procedure. Accessed at www.merriam-webster.com/dictionary/procedure on August 1, 2015.

Moss, C. M., & Brookhart, S. M. (2009). *Advancing formative assessment in every classroom: A guide for instructional leaders.* Alexandria, VA: Association for Supervision and Curriculum Development.

Naglieri, J. A., & Das, J. P. (1997a). *Cognitive assessment system.* Itasca, IL: Riverside.

Naglieri, J. A., & Das, J. P. (1997b). *Cognitive assessment system: Interpretive handbook.* Itasca, IL: Riverside.

Naglieri, J. A., & Pickering, E. B. (2010). *Helping children learn: Intervention handouts for use in school and at home* (2nd ed.). Baltimore: Brookes.

Naglieri, J. A., & Rojahn, J. (2004). Construct validity of the PASS theory and CAS: Correlations with achievement. *Journal of Educational Psychology, 96*(1), 174–181.

National Center for Children in Poverty. (n.d.). *Child poverty.* Accessed at www.nccp.org/topics/childpoverty.html on June 3, 2015.

National Association for Gifted Children. (n.d.). *Gifted education in the U.S.* Accessed at www.nagc.org/resources-publications/resources/gifted-education-us on June 3, 2015.

National Institute of Mental Health. (n.d.). *What is attention deficit hyperactivity disorder (ADHD, ADD)?* Accessed at www.nimh.nih.gov/health/topics/attention-deficit-hyperactivity-disorder-adhd/index.shtml on June 3, 2015.

Nelson, K., & Fivush, R. (2004). The emergence of autobiographical memory: A social cultural developmental theory. *Psychological Review, 111*(2), 486–511.

Oatly, K., & Nundy, S. (1996). Rethinking the role of emotions in education. In D. R. Olson & N. Torrance (Eds.), *The handbook of education and human development: New models of learning, teaching, and schooling.* Cambridge, MA: Blackwell.

Payton, J., Weissberg, R. P., Durlak, J. A., Dymnicki, A. B., Taylor, R. D., Schellinger, K. B. (2008, December). *The positive impact of social and emotional learning for kindergarten to eighth-grade students: Findings from three scientific reviews.* Chicago: Collaborative for Academic, Social, and Emotional Learning.

Pearson, P. D., & Gallagher, M. C. (1983). The instruction of reading comprehension. *Contemporary Educational Psychology, 8*(3), 317–344.

Reznitskaya, A., Anderson, R. C., & Kuo, L.–J. (2007). Teaching and learning argumentation. *Elementary School Journal, 107*(5), 449–472.

Rice, H. (2010). Fatalism. In E. N. Zalta (Ed.), *Stanford encyclopedia of philosophy* (Spring 2013 ed.). Accessed at http://plato.stanford.edu/archives/spr2013/entries/fatalism on February 5, 2015.

Ricci, C. (2015, April 13). Mindfulness very gently moving around the world's classrooms. *The Age.* Accessed at www.theage.com.au/national/education/mindfulness-very-gently-moving-around-the-worlds-classrooms-20150412-1mf5wg.html on June 3, 2015.

Rolheiser, C., & Ross, J. A. (2001). Student self-evaluation: What research says and what practice shows. In R. D. Small & A. Thomas (Eds.), *Plain talk about kids* (pp. 43–57). Covington, LA: Center for Development and Learning.

Roosevelt, T. (1910, April 23). *Citizenship in a republic.* Speech delivered at the Sorbonne, Paris, France. Accessed at http://design.caltech.edu/erik/Misc/Citizenship_in_a_Republic.pdf on February 12, 2015.

Ross, J. A. (2006). The reliability, validity, and utility of self-assessment. *Practical Assessment, Research, and Evaluation, 11*(10), 1–13. Accessed at http://hdl.handle.net/1807/30005 on February 12, 2015.

Ross, J. A., Rolheiser, C., & Hogaboam-Gray, A. (2002). Influences on student cognitions about evaluation. *Assessment in Education: Principles, Policy and Practice, 9*(1), 81–95.

Rule, N. O., Freeman, J. B., & Ambady, N. (2011). Brain and behavior in cultural context: Insights from cognition, perception, and emotion. In S. Han & E. Poeppel (Eds.), *Culture and identity: Neural frames of social cognition* (pp. 109–122). New York: Springer.

Schmitz, J. (2003). *Cultural orientations guide: The roadmap to building cultural competence* (3rd ed.). Princeton, NJ: Princeton Training Press.

Schwartz, K. (2014, January 17). *Low-income schools see big benefits in teaching mindfulness.* Accessed at ww2.kqed.org/mindshift/2014/01/17/low-income-schools-see-big-benefits-in-teaching-mindfulness on February 12, 2015.

Schwartz, M. S., Sadler, P. M., Sonnert, G., & Tai, R. H. (2008). Depth versus breadth: How content coverage in high school science courses relates to later success in college science coursework. *Science Education.* Accessed at http://curry.virginia.edu/uploads/resourceLibrary/depth_versus_breadth.pdf on February 5, 2015.

Seidel, T., Rimmele, R., & Prenzel, M. (2005). Clarity and coherence of lesson goals as a scaffold for student learning. *Learning and Instruction, 15*(6), 539–556.

Selfridge, R. J., & Sokolik, S. L. (1975). A comprehensive view of organizational development. *MSU Business Topics, 23*(1), 46–61.

Shenk, D. (2010). *The genius in all of us: Why everything you've been told about genetics, talent, and IQ is wrong*. New York: Doubleday.

Simonson, L. (1993). *Superman: The Man of Steel* (Vol. 21). New York: DC Comics.

Sinek, S. (2009a, September). *How great leaders inspire action* [Video file]. Accessed at www.ted.com/talks /simon_sinek_how_great_leaders_inspire_action?language=en on July 23, 2015.

Sinek, S. (2009b). *Start with why: How great leaders inspire everyone to take action*. New York: Portfolio.

Solomon, D., Battistich, V., Watson, M., Schaps, E., & Lewis, C. (2000). A six-district study of educational change: Direct and mediated effects of the Child Development Project. *Social Psychology of Education. 4*(1), 3–51.

Sonbuchner, G. M. (1991). *Help yourself: How to take advantage of your learning styles*. Syracuse, NY: New Readers Press.

Sousa, D. A. (2006). *How the brain learns* (3rd ed.). Thousand Oaks, CA: Corwin Press.

Sousa, D. A. (Ed.). (2010). *Mind, brain, and education: Neuroscience implications for the classroom*. Bloomington, IN: Solution Tree Press.

Stiggins, R. J., Arter, J. A., Chappuis, J., & Chappuis, S. (2007). *Classroom assessment for student learning: Doing it right—using it well*. Upper Saddle River, NJ: Pearson.

Storti, C. (1999). *Figuring foreigners out: A practical guide*. Yarmouth, ME: Intercultural Press.

Tharp, R. G. (1989). Psychocultural variables and constants: Effects on teaching and learning in schools. *American Psychologist, 44*(2), 349–359.

Triandis, H. C. (1988). Collectivism vs. individualism: A reconceptualization of a basic concept in cross-cultural social psychology. In G. K. Verma & C. Bagley (Eds.), *Cross-cultural studies of personality, attitudes, and cognition* (pp. 60–95). New York: St. Martin's Press.

Triandis, H. C. (1993). The contingency model in cross-cultural perspective. In M. M. Chemers & R. Ayman (Eds.), *Leadership theory and research: Perspectives and directions* (pp. 167–188). San Diego, CA: Academic Press.

Triandis, H. C. (1995). *Individualism and collectivism: New directions in social psychology*. Boulder, CO: Westview Press.

Trumbull, E., Rothstein-Fisch, C., Greenfield, P. M., & Quiroz, B. (2001). *Bridging cultures between home and school: A guide for teachers*. Mahwah, NJ: Erlbaum.

UGA Beyond the Arch. (2012, October 8). *Latino learning modules: Latino culture and cultural values*. [Video file] Accessed at www.youtube.com/watch?v=15jdTQIr7j4 on June 3, 2015.

U.S. Department of Education, National Center for Education Statistics. (2014, May). *The condition of education 2014*. Washington, DC: Author. Accessed at http://nces.ed.gov/pubs2014/2014083.pdf on June 3, 2015.

Van der Kolk, B., McFarlane, A. C., & Weisaeth, L. (Eds.). (2007). *Traumatic stress: The effects of overwhelming experience on mind, body, and society*. New York: Guilford Press.

Volunteer Alberta. (2012). *Cultural values*. Accessed at http://volunteeralberta.ab.ca/intersections/staff/building-cultural-knowledge/cultural-values on June 6, 2015.

Vygotsky, L. S. (1978). *Mind in society: The development of higher psychological processes*. Cambridge, MA: Harvard University Press.

Weaver, G. R. (1986). Understanding and coping with cross-cultural adjustment stress. In R. M. Paige (Ed.), *Cross-cultural orientation: New conceptualizations and applications*, (pp. 175–192). Lanham, MD: University Press of America.

Weinstein, C. S. (2006). *Middle and secondary classroom management: Lessons from research and practice* (3rd ed.). New York: McGraw-Hill.

Wiggins, G., & McTighe, J. (1998). *Understanding by design*. Alexandria, VA: Association for Supervision and Curriculum Development.215

Willis, J. (2006). *Research-based strategies to ignite student learning: Insights from a neurologist and classroom teacher*. Alexandria, VA: Association for Supervision and Curriculum Development.

Willis, J. (2007). *Brain-friendly strategies for the inclusion classroom: Insights from a neurologist and classroom teacher*. Alexandria, VA: Association for Supervision and Curriculum Development.

Wong, H. K., & Wong, R. T. (2001). *The first days of school: How to be an effective teacher* (4th ed.). Mountain View, CA: Wong.

Yousafzai, M. (2013, July 12). Our books and our pens are the most powerful weapons. *The Guardian*. Accessed at www.theguardian.com/commentisfree/2013/jul/12/malala-yousafzai-united-nations-education-speech-text on February 12, 2015.

Zwiers, J., & Crawford, M. (2011). *Academic conversations: Classroom talk that fosters critical thinking and content understandings*. New York: Stenhouse.

INDEX

You've Got to Reach Them to Teach Them: Hard Facts About the Soft Skills of Student Engagement
Mary Kim Schreck
Navigate the hot topic of student engagement with a true expert. Become empowered to demand an authentic joy for learning in your classroom. Real-life notes from the field, detailed discussions, practical strategies, and space for reflection complete this essential guide to student engagement.
BKF404

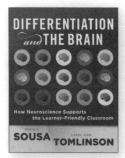

Differentiation and the Brain: How Neuroscience Supports the Learner-Friendly Classroom
David A. Sousa and Carol Ann Tomlinson
Examine the basic principles of differentiation in light of educational neuroscience research that will help you make the most effective curricular, instructional, and assessment choices. Learn how to implement differentiation so that it achieves the desired result of shared responsibility between teacher and student.
BKF353

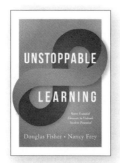

Unstoppable Learning: Seven Essential Elements to Unleash Student Potential
Douglas Fisher and Nancy Frey
Discover how systems thinking can enhance teaching and learning schoolwide. Examine how to use systems thinking—which involves distinguishing patterns and considering short- and long-term consequences—to better understand the big picture of education and the intricate relationships that impact classrooms.
BKF662

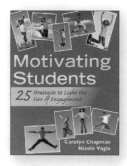

Motivating Students: 25 Strategies to Light the Fire of Engagement
Carolyn Chapman and Nicole Dimich Vagle
Learn why students disengage and how to motivate them to achieve success with a five-step framework. Research-based strategies and fun activities, along with tips and troubleshooting advice, show how to instill a lasting love of learning in students of any age.
BKF371

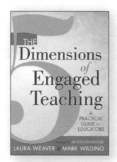

The Five Dimensions of Engaged Teaching: A Practical Guide for Educators
Laura Weaver and Mark Wilding
Engaged teaching recognizes that educators need to offer more than lesson plans and assessments for students to thrive in the 21st century. Equip your students to be resilient individuals, able to communicate effectively and work with diverse people.
BKF601

Wait! Your professional development journey doesn't have to end with the last pages of this book.

We realize improving student learning doesn't happen overnight. And your school or district shouldn't be left to puzzle out all the details of this process alone.

No matter where you are on the journey, we're committed to helping you get to the next stage.

Take advantage of everything from **custom workshops** to **keynote presentations** and **interactive web and video conferencing**. We can even help you develop an action plan tailored to fit your specific needs.

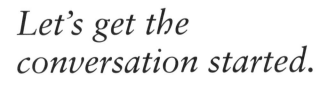

Let's get the conversation started.

Call 888.763.9045 today.